Proxemic Interactions:

From Theory to Practice

Synthesis Lectures on Human-Centered Informatics

Editor
John M. Carroll, *Penn State University*

Human-Centered Informatics (HCI) is the intersection of the cultural, the social, the cognitive, and the aesthetic with computing and information technology. It encompasses a huge range of issues, theories, technologies, designs, tools, environments and human experiences in knowledge work, recreation and leisure activity, teaching and learning, and the potpourri of everyday life. The series will publish state-of-the-art syntheses, case studies, and tutorials in key areas. It will share the focus of leading international conferences in HCI.

Proxemic Interactions
Nicolai Marquardt and Saul Greenberg
March 2015

An Anthropology of Services: Toward a Practice Approach to Designing Services
Jeanette Blomberg and Chuck Darrah
March 2015

Contextual Design: Evolved
Karen Holtzblatt and Hugh Beyer
October 2014

Constructing Knowledge Art: An Experiential Perspective on Crafting Participatory Representations
Al Selvin and Simon Buckingham Shum
October 2014

Spaces of Interaction, Places for Experience
David Benyon
September 2014

Mobile Interactions in Context: A Designerly Way Toward Digital Ecology
Jesper Kjeldskov
July 2014

Working Together Apart: Collaboration over the Internet
Judith S. Olson and Gary M. Olson
November 2013

Surface Computing and Collaborative Analysis Work
Judith Brown, Jeff Wilson, Stevenson Gossage, Chris Hack, and Robert Biddle
August 2013

How We Cope with Digital Technology
Phil Turner
July 2013

Translating Euclid: Designing a Human-Centered Mathematics
Gerry Stahl
April 2013

Adaptive Interaction: A Utility Maximization Approach to Understanding Human Interaction with Technology
Stephen J. Payne and Andrew Howes
March 2013

Making Claims: Knowledge Design, Capture, and Sharing in HCI
D. Scott McCrickard
June 2012

HCI Theory: Classical, Modern, and Contemporary
Yvonne Rogers
May 2012

Activity Theory in HCI: Fundamentals and Reflections
Victor Kaptelinin and Bonnie Nardi
April 2012

Conceptual Models: Core to Good Design
Jeff Johnson and Austin Henderson
November 2011

Geographical Design: Spatial Cognition and Geographical Information Science
Stephen C. Hirtle
March 2011

User-Centered Agile Methods
Hugh Beyer
2010

Experience-Centered Design: Designers, Users, and Communities in Dialogue
Peter Wright and John McCarthy
2010

Experience Design: Technology for All the Right Reasons
Marc Hassenzahl
2010

Designing and Evaluating Usable Technology in Industrial Research: Three Case Studies
Clare-Marie Karat and John Karat
2010

Interacting with Information
Ann Blandford and Simon Attfield
2010

Designing for User Engagement: Aesthetic and Attractive User Interfaces
Alistair Sutcliffe
2009

Context-Aware Mobile Computing: Affordances of Space, Social Awareness, and Social Influence
Geri Gay
2009

Studies of Work and the Workplace in HCI: Concepts and Techniques
Graham Button and Wes Sharrock
2009

Semiotic Engineering Methods for Scientific Research in HCI
Clarisse Sieckenius de Souza and Carla Faria Leitão
2009

Common Ground in Electronically Mediated Conversation
Andrew Monk
2008

Proxemic Interactions: From Theory to Practice
Nicolai Marquardt and Saul Greenberg

ISBN: 978-3-031-01080-4 print
ISBN: 978-3-031-02208-1 ebook

DOI 10.1007/978-3-031-02208-1

A Publication in the Springer series
SYNTHESIS LECTURES ON HUMAN-CENTERED INFORMATICS #25
Series Editor: John M. Carroll, Penn State University

Series ISSN 1946-7680 Print 1946-7699 Electronic

Proxemic Interactions:
From Theory to Practice

Nicolai Marquardt
University College, London

Saul Greenberg
University of Calgary

SYNTHESIS LECTURES ON HUMAN-CENTERED INFORMATICS #25

ABSTRACT

In the everyday world, much of what we do as social beings is dictated by how we perceive and manage our interpersonal space. This is called proxemics. At its simplest, people naturally correlate physical distance to social distance. We believe that people's expectations of proxemics can be exploited in interaction design to mediate their interactions with devices (phones, tablets, computers, appliances, large displays) contained within a small ubiquitous computing ecology. Just as people expect increasing engagement and intimacy as they approach others, so should they naturally expect increasing connectivity and interaction possibilities as they bring themselves and their devices in close proximity to one another. This is called *Proxemic Interactions*.

This book concerns the design of proxemic interactions within such future proxemic-aware ecologies. It imagines a world of devices that have fine-grained knowledge of nearby people and other devices—how they move into range, their precise distance, their identity, and even their orientation—and how such knowledge can be exploited to design interaction techniques.

The first part of this book concerns theory. After introducing proxemics, we operationalize proxemics for ubicomp interaction via the Proxemic Interactions framework that designers can use to mediate people's interactions with digital devices. The framework, in part, identifies five key dimensions of proxemic measures (distance, orientation, movement, identity, and location) to consider when designing proxemic-aware ubicomp systems. The second part of this book applies this theory to practice via three case studies of proxemic-aware systems that react continuously to people's and devices' proxemic relationships. The case studies explore the application of proxemics in small-space ubicomp ecologies by considering first person-to-device, then device-to-device, and finally person-to-person and device-to-device proxemic relationships. We also offer a critical perspective on proxemic interactions in the form of "dark patterns," where knowledge of proxemics may (and likely will) be easily exploited to the detriment of the user.

KEYWORDS

proxemic interactions, proxemics, embodied interaction, location and orientation awareness, natural user interfaces, ubiquitous computing, human computer interaction

Contents

Acknowledgments xv

Videos xvii

Figure Credits xix

1   Introduction 1
   1.1   Proxemics 2
   1.2   Proxemics Applied to Ubicomp Interactions 3
   1.3   Audience for this Book 6

   Part I: Proxemics and Ubiquitous Computing 7

2   Ubicomp in Brief 9
   2.1   Envisioning Ubiquitous Computing 9
   2.2   Situating Computing in People's Everyday Environments 11
   2.3   Embodied Interaction 12
   2.4   Context-Aware Computing 13
   2.5   Ubicomp Systems Considering Spatial Relationships 16
      2.5.1   Sensing Devices 17
      2.5.2   Sensing People 20
      2.5.3   Sensing Both People and Devices 24
   2.6   Conclusion 28

3   Proxemic Interactions Theory 31
   3.1   Personal Space 32
   3.2   Hall's Proxemics 33
   3.3   Environment: Fixed and Semi-Fixed Features 35
   3.4   Size and Shape of Interpersonal Distance Zones 36
   3.5   Orientation 37
   3.6   Compensation, Balance, and Privacy 37
   3.7   Discrete vs. Continuous Distances 38
   3.8   The Focused Encounter: F-formations 38
   3.9   Proxemic Theories as Analytical Lenses in Interaction Design 41
   3.10   Summary 41

4   Operationalizing Proxemics for Ubicomp Interaction **43**
   4.1   Proxemic Dimensions   43
      4.1.1   Distance   44
      4.1.2   Orientation   45
      4.1.3   Movement and Motion   46
      4.1.4   Identity   46
      4.1.5   Location   47
   4.2   Applying Dimensions to Ubicomp Interaction Design   47
   4.3   Conclusion   49

5   Exploiting Proxemics to Address Challenges in Ubicomp Ecologies **51**
   5.1   Ubicomp Interaction Design Challenges   51
   5.2   Revisiting Challenge 1: Revealing Interaction Possibilities   53
      5.2.1   Reacting to the Presence and Approach of People   53
      5.2.2   Transition from Awareness to Interaction   54
      5.2.3   Spatial Visualizations of Ubicomp Environments   55
   5.3   Revisiting Challenge 2: Directing Actions   55
      5.3.1   Discrete Distance Zones for Interaction   55
      5.3.2   Considering Attention and Orientation   56
      5.3.3   Considering Location Features   56
      5.3.4   Considering Motion Trajectories   57
      5.3.5   Adapt to Number of Nearby Devices   57
   5.4   Revisiting Challenge 3: Establishing Connections between Devices   57
      5.4.1   Connection as a Consequence of Close Proximity   58
      5.4.2   Progressive Connection Process   58
   5.5   Revisiting Challenge 4: Providing Feedback   58
      5.5.1   Adjusting Feedback Output   59
      5.5.2   Selecting Appropriate Feedback Modality   59
      5.5.3   Proxemic-Dependent Reveal of Feedback   59
   5.6   Revisiting Challenge 5: Preventing and Correcting Mistakes   59
      5.6.1   Inverting Actions   59
      5.6.2   Explicit Action to Undo   60
      5.6.3   Proxemic Safeguards   60
   5.7   Revisiting Challenge 6: Managing Privacy and Security   60
      5.7.1   Proximity-Dependent Authentication   61
      5.7.2   Distance-Dependent Information Disclosure   61
      5.7.3   Proxemic-Aware Privacy Mechanisms   61

5.7.4   Considering People's Expectations of Personal Space 62

5.8   Discussion and Conclusion 62

Part II: Exploiting Proxemics in Ubicomp Ecologies **65**

6   **Person/People-to-Device Proxemic Interactions** **67**

6.1   Scenario: The Proxemic Media Player Application 68

6.2   Incorporating the Fixed and Semi-Fixed Feature Space 72

6.3   Interpreting Directed Attention to People, Objects, and Devices 74

6.4   Supporting Fine-Grained Explicit Interaction 76

6.5   Continuous Movements vs. Discrete Proxemic Zones 78

6.6   The Gradual Engagement Pattern 79

6.7   Applying the Gradual Engagement Pattern: From Awareness
      to Interaction 80

6.8   Leveraging People's Identity 81

6.9   Mediating People's Simultaneous Interaction 82

    6.9.1   Merging Multiple Proxemic Distances 82

    6.9.2   Handling Conflicts 83

6.10 Other Example Applications 84

    6.10.1 ViconFace 84

    6.10.2 Proxemic Presenter 85

    6.10.3 Attentive Transparent Display for Museums 86

    6.10.4 Proxemic 3D Visualization System 87

    6.10.5 Proxemic-aware Pong 88

    6.10.6 Proxemic Peddler 89

    6.10.7 Spalendar 90

    6.10.8 Mediating Shoulder Surfing 91

6.11 Discussion and Conclusion 92

7   **Device-to-Device Proxemic Interactions** **93**

7.1   Applying Gradual Engagement to Cross-Device Information Transfer 94

7.2   Prior Work Applied to Gradual Engagement 97

    7.2.1   Awareness of Device Presence and Connectivity 98

    7.2.2   Revealing Exchangeable Content 98

    7.2.3   Transferring Digital Content 99

7.3   Stage 1: Awareness of Device Presence and Connectivity 99

    7.3.1   Proxemic-dependent Awareness 100

    7.3.2   Dynamic Notifications about Device Presence and Position 102

7.4 Stage 2: Reveal of Exchangeable Content 104
    7.4.1 Proximity-Dependent Progressive Reveal 104
    7.4.2 Implicit vs. Explicit Reveal 108
    7.4.3 Revealing Content on Personal vs. Public Devices 108
7.5 Stage 3: Techniques for Information Transfer between Devices 109
    7.5.1 Single Person Transfer: From Personal to Public Device 109
    7.5.2 Collaborative Transfer. 114
7.6 Other Example Applications 116
    7.6.1 ProxemiCanvas 116
    7.6.2 Multi-Device Viewer for Medical Images 117
    7.6.3 Proxemic Remote Controls 118
    7.6.4 Spatial Music Experience 119
    7.6.5 Tip-Me-Lens 119
    7.6.6 The Greeting Robot 120
7.7 Discussion 121
    7.7.1 Large Ecologies of People and Devices 121
    7.7.2 Gradual Engagement and Privacy 121
    7.7.3 Pattern Applied to Different Tracking Hardware 122
7.8 Conclusion 123

8 Considering Person-to-Person and Device-to-Device Proxemics **125**
8.1 Using Theory to Motivate Group Interaction Techniques 126
8.2 Design Study: Proxemics of People and Devices. 128
8.3 GroupTogether System: Detecting Federations 130
8.4 Interaction Techniques 131
    8.4.1 Tilt-to-Preview Selected Content 131
    8.4.2 Face-to-Mirror the Full Screen 132
    8.4.3 Portals. 133
    8.4.4 Cross-Device Pinch-to-Zoom 134
    8.4.5 Propagation through F-Formations 135
    8.4.6 A Digital Whiteboard as Part of an F-Formation 136
8.5 Discussion and Future Work 137
8.6 Conclusion 137

9 Dark Patterns **139**
9.1 Dark Patterns 139
9.2 The Captive Audience 140
9.3 The Attention Grabber 142

	9.4	Bait and Switch	144
	9.5	Making Personal Information Public	145
	9.6	We Never Forget	146
	9.7	Disguised Data Collection	148
	9.8	The Social Network of Proxemic Contacts/Unintended Relationships	149
	9.9	The Milk Factor	150
	9.10	Discussion	151
	9.11	Conclusion	153
10	**Conclusion**		**155**
	10.1	What Was Learnt	155
	10.2	Potential Directions for Future Work	157
		10.2.1 Defining Rules of Behavior	157
		10.2.2 Other Factors Influencing Proxemic Behavior	157
		10.2.3 Pattern Language of Proxemic Interactions	158
		10.2.4 Violating Proxemic Expectations	158
		10.2.5 Safeguarding Abuses	158
		10.2.6 Interactions in Large-Scale, Cluttered Ubicomp Ecologies	158
		10.2.7 Proxemic Interactions in Public Spaces, Buildings, Cities	159
		10.2.8 Technical Challenges	159
		10.2.9 Other Concerns	159
	10.3	The Future is Here	160
	10.4	Closing Remarks	160
	References		**161**
	Author Biographies		**177**

Acknowledgments

Many people participated in the intellectual foundations of this book. Our own efforts in Proxemic Interactions started several years ago, where we (Saul Greenberg as supervisor and Nicolai Marquardt as Ph.D. student) set this as a Ph.D. topic. As our work developed, so did the interest of other people in our Interaction Laboratory at the University of Calgary. When Marquardt created the Proximity Toolkit for rapid prototyping of proxemic systems, other students and researchers in our lab embraced it. They quickly developed their own projects on proxemics, ranging from quick and dirty explorations to full-blown research efforts. During this time, we developed a graduate course on the topic: students researched sub-topics, built systems, and added to our database of relevant background literature. The result was a research sub-culture, where Proxemic Interactions became an on-going topic of conversation and research. This rich environment added considerably to our own thinking about Proxemic Interactions.

We thank our collaborators and co-authors of joint publications which formed the basis of the content covered in this book. In particular, we would like to thank Till Ballendat, Sebastian Boring, Robert Diaz-Marino, Jakob Dostal, Ken Hinckley, Jo Vermeulen, and Miaosen Wang. We also thank all the other researchers and developers whose work we cite. Their work stimulated our own thoughts, and showed different ways of approaching and leveraging the idea of proxemics to interaction design. Dan Vogel and Ravin Balakrishnan's seminal paper and video on interactive public ambient displays (ACM UIST, 2004) was particularly inspiring: they planted the seed that eventually led to our own research explorations.

Videos

This book describes highly interactive systems built both by ourselves and others. Yet print is a poor way to show the dynamics of these systems. Fortunately, a subset of these systems is also illustrated by videos, many available on the Internet. We include a list of various videos produced not only by ourselves but by selected others, along with URLs to those videos. We highly recommend that readers look at these videos. When a video is available, we indicate that in our text by (see video: system name).

System or interaction technique name	Source
Tip-Me-Lens	Aseniero et al., 2013
http://grouplab.cpsc.ucalgary.ca/Publications/2013-TipMeLens-Report2013-1040-07	
Proxemic media player	Ballendat et al., 2010
http://grouplab.cpsc.ucalgary.ca/Publications/2010-ProxemicInteractions.ITS	
Shoulder surfing protection	Brudy et al., 2014b
http://grouplab.cpsc.ucalgary.ca/Publications/2014-MediatingShoulderSurfing.CHIVideos	
Spalender name	Chen et al., 2012
http://grouplab.cpsc.ucalgary.ca/Publications/2012-Spalendar.AVI	
Greetings Robot	Heenan et al., 2014
http://grouplab.cpsc.ucalgary.ca/Publications/2014-HRIGreetings.DIS	
Proxemic remote control	Lido et al., 2013
http://grouplab.cpsc.ucalgary.ca/Publications/2013-MobileProxemicControl-CHIVideo	
Proximity toolkit	Marquardt et al. 2011
http://grouplab.cpsc.ucalgary.ca/Publications/2011-ProximityToolkit.UIST	
Gradual engagement	Marquardt and Ballendat et al., 2012
http://grouplab.cpsc.ucalgary.ca/Publications/2012-GradualEngagement.ITS	
GroupTogether	Marquardt and Hinckley et al., 2012
http://grouplab.cpsc.ucalgary.ca/Publications/2012-GroupTogether.UIST	
Microseismic visualizer	Moustafa et al., 2013b
http://grouplab.cpsc.ucalgary.ca/Publications/2013-Microseismic-CHIVideo	
Proxemic Peddler	Wang et al., 2012
http://grouplab.cpsc.ucalgary.ca/Publications/2012-ProxemicPeddler.PervasiveDisplays	
ViconFace	Diaz-Marino and Greenberg 2010
http://grouplab.cpsc.ucalgary.ca/Publications/2010-ProximityToolkit.CHI	
Ambient display	Vogel et al. 2004
http://www.dgp.toronto.edu/~ravin/videos/uist2004_ambient.avi	

Figure Credits

Figures 1.1, 6.1, 6.2, 6.3. 6.4, 7.11: **From:** Ballendat, T., Marquardt, N., Greenberg, S., 2010. Proxemic Interaction: Designing for a proximity and orientation-aware environment, in: *Proceedings of the ACM Conference on Interactive Tabletops and Surfaces, ITS' 10*. ACM, New York, NY, USA, pp. 121–130. Copyright © 2010 ACM. DOI: 10.1145/1936652.1936676.

Figure 2.1: **From:** Weiser, M., 1991. The Computer for the 21st Century. *Scientific American* 265, 94–104. Copyright © 1991 Scientific American. Courtesy Nature Publishing Group.

And courtesy PARC.

Figure 2.2: **From:** Streitz, N., Prante, T., Müller-Tomfelde, C., Tandler, P., Magerkurth, C., 2002. Roomware©: the second generation, in: *Extended Abstracts on Human Factors in Computing Systems, CHI EA '02*. ACM New York, NY, USA, pp. 506–507. Copyright © 2002 ACM. Used with permission. DOI: 10.1145/506443.506452.

Figure 2.3: **From:** Want, R., Hopper, A., Falcão, V., Gibbons, J., 1992. The Active Badge Location System. *ACM Transactions on Information Systems* 10, 91–102. DOI: 10.1145/128756.128759.

And **From:** Schilit, B., Adams, N., Want, R., 1994. Context-Aware Computing Applications, in: *IEEE Workshop on Mobile Computing Systems and Applications*. IEEE, Los Alamitos, CA, USA, pp. 85–90. Copyright © 1994 IEEE. DOI: 10.1109/WMCSA.1994.16.

Figure 2.4: **From:** Ju, W., Lee, B.A., Klemmer, S.R., 2008. Range: exploring implicit interaction through electronic whiteboard design, in: *Proceedings of the ACM Conference on Computer Supported Cooperative Work, CSCW '08*. ACM, New York, NY, USA, pp. 17–26. Copyright © 2008 ACM. Used with permission. DOI: 10.1145/1460563.1460569.

Figure 2.5: **From:** Annett, M., Grossman, T., Wigdor, D., Fitzmaurice, G., 2011. Medusa: A Proximity-Aware Multi-Touch Tabletop, in: *Proceedings of the 24th Annual ACM Symposium on User Interface Software and Technology, UIST '11*. ACM, New York, NY, USA, pp. 337–346. Copyright © 2011 ACM. Used with permission. DOI: 10.1145/2047196.2047240.

Figure 2.6: **From:** Vogel, D., Balakrishnan, R., 2004. Interactive public ambient displays: transitioning from implicit to explicit, public to personal, interaction with multiple users, in: *Proceedings of the 17th Annual ACM Symposium on User Interface Software and Technology, UIST '04*. ACM, New York, NY, USA, pp. 137–146. Copyright © 2004 ACM. Used with permission. DOI: 10.1145/1029632.1029656.

Figure 2.7: Wilson, A.D., Benko, H., 2010. Combining multiple depth cameras and projectors for interactions on, above and between surfaces, in: *Proceedings of the 23nd Annual ACM Symposium on User Interface Software and Technology, UIST '10.* ACM, New York, NY, USA, pp. 273–282. Copyright © 2010 ACM. Used with permission. DOI: 10.1145/1866029.1866073.

Figure 2.8: **Based on:** Streitz, N., Prante, T., Röcker, C., Alphen, D. van, Magerkurth, C., Stenzel, R., Plewe, D., 2003. Ambient displays and mobile devices for the creation of social architectural spaces, in: *Public and Situated Displays—Social and Interactional Aspects of Shared Display Technologies, The Kluwer International Series on Computer Supported Cooperative Work.* Kluwer, Dordrecht, pp. 387–409. DOI: 10.1007/978-94-017-2813-3_16.

Figure 2.9: **From:** Bragdon, A., DeLine, R., Hinckley, K., Morris, M.R., 2011. Code space: touch + air gesture hybrid interactions for supporting developer meetings, in: *Proceedings of the ACM International Conference on Interactive Tabletops and Surfaces, ITS '11.* ACM, New York, NY, USA, pp. 212–221. Copyright © 2011 ACM. Used with permission. DOI: 10.1145/2076354.2076393.

And from: Sakurai, S., Itoh, Y., Kitamura, Y., Nacenta, M.A., Yamaguchi, T., Subramanian, S., Kishino, F., 2008. Interactive Systems. Design, Specification, and Verification, in: Graham, T.C., Palanque, P. (Eds.). Springer, Berlin, Heidelberg, pp. 252–266.

Figure 2.10: **From:** Marquardt, N., Diaz-Marino, R., Boring, S., Greenberg, S., 2011. The Proximity Toolkit: Prototyping proxemic interactions in ubiquitous computing ecologies, in: *ACM Symposium on User Interface Software and Technology, UIST'11.* ACM, New York, NY, USA, pp. 315–326. Includes video figure. DOI: 10.1145/2047196.2047238.

Figure 3.2: **From:** Hall, E.T., 1966. *The Hidden Dimension*, 1st ed. Doubleday, Garden City, NY Used with permission.

Figure 3.3: **From:** Kendon, A., 2010. Spacing and orientation in co-present interaction, in: Proceedings of Development of Multimodal Interfaces: Active Listening and Synchrony. Presented at the Lecture Notes in Computer Science, Springer, pp. 1–15. Copyright © 2010 Springer. Reprinted with the kind permission of Springer Science + Business Media. DOI: 10.1007/978-3-642-12397-9_1.

Figure 3.4: **From:** Marquardt, N., Hinckley, K., Greenberg, S., 2012. Cross-device interaction via micro-mobility and F-formations, in: *ACM Symposium on User Interface Software and Technology, UIST '12.* ACM, New York, NY, USA, pp. 13–22. Includes video figure. Copyright © 2012 ACM. DOI: 10.1145/2380116.2380121.

Figure 4.1: **From:** Marquardt, N. and Greenberg, S., 2012. Informing the Design of Proxemic Interactions. *IEEE Pervasive Computing*, 11(2): 14–23, April–June. Copyright © 2012 IEEE. DOI: 10.1109/MPRV.2012.15.

Figure 6.20: **From:** Chen, X., Boring, S., Carpendale, S., Tang, A., Greenberg, S., 2012. SPALENDAR: Visualizing a Group's Calendar Events over a Geographic Space on a Public Display, in: *Proceedings of the 11th International Working Conference on Advanced Visual Interfaces, AVI '12*. ACM. Copyright © 2012 ACM. DOI: 10.1145/2254556.2254686.

Figure 6.21: **From:** Brudy, F., Ledo, D., Greenberg, S., Butz, A., 2014a. Is anyone looking? Mitigating shoulder surfing on public displays through awareness and protection, in: *Proceedings of the 3rd International Symposium on Pervasive Displays, PerDisp '14*, ACM, New York, NY, USA, pp. 1–6. Copyright © 2014 ACM. DOI: 10.1145/2611009.2611028.

Figures 7.1, 7.7, 7.8, 7.10, 7.13, 7.14, 7.17, 7.19, 7.20: **From:** Marquardt, N., Ballendat, T., Boring, S., Greenberg, S., Hinckley, K., 2012. Gradual engagement between digital devices as a function of proximity: From awareness to progressive reveal to information transfer, in: *Proceedings of Interactive Tabletops and Surfaces, ITS '12*, ACM, New York, NY, USA, pp. 31-40. Includes video figure. Copyright © 2012 ACM. DOI: 10.1145/2396636.2396642.

Figure 7.25: **From:** Aseniero, B.A., Tang, A., Carpendale, S., Greenberg, S., 2013. Showing Real-time Recommendations to explore the stages of Reflection and Action (No. 2013-1040-07). Technical Report #2013-1040-07, Department of Computer Science, University of Calgary, Calgary, Alberta, Canada. Includes video figure.

Figure 7.26: **From:** Heenan, B., Greenberg, S., Aghel Manesh, S. and Sharlin, E., 2014. Designing Social Greetings in Human Robot Interaction, in: *Proceedings of the ACM Conference on Designing Interactive System, ACM DIS '14*, ACM, New York, NY, USA, pp. 855–864. Includes video figure. Copyright © 2014 ACM. DOI: 10.1145/2598510.2598513.

Figure 8.3–8.8: **From:** Marquardt, N., Hinckley, K., Greenberg, S., 2012. Cross-device interaction via micro-mobility and F-formations, in: *ACM Symposium on User Interface Software and Technology, UIST '12*. ACM, New York, NY, USA, pp. 13–22. Includes video figure. Copyright © 2012 ACM. DOI: 10.1145/2380116.2380121.

Figures 9.1, 9.3, 9.4, and 9.5: **From:** Greenberg, S., Boring, S., Vermeulen, J., Dostal, J., 2014. Dark patterns in proxemic interactions: A critical perspective, in: *Proceedings of the ACM Conference on Designing Interactive Systems, DIS '14*. ACM, New York, NY, USA, pp. 523–532. Copyright © 2014 ACM. DOI: 10.1145/2598510.2598541.

Figure 9.2: Copyright © Captive Media; used with permission.

Figure 9.6: Copyright © N=5 Ad Agency, Amsterdam; used with permission.

CHAPTER 1

Introduction

"When you walk up to your computer, does the screen saver stop and the working windows reveal themselves? Does it even know if you are there? How hard would it be to change this? Is it not ironic that, in this regard, a motion-sensing light switch is 'smarter' than any of the switches in the computer [...]?"

Bill Buxton, "Living in Augmented Reality" (Buxton, 1997)

Over the last two decades, Mark Weiser's (1991) vision of *Ubiquitous Computing* (ubicomp) as the next era of interacting with computers has increasingly become commonplace through the rising number of digital devices present in people's everyday life. *Ubicomp ecologies* are emerging (e.g., Figure 1.1), where people regularly use their portable personal devices (e.g., phones, tablets), interact with information appliances (e.g., digital picture frames, game consoles), and collaborate with large surfaces (e.g., digital whiteboards) within a given context. But Weiser's vision went beyond the mere *individual* devices. He predicted seamlessly accessible technologies of calm computing that "weave themselves into the fabric of everyday life, until they are indistinguishable from it" (Weiser, 1991) and "engage both the center and periphery of our attention" (Weiser and Brown, 1996). Unfortunately this vision does not yet exist, for there are still considerable problems that make interaction with devices in such ubicomp ecologies far from seamless. In practice, using multiple devices in *concert* is often tedious and requires executing complicated interaction sequences (Cooperstock et al., 1997).

For example, consider the digital ecology of the living room shown in Figure 1.1. While the devices within it are network-enabled, actually configuring, interconnecting, and transferring content between these devices is painful without extensive knowledge. Even when devices are connected, performing tasks between them is usually tedious—for example, navigating through network and local folders to find and exchange files. In practice, people rarely go through the effort. This means that, from a person's perspective, the vast majority of devices are blind to the presence of other devices. What makes this even more problematic is that these devices are also blind to the non-computational aspects of the ubicomp ecology, which may affect their intended use. Devices do not recognize *people* that are present, such as whether only a single person is interacting with the device vs. a group of people that could work collaboratively over those devices. They do not recognize *non-digital* objects, such as a person holding a physical object in their hand that could determine the intended interaction with the device. They do not recognize *spatial relations*, such as a person sitting on a chair facing a screen from a distance, from which we could infer that the person's attention is focused on the screen. And devices also do not recognize the *spatial layout of the environment* (e.g., position of walls or doorways), which could help to determine if another wirelessly connected device is in the same or an adjacent room, or to know when a person is entering the room through a door so the system can activate itself.

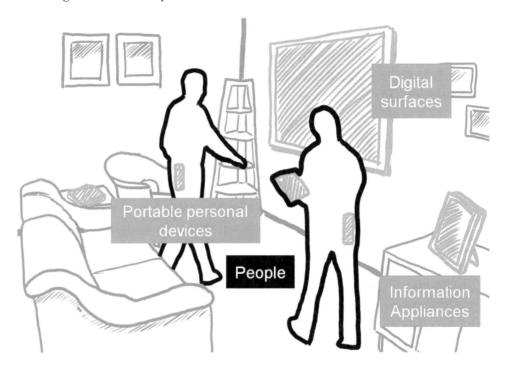

Figure 1.1: People, devices, and non-digital objects are part of a small-space ubiquitous computing ecology (Ballendat et al., 2010).

This book argues that computational knowledge of spatial relationships between people and the devices or objects around them could be leveraged in ubicomp interaction design. However, we first need a better understanding about how people use the space around them. A seminal theory analyzing and describing people's use of interpersonal space when interacting with others is Edward Hall's *proxemics*, introduced here but presented in more detail in Chapter 3.

1.1   PROXEMICS

In everyday life, the spatial relationships between ourselves and the other people or objects around us are important for how we engage, interact, and communicate. People often use changes of spatial relationships—such as interpersonal distance or orientation—as an implicit form of communication. For instance, we keep certain distances to others depending on familiarity, we orient toward people when addressing them (e.g., see the informal circles of collaboration in Figure 1.2), we move closer to objects we are interested in, and we stand or sit relative to others depending on the task at hand. *Proxemics*, a term coined by anthropologist Edward Hall, is one of the seminal theories about people's perception and use of interpersonal distances to mediate their interactions with other people (Hall, 1966).

Figure 1.2: People often implicitly adapt proxemic variables (e.g., distance or orientation) when interacting with others, as shown in these small group formations during conversations.

Hall's studies revealed patterns in how certain physical distances correlate to social distance when people interact. Other observations further refined this understanding of people's use of spatiality. For example, spatial features of the environment (e.g., location of walls, doors, furniture) influence people's use of proxemics. A person's orientation relative to others is another driving factor in how people greet and communicate with one another. Overall, proxemics mediate many aspects of social interaction. For example, it influences casual and serendipitous encounters (Kraut et al., 1988), is a nuance in how people greet one another (Kendon, 1990), and is a major factor in how people arrange themselves for optimal small group collaboration via spatial-orientational maneuvering (Kendon, 2010; Sommer, 1969).

1.2   PROXEMICS APPLIED TO UBICOMP INTERACTIONS

The key idea elaborated in this book is that we can leverage information about people's and devices' fine-grained proxemic relationships for the design of novel interaction techniques in ubicomp ecologies.

The overarching goal of this book is to inform the design of future *proxemic-aware devices* that—similar to people's natural expectations and use of proxemics—allow increasing connectivity and interaction possibilities when in proximity to people, other devices, or objects. Toward this goal, we explore how the fine-grained knowledge of proxemic relationships between the entities in small-space ubicomp ecologies (people, devices, objects) can be exploited in interaction design.

For example, in Figure 1.3 left, we see that one person in the room has a spatial relationship with other room entities: people, the devices (the whiteboard, the tablet, the mobile devices carried by both people, the various information appliances in the room), and non-digital objects (room boundaries, furniture). What can we do in terms of interaction if the ubicomp ecology knew about these spatial relationships? For example, in Figure 1.3 right, the ecology may detect that the person holding their tablet is approaching the digital whiteboard. As a consequence, it may automatically connect the tablet and the whiteboard, readying it for information sharing and exchange. The whiteboard may show progressively more detail about the information it is displaying as the person approaches it. Both tablet and whiteboard may show interface features allowing information from one device to be easily transferred to the other. Interaction methods can be tuned to best fit how far away the person is from the whiteboard, e.g., pointing while at a distance, touching when within reach. This book will explore these and many other possibilities.

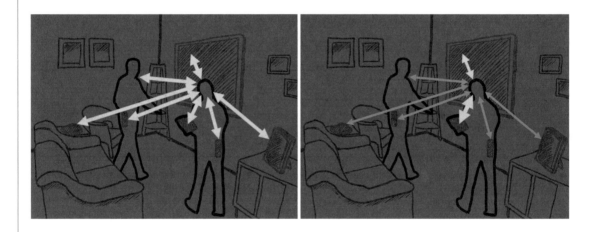

Figure 1.3: Interactions in ubicomp ecologies (cf. to Figure 1.1): (left) many possible interaction possibilities around a person, where (right) knowledge about proxemic relationships can be leveraged to identify devices more likely for possible interactions.

Over a decade ago, Vogel and Balakrishnan (2004) seminal research started exploring the use of proxemic relationships to drive people's interactions with large public displays (see video: ambient display). Other early pioneers continued in this vein, such as Ju et al.'s (2008) use of proxemics to mediate between implicit and explicit interactions. Yet despite the contextual rich information of proxemics and the opportunities presented by people's natural understanding of them, so far only a relatively small number of research installations incorporate knowledge about spatial relationships within ubicomp interaction design. Of those systems that do, most do not yet consider the fine nuances of distance, orientation, movement, location, and identity in people's and devices' proxemic relationships. Thus this book delves into Proxemic Interactions more deeply, where it explores further nuances and applications of proxemics to ubicomp interaction design.

In order to keep the scope of this book manageable, we primarily focus on the study of applying proxemics to interactions in *ecologies of people and devices* in *small space ubicomp environments*. This includes small- to medium-sized indoor rooms, such as a living room at home, or meeting rooms at the office. Figure 1.4 provides an example room layout and its entities. Later chapters in this book will selectively focus on proxemic relationships between the following entities:

- People (single person to small groups, i.e., 1–4 people)

- Large interactive digital surfaces (e.g., whiteboard)

- Information appliances (e.g., digital picture frames)

- Personal portable devices (e.g., phone, tablet computer)

- Non-digital objects (e.g., magazines, pens)

- Fixed features (e.g., walls) and semi-fixed features (e.g., furniture) of the environment

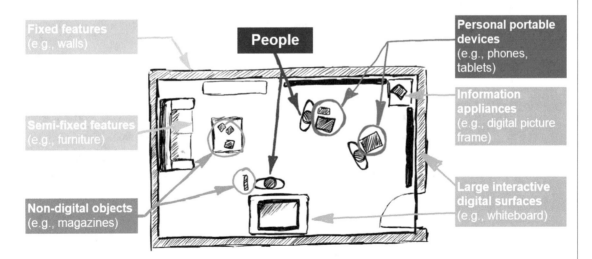

Figure 1.4: Ubicomp ecology with multiple people interacting with personal portable devices, information appliances, large digital surfaces, and non-digital objects.

Within this context, we ask how we can exploit the fine-grained knowledge of proxemic relationships (which we operationalize in Chapter 3 as distance, orientation, movement, location, and identity) between people, digital devices, non-digital objects, and the surrounding environment to mediate ubicomp interactions. In particular, the book is divided into two parts that elaborate two primary themes.

1. Part I. We operationalize proxemic theories for ubicomp interaction design in the framework of Proxemic Interactions.

2. Part II. We describe the design and implementation of three explorative case studies probing into the design space of Proxemic Interactions in small space ubicomp ecologies—and therewith applying the operationalized proxemic theories.

There are, of course, important topics this book does not cover in detail. First, we recognize that ubicomp systems designed for public spaces and building- and city-wide deployments could also leverage proxemics. While this book can help inform some of that design, we leave it to others to pursue the nuances of those different spaces. Second, Proxemic Interactions require our computers and devices to somehow sense spatial relationships between entities in the environment: people, devices, and even non-digital objects. There are various technologies and infrastructure that can perform that sensing, and these are used by the various systems described in the book. However, we do not elaborate on the sensing technologies for various reasons: space is limited; the various technologies currently used are all limited in their own way, and we expect new technologies to be introduced in the near future. Even so, the pointers we provide to source references should suffice for those interested in using, reproducing, or researching such sensing systems.

1.3   AUDIENCE FOR THIS BOOK

The primary audience for this book is ubicomp developers, human-computer interaction researchers, interaction designers, and indeed anyone interested in novel ways of interacting with technology.

The book provides sufficient background to bring you, its reader, up to speed. If you have no knowledge of proxemics and just passing knowledge of ubiquitous computing, the first part of this book will explain what proxemics is and how it relates to ubicomp design. If you do have expertise in the area, you will find that the details provided along with pointers to related work will give you a rich intellectual basis for considering and applying proxemics to both research and product design.

The book is based on various social theories of proxemics, which by themselves may be insufficient to guide design. Consequently the book operationalizes proxemics as dimensions that can be sensed and managed by a computer, which will help you as a practitioner, developer, or interaction designer apply proxemics to your own system creation. Part II of the book gives three case study designs along with myriads of novel interaction techniques based on proxemics. These make Proxemic Interactions design concrete. Overall, we hope this will inspire and inform your design processes for building ubicomp systems.

PART   I

Proxemics and Ubiquitous Computing

In this first part of the book we investigate proxemic theory and how it can be operationalized for ubicomp interaction design. First, in Chapter 2 we survey related work in ubiquitous computing and context-aware computing, and review previous work considering spatial information for ubicomp interfaces. Next, in Chapter 3 we lay out the foundation of Proxemic Interactions in ubicomp, with a survey of seminal theories of proxemics and personal space. In Chapter 4, we operationalize proxemics for ubicomp through the Proxemic Interactions framework, which identifies five key dimensions of proxemic measures most relevant for ubicomp interaction design. Last, in Chapter 5 we describe how to leverage proxemics in system design to mitigate six particular ubicomp interaction design challenges.

CHAPTER 2

Ubicomp in Brief

"The most profound technologies are those that disappear. They weave themselves into the fabric of everyday life, until they are indistinguishable from it."

Mark Weiser (1991)

This chapter provides a brief introduction to interactive ubicomp ecologies, which in turn frames the rest of this book. Sections 2.1 and 2.2 introduce ubiquitous computing. Because ubicomp is a large area, our introduction quickly narrows to work that relates to the book's focus of interactions in ubiquitous computing ecologies. In particular, Sections 2.3 and 2.4 briefly survey two seminal concepts in ubiquitous computing: embodied interaction and context awareness. Section 2.5 reviews historic ubicomp research projects that incorporate some kind of spatial or proxemic information to mediate people's interaction with ubicomp systems.

2.1 ENVISIONING UBIQUITOUS COMPUTING

Over twenty years ago, in his *Scientific American* article Mark Weiser characterized the past, present, and future of modern computing (Weiser, 1991). He described how computer usage had already evolved from mainframe computing (one computer shared by many people) to personal computing (one person sits in front of one computer). He then predicted that the next major shift of how people would use computers would be toward *ubiquitous computing*, where each person has routine access to many digital devices. He foresaw that these digital technologies would be linked by networks, where devices would be available in a variety of form factors and sizes that would suit the task at hand. He also predicted that the number of devices available to people would increase dramatically over time.

Weiser and his colleagues at PARC designed a set of devices to illustrate his ubicomp concepts, and to serve as a sandbox for further exploration. Notably, he described device characteristics as arising in part from their quite different size scales (Weiser, 1991): the yard-scale immovable large interactive *LiveBoards* (Figure 2.1, left), the foot-scale portable notebook-sized *ParcPads* (Figure 2.1, bottom left), and the smaller handheld sized *ParcTabs* at the inch-scale (Figure 2.1, right). All were linked via a wireless network. Weiser's basic idea was that each device was designed and made readily available so that people could choose the kind of technology that best fit the task at hand, e.g., using the LiveBoard for discussing digital content in a group, or using the Parcpad to add private annotations to a document.

Figure 2.1: PARC's early test bed for ubicomp exploration: (left) LiveBoard in the background and a person using the ParcPad in the foreground; (right) the ParcTab handheld device (Source: *Scientific American* article by Weiser (1991) and Xerox PARC, available in the PARC newsroom media library with credit to Brian Tramontana: http://www.parc.com/newsroom/media-library.html).

It may seem that Weiser's vision has been realized given today's availability and use of devices such as smartphones, tablet computers, net-aware digital cameras, photo-frames, interactive whiteboards, digital tabletops, and so on. Yet his vision went beyond device availability.

Importantly, Weiser predicted the move of computing technology into people's everyday surroundings, embedded in all kinds of everyday objects and spaces, and eventually becoming invisible tools. The characteristic of invisibility in this context meant that the tool does not intrude on people's consciousness so that they could "focus on the task, not the tool" (Weiser, 1994). A second key concept of ubicomp was to allow *seamless interactions*. As defined by Ishii et al. (1994), seamless design pursues two goals: *continuity with existing work practices* so people can keep doing what they are skilled at doing, and *smooth transitions between functional spaces* so people can shift easily between modes. Later, Ishii and Ullmer (1997) summarize this concept as the seamless couplings between the physical and the digital world (or short: "seamless couplings of bits and atoms"). To partially realize seamlessness, Weiser and Brown proposed "calm" technology that "engages both the center and periphery of our attention" (Weiser and Brown, 1996). That is, according to Weiser's vision, information technology should be accessible around people at the place where it is needed, and should reside invisibly in the background until the moment *when* it is required. Weiser emphasized that ubiquitous computing "takes into account the natural human environment and allows the computers themselves to vanish into the background" (Weiser, 1991).

It is these parts of Weiser's vision—the seamless interaction with the disappearing and calm technology, the fluent transitions between foreground engaging activity and background peripheral perception—that is still missing from people's everyday experience with ubicomp technology. People carry mobile phones between them. Desktop and laptop computers abound. Large displays and digitally controlled appliances are increasingly commonplace. Yet they largely exist as separate devices. For those that can be interconnected, the interface to do those connections are, at best, quite awkward. Still, progress has been made. As the next few sections show, researchers have developed, refined, and nuanced concepts of ubicomp.

2.2   SITUATING COMPUTING IN PEOPLE'S EVERYDAY ENVIRONMENTS

The vision of ubiquitously available technology in our environments and embodied interaction was highly influential for later technology explorations.

For example, researchers further refined interaction concepts in so-called *multi-display environments* (MDEs), where displays of diverse form factors allow access to (and interaction with) digital information in everyday environments. Previous research has shown how such an "ecosystem of displays" (Terrenghi et al., 2009) can support various collaborative activities—mostly in office environments. Because of their device heterogeneity, MDEs can be beneficial for group collaboration, for example by allowing the division and organization of tasks across devices, and choosing the type of device/screen that best fits to the task at hand. A core idea between these systems is that information can be easily moved between and across these displays in a near-seamless manner.

To illustrate, *interactive landscape* (i-Land) by Streitz et al. (1999) was one of the early explorations of interactions in multi-display environments, where it considered people's interaction in the environment as a whole (Figure 2.2). As part of the interactive furniture they introduced chairs with integrated computers (*ComChairs*), multiple connected interactive walls (*DynaWall*), and tabletops for collaboration (*InteracTable*) (Streitz et al., 1999). A significant focus in their research was the seamless transfer of digital content between all entities. Within the three displays comprising the DynaWall (Figure 2.2 top), people could move information across the displays as if it were a single unit. Moving information between the interactive furniture was done differently. A person used physical objects identified by the system, where each object could act as a virtual container to represent digital data. To bring digital information from one device to another, a person placed the physical object next to any of the digitally augmented furniture (on the so-called *Bridge*) to associate information with the object. When bringing the object then to another device, the system would open the corresponding linked digital information on the screen (Streitz et al., 2002). A later addition to i-Land was the ConnecTable (Tandler et al., 2001), a pen-based small table. While each ConnecTable could be used individually, two people wishing to do tightly coupled work could create a single homogeneous interactive digital workspace simply by abutting two ConnecTables together (as shown in in Figure 2.2, left side), which would automatically connect the displays. The way ConnecTables leveraged their physical spatial relationship to establish a digital connection makes them a notable early—albeit restricted—example of Proxemic Interactions.

Figure 2.2: i-Land multi-display environment (Source: Streitz et al., 2002).

There are myriads of researchers who have explored various interaction challenges in MDEs (e.g., Nacenta et al. 2005, 2009; Biehl and Bailey 2004; Wigdor et al. 2006; Terrenghi et al. 2009). MDEs such as i-Land provide good examples that address a particular niche in ubicomp technology, where it attempts to minimize the seams between the displays of multiple but different devices. Some of the work in Proxemic Interactions, as described in later chapters, also contributes to MDEs, but—as with the ubicomp vision—is broader than that.

2.3   EMBODIED INTERACTION

Dourish's (2001a) theory of *embodied interaction* expands upon the ubicomp concept of situating technology in people's everyday environment. He brought together the core ideas of phenomenology theory, social computing, and tangible user interfaces, where he emphasized the importance of designing technology that exploits human skills and experiences that take place in their world (Dourish, 2001a). Extending the ubicomp vision, the goal of embodied interaction is to build technology that is seamlessly integrated into people's everyday *practices*. People should not act on technology but instead through the technology, to perform their task at hand. The technology should be seamlessly integrated not only into the physical environment but also *embedded in people's social practices*. A fundamental concept of embodied interaction is therefore the technology's "presence and participation in the world" (Dourish, 2001b), and the consideration of the associated meanings of the actual *place* in *space* where the interaction takes place (Harrison and Dourish, 1996).

Dourish (2001b) emphasizes that embodied interaction's notion of seamless integration requires bridging the gap between the digital and physical world. He makes specific reference to Ishii and Ullmer's concept of *tangible user interfaces*, or TUIs (Ishii and Ullmer, 1997). TUIs integrate both digital input and output into graspable, physical objects. When well designed, these interfaces draw on people's natural skills and abilities when interacting with physical world objects. They emphasize that an important characteristic of TUIs is the seamless integration of technology with the physical environment (where they refer to Weiser's use of *invisibility* of technology), but also that the systems allow for "seamless transition of the user's interaction between background and foreground information." Under the covers, these systems use a variety of *sensors* (e.g., motion, touch) to gather input, and *actuators* (e.g., motors, solenoids) to manipulate the physical object to form output. For example, Ishii and his students developed *inTouch* to provide haptic interpersonal communication over distance (Brave et al., 1998). Each inTouch device comprises three cylindrical wooden rollers. When a person moves the rollers on one device (detected by position sensors), that motion is replicated on the other device (actuated by high precision motors). These devices are two-way, where both people can manipulate their device concurrently, yet feel the other's movement via force feedback. The concept of TUIs, however, goes beyond digitally connecting two physical devices, as TUIs can also mediate interaction between digital and physical entities. For instance, Ullmer et al. (1998) uses physical tokens to allow easy transfer of digital media between devices. Underkoffler and Ishii (1999) uses the placement of physical miniature buildings to control and augment a digital urban planning simulation on a tabletop display.

Dourish emphasizes other aspects of embodied interaction. He believes that embodied interaction recognizes multiple people, where he points to the field of Computer Supported Cooperative Work (CSCW). Furthermore, he emphasizes how embodied interaction is a way of looking at the world: "embodied interaction is not a technology or a set of rules. It is a perspective on the relationship between people and systems. The question of how it should developed, explored, and instantiated remain open research questions" (Dourish, 2001a).

Our own exploration of proxemics in ubicomp is a part of embodied interaction, in that we ground our designs on theories about people's implicit understanding, practices, and use of proxemics in everyday situations, and carefully translate these principles to ubicomp system design.

2.4   CONTEXT-AWARE COMPUTING

Context-aware computing relates to embodied interaction and ubicomp. The basic idea is that some kind of context-aware sensing method provides devices (or the architecture controlling them) with knowledge about the situation around them. Using that knowledge, devices infer where they are in terms of social action, and then act accordingly to that context (Schilit et al., 1994).

Early research in context-awareness began with the integration of sensing capabilities, ultimately to give ubicomp systems sufficient information to recognize and react to situational context changes (Antifakos and Schiele, 2002; Dey et al., 2001). An example of a context-aware device would be a mobile phone that can decide whether to ring depending on a person's current location (e.g., avoid ringing when in the cinema or a meeting in the office) (Coulouris et al., 2011). Often, context-aware systems infer the contextual information (e.g., location) from relatively simple measured properties such as noise levels, temperature, light, time, or acceleration. Strategies have been applied to fuse these diverse sensor measurements together in order to get more reliable results for inferring context (Antifakos and Schiele, 2002). Schilit et al. (1994) identified three important aspects of context: "where you are, who you are with, and what resources are nearby." This extends the understanding of context to not only include location information of the person or device itself, but to consider the presence of people and resources in the environment as well.

Figure 2.3: Context-aware computing: (left) Active Badge and (right) its application in practice: people's badges are detected to determine their presence in three different rooms (Source: Xerox PARC, Want et al., 1992, and Schilit et al., 1994).

ActiveBadge (Figure 2.3 left) was an early enabling technology exploring the practice of context- and location-aware computing concepts (Want et al., 1992). The sensing aspect of the system is relatively simple: it determines the room people are in by transmitting signals via infrared to the tags—called ActiveBadges—that people wear (Figure 2.4), where that information is received by receivers in the room. Yet even this basic information can be used to good effect. In particular,

Schilit et al. (1994) later describe four novel techniques that consider this information about people's location (e.g., as sensed by the Active Badge sensor, as shown in Figure 2.3 right) to drive interactions. First, the *proximate selection* technique filters nearby devices based on their location (e.g., showing all nearby devices that are in the same room as a person). Second, *contextual reconfiguration* changes a device's configuration based on its current location (e.g., automatically making a nearby printer the default one). Third, with the *contextual information* technique the device's interface changes automatically when entering a new location (e.g., showing a list of discounted products when a person enters a store). Fourth, *context triggered actions* can be set to activate commands when entering a pre-defined location (e.g., reminding a person to look for a particular book the next time they are in a library). Overall, these interaction strategies summarize the core of interactions applied in many context-aware computing systems. As with ActiveBadges, many research projects primarily focus on *location* information (Oulasvirta and Salovaara, 2009), either by sensing it directly or by inferring location information from other sensed properties.

A particular category of context-aware systems are *reactive environments* (Buxton, 1997; Cooperstock et al., 1997). The fundamental idea of reactive environments is to design spaces that—by sensing people and device presence and movement—can infer the context of use and leverage that information to proactively perform certain system actions. Buxton illustrates the concept of reactive environments with an example that maps a simple sensed state in the physical world to control behaviors in the digital world (Buxton, 1997). The *DoorMouse* sensor detects whether the door of an office is currently open or closed. This current state of the physical door (open/closed) is then directly mapped to the digital world, where it either allows or prevents a person to be interrupted with incoming messages or video calls on their computer. This simple design allows the technology to preserve some of the social protocols of the physical world (i.e., closing the door for not being disturbed) across to the digital realm. In another example, Cooperstock et al. (1997) built a reactive meeting room that automatically adapts the lights to a person's preference, displays a calendar overview, and reconfigures the audio and video equipment to address the presenter's needs. *Sentient computing* describes a similar concept for environments that reconfigures devices in reaction to the people using the device (Addlesee et al., 2001). As one example, the system determines when a person is in close proximity to a desktop computer and automatically opens the last desktop session of that user—and closes it automatically when leaving (a concept introduced earlier as teleporting application states across devices by Bennett et al., 1994).

The question of how to implement such reactive environments or context-aware applications, and how to design adequate rules of behavior, remains an active challenge of ubicomp research. Creating context-aware applications that match the environment and people's understanding of the situation is a critical yet highly difficult task for ubicomp developers. For example, Greenberg emphasizes that context is a dynamic construct that it is not always stable, and that similar-looking contextual situations may actually differ dramatically in their meaning to the people involved

(Greenberg, 2001). He states how this is partially due to the fact that not all information that defines a certain social context can be sensed by the system, such as: people's history of interaction, their emotions, or their current objectives (Greenberg, 2001). Consequently, creating the rules of behavior for context-aware systems (i.e., the rules that determine the system actions based on sensed properties) is not just difficult, but sometimes even impossible (especially when errors cannot be tolerated). Greenberg warns not to "trivialize context," which could lead to inappropriate and frustrating applications. As partial solutions, he suggests that the rules of behavior should avoid invoking risky system actions that the system should provide clear feedback of what it is doing, and that manual override should be possible in case the system gets it wrong. Others have also questioned the overly ambitious goals of using sensors to infer comprehensive context models fully describing social situations (e.g., Oulasvirta and Salovaara, 2009; Rogers, 2006). The challenges faced by context-aware system designers was even compared with the problems encountered in strong artificial intelligence research (AI), where the goal was to build intelligent computer systems that match or exceed human intelligence (Erickson, 2002; Rogers, 2006).

Our research toward Proxemic Interactions relates in several regards to the research in ubiquitous computing, embodied interaction, and context-aware computing. Like many ubicomp systems, we also envision systems that, in part, react proactively to sensed properties in the environment, and believe that these system designs can lead to more seamless and fluent interactions of people with their surrounding devices.

We now sample related work that considers some form of spatial sensing (either devices, or people, or both) to drive people's interaction with their surrounding technology in such context-aware systems.

2.5   UBICOMP SYSTEMS CONSIDERING SPATIAL RELATIONSHIPS

We are not the first to advocate sensing of spatial relationships and proxemics to ubicomp system design. In this section, we review selections of related ubicomp system designs that consider some form of spatial or proxemic information in the design of interactive applications. It is important to note that the primary focus of this section is to provide a structured general overview of the field. More detail will emerge in other chapters, where we will refer back to many of these systems later to discuss how these systems consider particular nuances of proxemic information in interaction design.

Because this book focuses on systems that operate in indoor ubicomp environments, we exclude broader area ubicomp deployments, such as interactive systems using Global Positioning System (GPS) receivers to determine the position of a person in a city (e.g., as done by Abowd et al., 1997). However, we try to be broader than specific interactive features that may be afforded by spatial relationships, e.g., Chong et. al.'s (2014) good but narrower survey of techniques supporting spontaneous device relationships. Most of the systems and interaction techniques we do survey in this section focus on a particular subset of the entities comprising ubicomp ecologies (e.g., interactions between devices, or between one person and a device). We see these works as providing fundamental building blocks for creating interaction designs considering the full ubicomp ecology.

This survey is structured into three major parts as shown in Table 2.1. The first part (Table 2.1a) lists related work that considers the spatial relationships of devices. From bottom to top the systems or techniques are ordered according to their fidelity of tracked spatial information: detecting device presence at discrete distances (Table 2.1b), continuous distance between devices (Table 2.1c), or continuous distance and orientation (Table 2.1d). The next part (Table 2.1e) lists systems that sense people's presence. From left to right the projects are again ordered according to their tracking fidelity: detecting people's presence at discrete distances (Table 2.1f), continuous distance (Table 2.1g), or continuous distance and orientation (Table 2.1h). Finally, in the third part we survey projects considering the spatial relationships of both people and devices in the full ubicomp ecology.

2.5.1   SENSING DEVICES

A major problem in Ubicomp is how to control the interconnectivity of devices. This is especially problematic for mobile devices that may appear and disappear over time in an unpredictable manner, and that may not be known to the system before its first appearance. Consequently, various researchers have developed methods that involve sensing the close proximity of one device to other device(s) to mediate the establishment of inter-device connections and (typically) to then transfer digital content between these devices over that connection. Most approaches do require some form of limited a priori connectivity to coordinate this recognition, perhaps between devices or as mediated by a cloud network synchronization.

This section reviews such device-to-device work, as summarized in part (a) in Table 2.1. The review progresses from devices that just sense each other's presence at discrete distances (Table 2.1b), to those that recognize continuous distances (Table 2.1c), and finally to those that sense and react to devices continuously changing distance and orientation (Table 2.1d).

Sensing devices' presence at discrete distances (Table 2.1b). A first class of techniques uses one or multiple discrete spatial zones—which often depends on the sensing technology used—to both initiate connectivity and to mediate the information exchanged between devices. A connection is automatically triggered when the spatial regions between devices overlap, i.e., to trigger the presence of one another. For example, Want et al. introduced a method that lets a device react to the presence of nearby devices or non-digital physical objects (Want et al., 1999). By attaching RFID tags to books, paper, or watches, a digital device equipped with an RFID reader is able to trigger

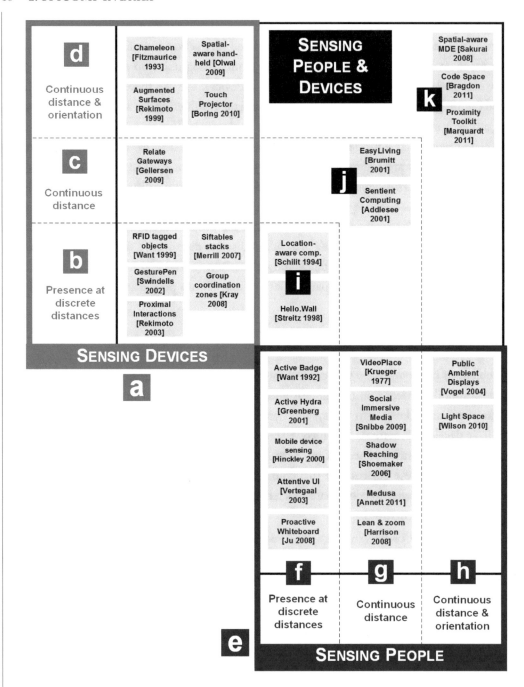

Table 2.1: Overview of related work of ubicomp research considering spatial information, categorized by type of tracked entity (people, device, and people + devices) and fidelity of sensed spatial information.

certain activities as soon as these tagged objects come into sensor range. Similarly, the *Siftables* (small micro displays) detect proximity of other nearby devices when stacking them in a pile or placing them next to each other (Merrill et al., 2007). These techniques are powerful for connecting devices that are in very close proximity or—like in many cases—are even directly touching one another. Other techniques sense a device's presence from a larger distance. For example, Rekimoto et al. (2003) combined RFID and infrared for establishing seamless device connectivity. Swindells et al. (2002) introduced a technique that worked from a larger distance, where he applied it to the *gesturePen* for initiating remote pointing for device selection (i.e., by pointing the pen directly at a device selects it).

Instead of using one distance threshold to determine inter-device connectivity, later research explored using multiple discrete zones. For example, Kray et al.'s (2008) *group coordination negotiation* introduced multiple spatial regions around mobile phones. Their scenario exploited these regions to negotiate exchange of information with others and to visualize the regions on a tabletop. Depending on how devices were moved in and out of three discrete regions, the transfer of media data between the devices is initiated.

Sensing devices' continuous distance (Table 2.1c). A second class of techniques uses distances as a continuous measure, but does not sense the orientation of devices. For example, Gellersen et al.'s (2009) RELATE Gateways provided a spatial-aware visualization of nearby devices, which included their approximate distance and direction relative to the device. A graphical map showed the spatial room layout, and icons indicated the position of other nearby devices. Alternatively, and similar to Rekimoto et al. (2003), icons at the border of a mobile device screen represented the type and position of surrounding devices.

Sensing devices' continuous distance and orientation (Table 2.1d). A third class of techniques uses continuous measures of distances and orientation. Researchers for example considered how a spatially aware mobile device would interact with other surrounding devices.

Notably, Chameleon (Fitzmaurice, 1993) was a palmtop computer aware of its position and orientation (with 6° of freedom). Fitzmaurice explored the use of the Chameleon device to access 3D information spaces, such as to support people's interaction in libraries with digitally tagged bookshelves that the device could sense and react to. The Chameleon also allowed spatial navigation in a local virtual space by moving the handheld device in a two-dimensional area (e.g., for panning a digital map that is larger than the display of the handheld device).

Olwal and Feiner (2009) later refined this technique. They explored the use of spatially aware handhelds for high-precision interaction on large displays, with the advantage of having higher resolution visual output on the mobile device and a more consistent task performance. Similarly, *TouchProjector* (Boring et al., 2010) also tracks the precise distance and orientation of a mobile device relative to other nearby digital surfaces. By doing so, it enables people to interact with remote screens through a live video displayed on their mobile device.

Augmented Surfaces (Rekimoto and Saitoh, 1999) demonstrate how the tracking of spatial relationships and orientation between devices allows techniques such as *hyperdragging* of content across devices, where a person can begin a mouse drag operation on one device, and continue the operation seamlessly onto another device to drop the information.

2.5.2   SENSING PEOPLE

Next, we review related work where systems sense and react to the presence of a nearby person or multiple people (Table 2.1e).

Sensing people's presence in discrete zones (Table 2.1f). A first class of projects in ubicomp react to the sensed presence of people as a binary state, i.e., if a person is in a particular room or not. One of the earliest of such systems is *ActiveBadge* (Want et al., 1992). As we mentioned earlier, a person wears a small electronic name tag that communicates its position through infrared signals to surrounding receivers (e.g., mounted to the ceiling). This made it possible to build applications that leverage the fact that the system knows the presence and identity of an individual within a particular room. For instance, an application could forward phone calls appropriately to another room when a person is not at their desk (Want et al., 1992) or guide a person through a building (Abowd et al., 1997).

Hinckley et al. (2000) built another example of a device capable of detecting a person's presence—though at a smaller scale. They integrated a front-facing proximity range sensor into a mobile phone, allowing the device to determine the close presence or absence of a person's head. The display was then deactivated when the device sensed the close proximity to a person's head. Researchers have also considered a person's eye gaze direction as a measure that indicates a person's presence and focus to a particular device (Vertegaal and Shell, 2008). *Attentive User Interfaces* (AUIs) describe this research approach, where a system is monitoring a person's eye gaze to determine what device the user is attending to. This technique allows designing systems that only become activated (or receive input from a user) when the person is directly looking toward them. Therefore, attentive user interfaces are a suitable approach to direct a person's multimodal commands (like speech and hand gestures) to the correct device receiving these commands.

Other projects track people's presence in one of multiple discrete zones around a device. Greenberg and Kuzuoka (2001) designed the *ActiveHydra* device to demonstrate a responsive media space detecting people's presence. The device determines a person's distance (in one of three discrete zones) to the communication device to control the fidelity of the audio and video link between two remote collaborators. When looking at the device from a large distance, the screen updates at a low frame rate and only gives glimpses of the remote collaborator's location. When moving closer, the video changes to normal quality, but leaves the audio deactivated to preserve privacy. The audio channel is activated only when both people move directly in front of the device—and thus emulates a face-to-face conversation.

In a related approach, the *Range* system (Ju et al., 2008) divides the interaction space around a digital whiteboard into four discrete interaction zones (Figure 2.4). These zones correspond to certain transitions of how the system implicitly reacts to a person standing and interacting with the digital whiteboard from a particular distance: for example, ink strokes are clustered when standing at a distance, and the whiteboard clears up space in the center of the display when a person approaches the board to add new content. Ju and her colleagues discuss a framework that categorizes these transitions along the dimensions of *implicit to explicit* and *foreground to background* interaction.

Sensing people's continuous distance (Table 2.1g). A second class of systems sense and react to the continuous distance of nearby people to mediate interactions.

For example, some systems allow full body interaction with a large surface through continuous position sensing. With Kruger et al.'s (1985) *Videoplace*, people use their silhouettes (captured by a vision system onto the display) to directly interact with display's digital content. Later, Snibbe and Raffle (2009) built *social immersive media* installations—letting people playfully interact with digital projections on a large wall display or on the floor. This was developed further with the *shadow reaching technique* (Shoemaker et al., 2007), that allows similar interaction through real or virtual shadows. The shadows of a person can function as a magic lens modifying displayed content. In all three projects, the presence and movement of the person's body directly in front of the interactive screen is an essential part of the interaction technique itself.

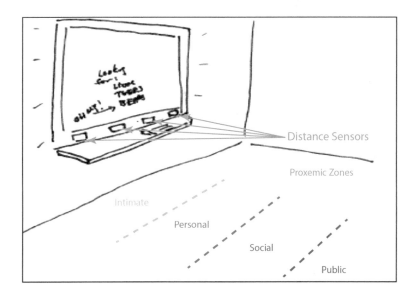

Figure 2.4: Four proxemic zones with Range digital whiteboard (Source: Ju et al., 2008).

The *Medusa* tabletop (Annett et al., 2011) introduced a method for continuous proximity sensing for detecting nearby people standing around a horizontal tabletop display. Inferring the position of where people stand around the tabletop allowed them to build applications that: automatically reorient content on the screen to the direction of the person; show control widgets when approaching the screen with a hand; or hiding personal content once a second person approaches. Remarkably, the system is built by using an array of 138 IR proximity sensors mounted in several layers around the tabletop (Figure 2.5).

Figure 2.5: Proximity-aware multi-touch tabletop (source: Annett et al., 2011).

At a desktop computer, the *lean and zoom* technique (Harrison and Dey, 2008) illustrates how to use continuous measurements of a person's distance to a desktop computer screen adapting the view of displayed content. The smaller the distance becomes between a person's head and the screen, the more the application zooms into the displayed content.

Sensing people's continuous distance and orientation (Table 2.1h). A third class of devices explores the design of systems recognizing the continuous distance and orientation of one person or multiple people in space. For example, Vogel and Balakrishnan (2004) designed a public ambient display reacting to a person's distance and body orientation relative to the display (see video: ambient display). They map discrete zones to four modes of interaction (similar to Hall's proxemic zones), moving from ambient display, to implicit, subtle, and personal interaction (Figure 2.6 left). Importantly, the project explores the possible ways a person's interaction with the ambient display can be mediated by moving in and out of these discrete zones, along with sensing and using a person's body orientation. Their system also recognizes a set of 3D hand gestures, used by a person to explicitly control the displayed content (Figure 2.6 right). A major idea in their work is that interaction from afar is public and implicit, and becomes more private and explicit as people move toward the surface. They illustrate their concept with a digital calendar application (Figure 2.6 right) that reveals more detailed and personal information when a person moves closer, that hides the information immediately when the person turns around, and that recognizes the presence of multiple people in front of the display and changes the displayed content accordingly.

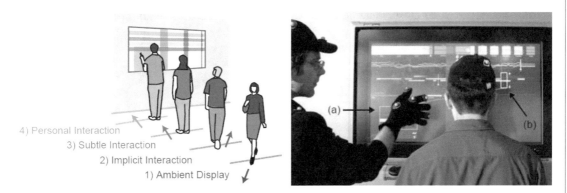

Figure 2.6: Interaction with public ambient displays (Source: Vogel and Balakrishnan, 2004).

Figure 2.7: Tracking people's movements in a ubicomp environment with LightSpace (Source: Wilson and Benko, 2010).

More recently, *LightSpace* describes novel interactions of one or multiple people in a ubicomp ecology (Wilson and Benko, 2010). Because the system tracks the people moving in space with ceiling-mounted cameras (Figure 2.7 left), a person can, for example, transfer a digital picture from one display to another by simply touching both the digital object and the destination surface simultaneously (Figure 2.7 right). Alternatively, a person can pick up virtual objects by sweeping them into their hands, dropping the virtual object onto another digital surface by touching it, or even passing an object to another person by dropping it into their hands. Importantly, the project explores interactions that leverage people's position and gestures *between* the interactive multi-touch surfaces where "the room becomes the computer" (Wilson and Benko, 2010).

2.5.3   SENSING BOTH PEOPLE AND DEVICES

The last category of systems (Table 2.1i–k) that considers both people's and devices' spatial relationships is in particular closely related to our own research goal of mediating people's interactions in a *complete ubicomp ecology*.

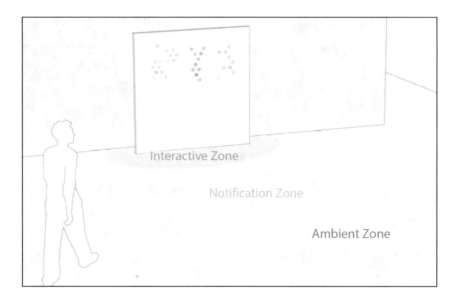

Figure 2.8: Presence of people and devices in discrete distance zones affects the interaction with Hello. wall (based on: Streitz et al., 2003).

Sensing people and devices' presence at discrete distances (Table 2.1i). A first class of systems recognizes the presence of devices or people in an environment. Schilit et al.'s (1994) location-aware interaction techniques extend the earlier work of ActiveBadges (that focused on tracking people) to combine the system's knowledge of a person's location with the knowledge of surrounding mobile and stationary devices. The system then, for example, uses this information to facilitate selection of nearby devices (e.g., the closest printer), or to reconfigure nearby technology (e.g., dim the lights according to personal preferences). Other research projects track people and their devices' presence in *discrete distance zones* around large displays to adapt the modes of interaction. For example, *Hello.wall* (Streitz et al., 2003) introduces the notion of "distance-dependent semantics," where the distance of a person to the interactive wall defines the possible forms of interaction and the kind of information shown on both the wall display and a person's mobile device. The project technically detects people and their devices in three discrete spatial zones around the display (using a sensing mechanism of RFID tags), and moves from ambient information, to notification, and direct interaction that links the mobile device to the large surface (shown in Figure 2.8).

Sensing people's and devices' continuous distances (Table 2.1j). A second class of systems considers continuous information about people's and devices' position. The intelligent home environment of the *EasyLiving* project (Brumitt et al., 2000b) leverages information about the current position of people and devices to, for example, provide a customized interface on a person's mobile device to control nearby devices (e.g., adjusting the lights), or to automatically activate devices based on a person's presence (e.g., playing the preferred music of a person on nearby speakers). To allow the design of such interactions, the project introduced the concept of creating a geometric model between entities in space that is updated with data gathered by fusing multiple sensor sources (e.g., computer vision and radio sensing). The software then takes this geometric model to check the position of a particular person, and updates interfaces or starts and stops services accordingly (Brumitt et al., 2000a). As mentioned earlier in Section 2.4, the sentient computing strategy applied a similar technological design to facilitate people's interactions in office spaces (Addlesee et al., 2001). For example, mobile devices automatically reconfigure themselves depending on who picks them up.

Sensing people's and devices' continuous distance and orientation (Table 2.1k). A third class of devices considers both people's and devices' continuous distance and orientation to mediate interactions.

First, systems leverage knowledge about these precise relationships to facilitate people's navigation and use of multiple screens in ubicomp ecologies. For example, Sakurai et al.'s (2008) middleware for MDEs generates perspective-corrected output on all screens surrounding a person to facilitate mouse cursor navigation across these screens. The cross-display mouse movement technique itself is related to hyperdragging (Rekimoto and Saitoh, 1999) we mentioned earlier, except that only the knowledge about the exact relationship between a person's head to the surrounding displays and devices enables the accurate perspective correction of this approach (Figure 2.9 left).

Second, Bragdon et al. (2011) build on the concept of spatially aware environments, where they contribute the Code Space system (Figure 2.9 right) supporting developer's code review meetings. Their novel *touch + air hybrid gestures* allow people to access, control, and share information across multiple personal devices and large surfaces. As part of their set of cross-device interactions a person can, for example, share content from a notebook computer onto a large display by touching the notebook's screen with one hand while pointing toward large wall display with their other hand. Most importantly, these hybrid techniques only become possible because the system considers the spatial relationships between people and their devices.

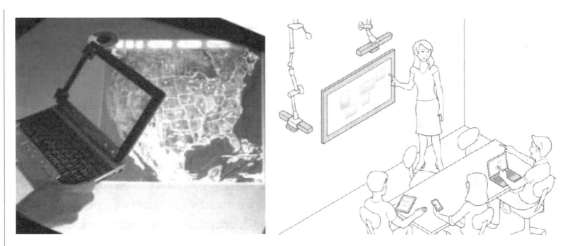

Figure 2.9: Tracking continuous distance and orientation between people and their devices in ubicomp ecologies: MDE middleware (source: Sakurai et al., 2008) and CodeSpace (source: Bragdon et al., 2011).

Figure 2.10: Left: three entities—person, tablet, and vertical surface; center: proxemic relationships between entities, e.g., orientation, distance, pointing rays; right: visualizing these relationships in the Proximity Toolkit's visual monitoring tool (Marquardt et al., 2011).

Finally, our own Proximity Toolkit (Marquardt et al., 2011; Marquardt, 2013; Diaz-Marino and Greenberg, 2010) facilitates the developer's access to essential aspects of proxemic relationships in ubicomp ecologies (see video: proximity toolkit). The toolkit collects and transforms raw tracking data gathered from various hardware sensors into rich high-level proxemic information accessible via an event-driven object-oriented API. That is, the toolkit allows programmers to easily access accurate distance, orientation, movement, identity, and location information of people, objects, and devices in the ubicomp ecology. While entities can be tracked individually, the toolkit allows easy definition and later access to particular proxemic relationships between particular entities (e.g., by defining the relationship between a particular person and a digital display). The Proximity Toolkit also includes a visual monitoring tool that displays the physical environment as a live 3D scene and shows the proxemic relationships between entities within that scene. An example is illustrated in

Figure 2.10, where proxemic relations between the person, tablet, and the interactive vertical surface are being tracked and automatically visualized.

Further technical detail about the Proximity Toolkit is warranted, as it was used to implement the majority of projects described in later chapters. The toolkit's tracking mechanism is achieved through a plug-in architecture, where it can incorporate various types of tracking hardware. Although several modules exist (e.g., for the Microsoft Kinect and OptiTrack), we primarily rely on our VICON motion capture hardware and software plug-in module. VICON is a commercial-grade camera-based system that tracks the 3D positon of reflective infrared markers with high precision. It is used primarily by the 3D animation industry, where animated characters are modelled after the tracked facial and body movements of real actors. Objects (entities) can also be tracked as a whole by identifying particular configurations of markers placed on that object. The Proximity Toolkit transforms the information returned by the tracking software into many proxemic variables, roughly divided into three categories as listed below.

Individual entity returns the individual properties of an entity. Example properties include:

- Name: identifier of the tracked entity;

- IsVisible: if the entity is visible to the tracking system;

- Location: 3D positon in world coordinates (contextual location information is held in a different property);

- Velocity/Acceleration: current velocity and acceleration defining the entity's movement;

- RotationAngle/Roll/Azimuth/Incline: orientation in the horizontal plane parallel to the ground, and in 3-space;

- Pointers: access to all pointing rays (e.g., forward, backward); and

- Markers/Joints: access to individual tracked markers or joints.

Relations between two entities returns the properties of how two entities, A and B, relate to one another. Example properties include:

- Distance between two entities A and B;

- ATowardB, BTowardA: whether entity A is facing B, and vice versa;

- Angle, HorizontalAngle: angle between front normal vectors or between horizontal planes;

- Parallel, ATangentalToB: geometric relationships between entities A and B;

- [Incline/Azimuth/Roll/Velocity/Acceleration] Difference: differences between A and B's particular properties;

- [X/Y/Z] VelocityAgrees / AccelerationAgrees: if A and B's velocities or accelerations are similar;

- Collides / Contains: relationships between the volumes surrounding A and B; and

- Nearest: the nearest point of A's volume relative to B.

Pointing relationships between A and B occur when one entity defines a forward face (a ray) that can point to another entity. Example properties include:

- PointsAt: pointing ray of A intersects with volume of B;

- PointsToward: A points in the direction of B (with or without intersection);

- IntersectionDegree: angle between the ray and front-facing surface of B;

- DisplayPoint: intersection point in B's screen / pixel coordinates;

- Intersection: intersection point in world coordinates;

- Distance: length of the pointing ray; and

- IsTouching: A is touching B (pointing ray length = 0).

As mentioned, the Proximity Toolkit provides the programmer with a visual monitoring tool that displays the scene (Figure 2.10). Using this visualization, the programmer can also specify interest in one or more of the properties above, which are then realized graphically within the scene. For example, Figure 2.10c illustrates the pointing ray and intersection of the tablet and the large display. The visual monitoring tool helps the programmer examine properties of potential interest as they move entities about. Subsequently, the programmer can programmatically track particular properties by registering callbacks to them through a conventional API, where property values are returned whenever they change. In most cases, programming is straight forward, as only a few particular properties of interest within particular project need to be tracked.

2.6   CONCLUSION

In this chapter we surveyed related work in the research area of ubiquitous computing most relevant to our proposed research of Proxemic Interactions. Similar to many of the projects surveyed in this chapter, we also envision systems that, in part, react proactively to sensed properties in the environment, and believe that these system designs can lead to more seamless and fluent interactions of people with their surrounding devices.

The work reported in this book does, however, differ in three important aspects to earlier research in context sensing, embodied interaction, and ubicomp.

First, instead of a general model of context through sensing, we focus primarily on very specific aspects relevant to proxemics: the distance, orientation, and other aspects defining the spatial relationships between people, devices, non-digital objects, and the environment they are in. With this, the proxemic dimensions we will identify in Chapter 4 are a *focused subset* of context-aware information. Our case studies of proxemic-aware systems in later chapters—while all considering the fine-grained knowledge about entities in ubicomp ecologies—then each focuses on a particular segment of the design space we discussed based on Table 2.1. First, we investigate person/people-to-device proxemics, then device-to-device proxemics, and finally consider both the proxemics between people and proxemics between devices in ubicomp interaction design.

Second, our Proxemic Interactions framework tries to leverage social expectations of people as described by proxemic theory (to be discussed later), i.e., that system reactions are in accordance to people's expectations.

Third, our focus differs in the granularity of spatial information we are interested in. Instead of knowing that a person or device is "in a room" as common in many context-aware systems, we are interested in finding out what technology designs are possible with more accurate, fine-grained measures of proxemics defining the relationships between entities: How close are people? Where exactly are devices located? How are people holding their devices? What is the orientation of people and devices, and are they facing each other? How fast is a person approaching a particular device? Similar to the richness of how these proxemic relationships affect our everyday interactions with other people, our belief is that we can mediate interactions with devices by considering proxemic relationships in ubicomp ecologies.

To gain a better understanding of exactly what kind of proxemic relationships are most relevant to consider, and how these could be measured in an interactive ubicomp system, our next two chapters distill the essential proxemic theories, and then operationalize those theories as proxemics applied to ubicomp interaction design.

CHAPTER 3

Proxemic Interactions Theory

The idea of integrating information of people's or devices' spatial relationships in interaction design is not new. However, this integration was only rarely done in the context of complete ubicomp ecologies comprising people, devices, and objects. Furthermore, the earlier work focused primarily on distance information (often only divided into discrete spatial regions), and had not factored in other fine-grained and nuanced aspects defining spatial relationships.

Before delving into the specifics of how we can integrate spatial relationships into interaction design, we need to better understand what we mean by spatial relationships, and how these might apply to interaction design. To begin this exploration, we review several seminal theories in sociology, psychology, and ethnology about people's understanding and use of the personal space around them. Based on this understanding we then operationalize these theories in Chapter 4 for ubicomp interaction design, and discuss the potential of applying nuances of these theories to address various ubicomp interaction design challenges in Chapter 5.

Within this context, the goal of the next few chapters is to inform and guide the design process of ubicomp developers in form of an operationalization of proxemics—that we call the Proxemic Interactions framework—in order to let developers create, invent, or discover novel proxemic-aware interaction techniques. The strengths of this framework are similar to generative theories (Rogers, 2004; Shneiderman, 2006) or interaction models (Beaudouin-Lafon, 2004), which (a) allow thinking in structured ways during the design process, (b) provide clear vocabulary for discussing designs, and (c) allow generating novel ideas through design dimensions and constructs. Rogers (2012) emphasizes that the appeal of generative theories "is their ability to account for technology-augmented behaviors and to inform new interventions to change behaviors that people care about — compared with the scientific theories that were intended to test predictions, and to make generalizations about human performance under controlled conditions." Our intention is not to provide a prescriptive set of guidelines or rules for the design of spatially aware ubicomp systems, but to introduce the Proxemic Interactions framework as a first-order approximation of how to apply proxemics to ubicomp interaction design.

This chapter sets the intellectual background for the Proxemic Interactions framework. It surveys seminal psychological and social theories about human spatial behavior that are most relevant for ubicomp interaction design. We begin by reviewing theories that we believe are relevant to inform ubicomp design. In particular, this research leverages insights from sociological concepts—most importantly the theories of personal space, proxemics, and F-formations.

3.1   PERSONAL SPACE

The term *personal space* was initially used in zoology for describing animal reactive behavior, and defined as the distance zone where animals
perform complex greeting, courting, and care-soliciting behaviors (Katz,
1937). The biologist Hediger later suggested that animals are surrounded
by "bubbles or balloons" that affect their spacing relative to other animals
around them (Hediger, 1950). He observed particular distances affecting animal behavior: most importantly the flight distance (that when

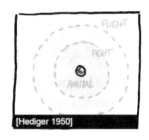

entered by a predator causes the animal to try to escape), and the smaller critical or fight distance
(when entered by a predator causes the animal to fight back). These distances were also influenced
by the animal species, their age, size, and gender.

Researchers later adopted the term personal space to the study
of human spatial behavior, and in particular *interpersonal relationships*.
Sommer (1959) describes personal space as the distance that one person places between themselves and other people around them. Personal
space is often described as an invisible boundary or bubble of space
surrounding a person (Altman, 1975). People's perception of changes
in the area of personal space around them influences how they engage,

interact, and communicate with others. A major part of psychology research primarily focused on
the protective function of personal space and people's use of this space as it is dictated by social
rules and norms (Aiello, 1987). People often react with resentment if these rules are broken—for
example if a stranger enters the boundaries of their personal space (Altman, 1975; Ciolek, 1983).

Even though studies of personal space are related to those of *territories*, there are important
differences (Altman, 1975; Sommer, 1959). While territories usually refer to a fixed geographical
location with clear boundaries, the personal space does not have a fixed location or any clearly
marked boundaries. Territoriality theory has been extended to explain how people partition shared
work areas, such as when a group works around physical or digital tables (Scott et. al., 2004; Scott
and Carpendale, 2010).

Personal space is typically defined as being an area around the body of a person, while territories are not (Bechtel and Churchman, 2002). The definition of personal space as an invisible
bubble surrounding a person has been controversial (Aiello, 1987). For example, Patterson (1975)
criticizes this definition as "unnecessary and probably misleading," as it implies stability where
actually a large variety of factors impact people's perception of personal space. Similarly, Knowles
(1989) argues that studies of discrete personal space distances makes the questionable assumption
that people's reactions to distance changes are *not* continuous. This is why further theoretical ap-

proaches were introduced for the study of human spatial behavior—perhaps most importantly the theory of proxemics.

3.2   HALL'S PROXEMICS

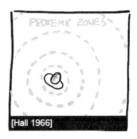

The anthropologist Edward Hall introduced *proxemics*[1] to define the "interrelated observations and theories of man's[2] use of space" (Hall, 1966). He focused in particular on the measurable distances between people as they interact. Most importantly, Hall went beyond the sole analysis of people's use of personal space as a protective measure. Instead, he conceptualizes personal space as a form of non-verbal and implicit communication, which he also refers to as the "silent language."

His theory—while emphasizing social and cultural differences—generally describes how people perceive, interpret, structure, and (often unconsciously) use the micro-space around them, and how this affects their interaction and communication with other nearby people. Hall believed that the theory of proxemics not only contributes to the study of people's interactions in daily life, but also helps us better understand "the organization of space in his houses and buildings, and ultimately the layout of his towns" (Hall, 1963).

Hall details how people perceive, interpret, and use proxemic cues, especially distance, to mediate relations to other people. In particular, he correlates physical distance to social distance between people. As illustrated in Figure 3.1, he categorizes this into four discrete distance zones that are also directly linked to people's perceived sensory information, and describes the primary types of activities corresponding to them [3]:

- Intimate (0–50cm), e.g., the distance of individuals in close relationship (or in an engaged argument as shown in Figure 3.2a). This is the distance that addresses the most sensory inputs: people can see the other close person, hear even a whisper, feel the heat or smell another person, and touch them. Normally people enter the intimate distance of another person only with permission (with exceptions due to environmental constraints, such as people standing very close in an elevator).

---

[1]   From the Latin root *prox-* (*proximitas*, meaning nearest or closest) and the suffix *-emic* (a term used by anthropologists to reflect a point of view in terms of the individual within a culture, and that also indicates links to terms in linguistic structuralism, such as systemic and phonemic); see (Nöth, 1995).

[2]   In his writings, Hall uses the term "man" to refer to both men and women, as it was a convention at that time (now ~50 years ago).

[3]   This particular distance categorization applies mostly to North American culture, but Hall also describes cultural differences of proxemics (and the zone distances in particular) that he observed with people of different cultures (e.g., Latin American, Asian, and European).

- Personal (0.5–1.2m), e.g., when interacting with friends or family (Figure 3.2b). At this distance "within arm's length" it is still possible to touch the other person, and people can speak at a lower volume to each other.

- Social (1.2–3.5m), e.g., the interaction in a more formal setting (Figure 3.2c). At this distance it is harder to reach out to touch another person, the voice is louder, and interactions are often more formal.

- Public (> 3.5m), e.g., the distance of a speaker to an audience (Figure 3.2d). At this distance people have to speak louder to address others, and the other primary sensory input is vision.

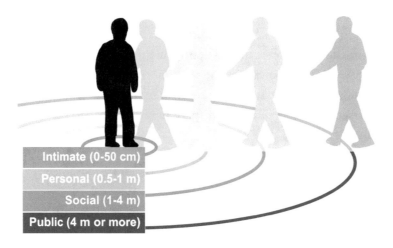

Figure 3.1: Hall's four discrete proxemic zones.

Hall further divides each into a near and far distance and collectively calls them the *dynamic space*. This space characterizes a progression of interactions ranging from highly intimate, to personal, to social, and to public (Hall, 1966). The four zone names are also suggestive of the kinds of relationship people consider within them: intimate distance for intimates (e.g., partners), personal for people who are close (e.g., friends), social for people in a professional relationships (e.g., colleagues), and public for addressing an unfamiliar or unknown group of people (e.g., audience of a talk).

Even though the boundaries of proxemic zones are invisible and often tacit, people's social responses to violations of expected behavior corresponding to each zone are perceived as real and concrete. Even through Hall emphasized distance as the most important factor in regards to proxemic behavior, we also acknowledged the effect of other variables such as orientation (explained shortly). While Hall mostly derives his theory from qualitative observations of human spatial behavior, later empirical studies confirmed the validity of Hall's qualitative ideas (Aiello, 1987).

Figure 3.2: Proxemic distances: (a) intimate, (b) personal, (c) social, (d) public (Source: Hall 1966).

3.3   ENVIRONMENT: FIXED AND SEMI-FIXED FEATURES

Proxemic behavior is not only affected by people's use of the immediate space around them, but also "the organization of space in his houses and building, and ultimately the layout of his towns" (Hall, 1963). In this context, Hall identified two other factors that influence people's use of proxemics (Hall, 1966). *Fixed features* include the immobile properties of the space, such as the layout of buildings and rooms, the walls, doors, and windows. *Semi-fixed features* include the spatial layout of elements in the space that can be moved (like furniture, chairs, or tables).

Hall noticed that the layout of the fixed features as well as the arrangement of elements in the semi-fixed feature space influence our use and perception of personal space. Particular layouts can be *sociofugal* (separating people) *vs. sociopetal* (bringing people together)—where he refers to earlier studies by Osmond (1957). A simple example is how chairs in a living room can be brought together into a sociopetal small circle to encourage intimate chat, or placed opposing each other to enforce a sociofugal dynamic.

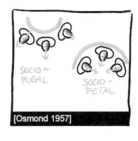

Although others have critiqued Hall's classification of personal space as being overly simple (e.g., commentaries reported in Hall, 1968), his work has become an influential seminal theory of studying personal space and is still being widely applied in psychology and sociology research to study, understand, and consider people's use and perception of personal space (Aiello, 1987; Bell et al., 2005). Since then (and summarized next), other theories added new perspectives that go beyond Hall's original distance-focused view of personal space.

3.4   SIZE AND SHAPE OF INTERPERSONAL DISTANCE ZONES

The exact ranges of interpersonal distance zones (or the single personal space distances) are not static. Even Hall noted that "the measured distances vary somewhat with differences in personality and environmental factors" (Hall, 1966). Later experimental psychological studies observed that the size of the personal space boundaries depends on a variety of factors, and that those are "continually open to modification" (Hayduk, 1985). For example, the following experiments (or surveys of multiple study results) observed changes of the personal space distance depending on the various factors.

- The environment. Factors that impact people's use of proxemics are, for example, room size, spatial layout, and room density (Evans et al., 1996) or the current lighting conditions (e.g., interpersonal closeness caused significantly less discomfort in high illuminated settings than in darker settings) (Adams and Zuckerman, 1991).

- The cultural background. Empirical studies mostly confirmed Hall's qualitative observations that people from contact cultures (Mediterranean and Latin backgrounds) sit and stand closer than people from noncontact Anglo Saxon cultures (Aiello, 1987).

- Gender and age. Studies showed that female pairs often stand closer than male pairs (Price and Dabbs, 1974), and that interpersonal distance increases from childhood age to adults (Aiello and Aiello, 1974).

- Relationship to the people around. Friendship and acquaintanceship decreases interpersonal distance (Sommer, 2002). Personality of people adds an additional effect. For example, people that are extroverted or affiliative tend to work in closer proximity (Gifford, 1997).

Further experimental studies also confirmed that the shape of personal space is not necessarily circular around a person, as it was often described in earlier work. For example, an elliptical shape was suggested, with longer distance at the front and smaller distances at the sides (Petri et al., 1974). This ellipse shape

also appears in other related studies about people's reaction to other people entering their perceived personal space (Adams and Zuckerman, 1991; Duke and Nowicki, 1972). Later, Sommer suggested an hourglass shape for the personal space, with the wider areas in front and back of a person, and narrower sides of the hourglass shape at the side of the person (Sommer, 2002).

3.5   ORIENTATION

Orientation generally describes how people face toward or away from each other, and this too affects proxemic relationships. Orientation, of course, affects people's perception of their surrounding personal space. Sommer (1969) studied people's preference of spatial seating arrangements and relative orientation around a table depending on the task at hand. Depending on the task, the majority of people tended to particular seating positions: face-to-face seating for competitive tasks, side-by-side

for cooperative tasks, and side-by-side or corner-to-corner during conversations. Sommer concludes that spatial arrangements and relative orientation that people choose during small group interactions are "functions of personality, task, and environment." This explains why structuring the semi-fixed feature space can have a "profound effect on behavior and […] this effect is measurable" (Hall, 1966). Others identified related patterns, where people's orientation to one another depends on the type of conversion and the social status of participants (Ciolek, 1983). Overall, these and other study experiments demonstrated the importance of considering orientation (and not just relative distance) when analyzing human interactions in close proximity.

3.6   COMPENSATION, BALANCE, AND PRIVACY

People constantly adjust their use of space to fit the presence of, and interactions with, others. This includes how people react to and try to overcome "invasions" or "violations" of their personal space. Some theories describe people's adaptation to given spatial circumstances, and how they try to maintain a certain comfort level or equilibrium in these situations (Baldassare, 1978). For example, the *intimacy equilibrium model* (Argyle and Dean, 1965) assumes that when people interact they always strive to maintain an overall balance toward a desired optimal proxemic distance. To achieve this balance, people might try to adapt proxemic variables such as distance, orientation, or eye contact, which the model describes as "inverse relationship between mutual gaze, a nonverbal cue signaling intimacy, and interpersonal distance" (Ciolek, 1983). For example, when a person stands too close to us, we might step back to maintain the equilibrium. If any of the variables cannot be changed in this particular situation (such as standing very close to others in an elevator), the change of *another variable* can be used to compensate (in the elevator example: changing orientation to face away while avoiding eye contact). Another predictive model formalizes equilibrium as an optimal proxemic distance, where it adds proxemic variables including identity and familiarity of the other person, and the type of interaction (Sundstrom and Altman, 1976). People also use personal space as a method to protect a certain level of privacy. Altman reframes this use as a dynamic boundary regulation process that controls privacy (Altman, 1975).

3.7   DISCRETE VS. CONTINUOUS DISTANCES

The analytical observations of human spatial relationships do not nec-essarily have to be classified into discrete zones (such as the single zone of personal space, or Hall's four proxemic zones). Aiello did not find ev-idence that people's reactions to changes in spacing/orientation happen at the zonal transition points (Aiello, 1987). This is in line with Knowles, who argues that any discrete category system makes the assumption that people's reactions to distance changes are *not* continuous (Knowles,

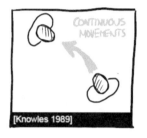

1989). Instead, Aiello suggests that "experiences occur more *gradually* as sensory inputs change from one distance zone to another." For example, the continuous position/orientation adjustments and movements that people do according to the intimacy equilibrium model (Argyle and Dean, 1965) explained earlier fit into this understanding of continuous changes of proxemic variables.

3.8   THE FOCUSED ENCOUNTER: F-FORMATIONS

Distance in and of itself is not a complete description of the social con-nectedness of co-located persons. Whereas Hall's notion of proxemics primarily concerns the impact of *distance* on the perceptions available to the organism—and hence the types of communications afforded—the study of *F-formations* further considers the physical arrangements that people adopt when they engage in focused conversational encounters. Specifically, F-formations (*Face- or Facing-Formations*) are a macro-level

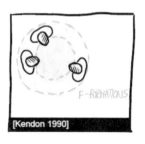

theoretical lens through which one observes small-group interactions (Ciolek and Kendon, 1980; Kendon, 2010, 1990).

F-formations consider the spatial relationships that occur as people arrange themselves during face-to-face interaction for optimal task-dependent communication and clarity of perception. A typical arrangement is a roughly circular cluster that contains 2–5 persons who are actively part of the group (see Figure 3.3 and Figure 3.4). The inner overlapping space of that circle (called *o-space*) is reserved for the main activity the group is pursuing. This inner space is formed by the overlap-

ping area of the transactional segments of each individual person that is part of the formation. These transactional segments are defined as the "space extending in front of a person which is the space he is currently using in whatever his current activity may be" (Kendon, 1990). In many cases this is the area in front of a person's body that can be reached with their hands, but can extend beyond that reach to further distances. The ring of space occupied by the people (*p-space*) determines group membership and it is where people are located. The surrounding region (*r-space*) buffers the group from the outside world. Thus persons who are nearby but not in the p-space are excluded from the fine-grained social circle that defines the F-formation. Still, the group monitors the r-space to see others who may be trying to join.

Figure 3.3: F-formations: (left) circular, (center) corner-to-corner, (right) face-to-face (source: Kendon, 2010).

Kendon describes specific procedures that take place when a person joins an existing F-Formation from within the r-space. For example, an approaching person in r-space may be greeted via eye contact, while a person who is facing away, even if close to the group, is not treated as a potential member.

F-formations are nuanced and not necessarily circular. Different relative body orientations—face-to-face, side-by-side, or corner-to-corner (see Figure 3.3)—afford different types of collaborative tasks: competitive, collaborative, or communicative, respectively (which directly relate to earlier observations by Sommer, 1959). As illustrated in Figure 3.5, further, more fine-grained spatial arrangements in F-formations can be differentiated, and classified into open and closed formations (the letters used to describe these formations are derived from the lines formed by the major box axis connecting the left and right shoulder of a person, and the connection line between the two people—for example, the letter "H" for two people standing face to face). Group size varies, but tends to be small. Freely forming groupings rarely surpass five persons; 95% are four persons or fewer, and more than half are dyadic (Dunbar et al., 1995). Gestures made or objects held within the o-space become the focus of conversation, whereas objects held down (in p-space) or outside the circle (in r-space) are excluded (Ciolek and Kendon, 1980).

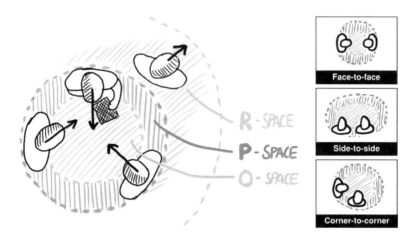

Figure 3.4: An F-formation consists of two or more persons engaged in joint activity. Their bodies define three, roughly circular, regions: the inner o-space, the ring of p-space, and the surrounding r-space (Marquardt et al., 2012b).

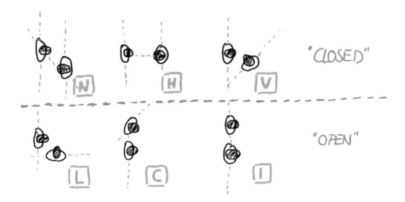

Figure 3.5: Types of F-formations.

Semi-fixed features around a person can also be part of the transactional segment of a person or multiple people. Kendon explains how semi-fixed features of a room (e.g., a TV that a person is looking at) or moveable objects (e.g., a piece of paper the person is writing on) can be the focus point of a transactional segment and influence the structure of

F-formations (Kendon, 2010). In this case, "spatial and postural orientation are […] excellent clues to major junctures in the flow of behavior" (Kendon, 2010).

3.9   PROXEMIC THEORIES AS ANALYTICAL LENSES IN INTERACTION DESIGN

In HCI research, theories of proxemics and F-formations have both been used as lenses to analyze individual or group interactions with interactive technology.

For example, F-formations have been used to analyze social interactions in crowded environments, for example by using the F-formations theory as a conceptual lens for analyzing social interactions of visitors in a tourist information center (Marshall et al., 2011). Later, the theory was also a fundamental part of a method to classify touch-less gestural interactions of medical doctors reviewing patient's digital images during surgeries (Mentis et al., 2012). So far, however, the F-formations theory has only rarely been applied to interaction technique design (Marquardt et al., 2012b, which will be described in Chapter 8).

In the context of interaction design, researchers have taken Hall's proxemic concepts and defined discrete zones around devices with implications of how these zones affect people's interactions. For example, we previously described how Vogel and Balakrishnan (2004) used four distance zones to define the possible interactions around an ambient display. Somewhat similarly, we described how Ju et al. (2008) illustrated how people's presence in four zones affected how an interactive whiteboard application reacted to people's implicit vs. explicit actions.

3.10   SUMMARY

In summary, the reviewed sociological and psychological theories (in particular personal space, proxemics, and F-formations) formalize an important phenomenon of people's everyday interactions: the perception and use of personal space during everyday encounters. They describe how factors such as distance and orientation play an important role in how people mediate their interactions with others, as well as how these factors change over time.

Yet in spite of proxemics being a fundamental part of social behavior, the fine-grained nuances of proxemics are only rarely considered in ubicomp interaction design. A few researchers have taken Hall's proxemic concepts and defined discrete zones around devices with implications of how these zones affect people's interactions (Vogel and Balakrishnan, 2004; Ju et al., 2008). However, only a few recent systems have considered other varied aspects of proxemics (e.g., distance, orientation, motion, continuous vs. discrete zones, fixed and semi-fixed features, etc.) between all entities of the ubicomp ecology: the people, devices, objects, and the surrounding environment.

In the context of ubicomp, the implication is that proximity becomes, in part, an estimation of people's desire to attend and communicate with one another via the devices they carry and—by extension—a desire of one or more people to interact with particular devices that surround them. In the next chapter we discuss how proxemic theories can be operationalized to inform the design of novel techniques for people's co-located interactions with digital devices in ubicomp ecologies.

CHAPTER 4

Operationalizing Proxemics for Ubicomp Interaction

The proxemic theories in Chapter 3 describe many different factors and variables that people use to perceive and adjust their spatial relationships with others. It is important to note that most of these theories describe people's relations to people, and not to devices. People likely make tacit judgements of proxemics based on not only primary factors (e.g., distance), but many others: subtle nuances such as the other person's body language, the social context of the moment, personal emotional state, social relationships, willingness to engage in conversation, and so on.

Even so, we argue that we can use these theories as a first-order approximation to apply proxemics to ubicomp design. That is, we can computationally sense and then exploit a few primary factors related to proxemics. While they won't afford the subtlety of interpersonal communication, we suggest that—in most cases—they will be "close enough" to allow devices in an ecology to express (somewhat) proxemic-aware behaviors and actions, and that people will respond accordingly.

As part of this approximation, we will identify five device-oriented proxemic dimensions—inputs and states that devices can sense and hold about proxemic relationships—which we believe are most relevant to operationalizing proxemics in ubicomp interaction (summarized in Figure 4.1). That is, they describe not only the fine-grained nuances in the relationships between people, but between all entities in ubicomp ecologies: people, digital devices, non-digital objects, and the features of the surrounding environment. We will then describe how these dimensions can be selectively used within a Proxemic Interactions framework.

4.1   PROXEMIC DIMENSIONS

The following five proxemic dimensions are directly derived from the theories we reviewed in Chapter 3. We note that these dimensions are a starting point, where they determine what we consider the foundational information that can be sensed computationally and applied to Proxemic Interactions. We anticipate that other dimensions will be identified in future work that can contribute to the nuances of designing Proxemic Interactions.

Figure 4.1: **Five key proxemic dimensions relevant for ubicomp interaction design** (Marquardt and Greenberg, 2012).

4.1.1   DISTANCE

Distance is a fundamental dimension of describing spatial relationships, where it relates directly to the theories of personal space and proxemics we reviewed earlier. Distance describes the measurable length between entities in the ecology: people, devices, objects, and fixed/semi-fixed features in the environment (Figure 4.2). Distances can be represented in many ways. For example, they can be precise measurements (e.g., 120 centimeters) or crude categorizations (e.g., zone

1). Distance can be described by either absolute positions, or by relative distances between entities.

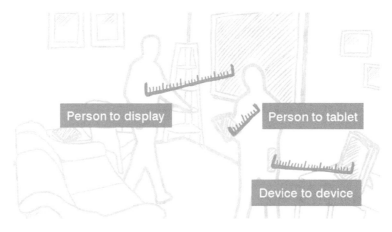

Figure 4.2: Examples of distance relationships in ubicomp ecologies (cf. to Figure 1.1).

Furthermore, distance can be updated at discrete levels or continuously. For example, a designer can consider discrete distance updates at a single threshold when in very close proximity (Figure 4.3a), when person or device enters a distance threshold at a larger distance (Figure 4.3b), or when an entity passes from one zone to another (Figure 4.3c)—such as with Hall's four proxemic zones (Hall, 1966). Alternatively, distance can be updated *continuously* as entities move in space (Aiello, 1987; Knowles, 1989), either as a linear mapping of distance to engagement (Figure 4.3d), or any other mapping such as a logarithmic function (Figure 4.3e). Discrete and continuous distances can also be intermixed, for example, such as defining discrete zones at far distances but shifting to continuous measures when a close threshold has been reached (such as shown in Figure 4.3f and g).

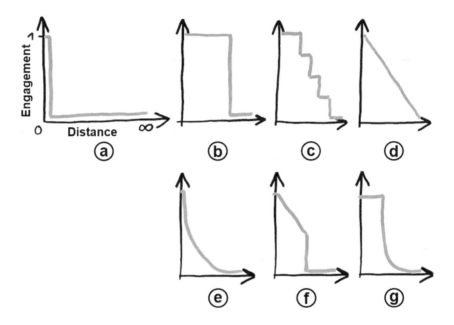

Figure 4.3: Using distance measures to determine a person's level of engagement with a ubicomp system: from discrete to continuous measures.

4.1.2   ORIENTATION

Orientation provides information about which direction an entity is facing. For people, this includes a person's body orientation (Sommer, 1969), but also the orientation of the face and limbs like arms or legs (which can be summarized in a body posture). It can also include the orientation of a person's gaze toward another entity (Argyle and Dean, 1965). For devices or objects, orientation might require a well-defined front (e.g., the front-facing side of a display), and  can also include further, more refined measures of orientation (e.g., the body, face, and gaze orientation of a humanoid robot).

Orientation can be relative between two or more entities, or absolute when relative to a fixed point in the environment. They can be described in both qualitative terms (e.g., "facing toward" or "facing away," Figure 4.4a) and quantitative terms (e.g., the measured angle, Figure 4.4b). Such quantitative descriptions can, for example, be expressed as pitch/roll/yaw angle of one object relative to another.

Given a known quantitative orientation, it is possible to determine where a ray cast from one entity would intersect with another entity (*ray casting*). Ray casting is useful, for example, to determine what a person is pointing at as they stretch out their arm to point at an object in the environment, or even what they are looking at (i.e., the focus of one's gaze) (Figure 4.4c, see arrows).

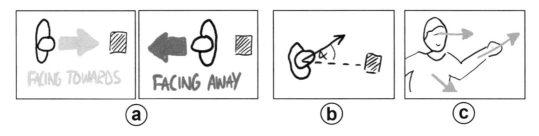

Figure 4.4: Considering orientation: (a) facing direction, (b) exact orientation angles, (c) orientation of a person's body, head, and arms.

4.1.3   MOVEMENT AND MOTION

Measurement of *movements* and *motion* lets us derive and understand the absolute or relative changes of position, orientation, speed (velocity), and acceleration of an entity over time (e.g., a person that is walking toward a device, or a device that is moved closer to another device).

These changes in movements, for example, reveal how a person is approaching a particular device or object, whether the person is speeding up or slowing down, and whether the person is changing directions. Different actions of the system can then be taken depending on (for example) the speed of motion, and/or whether one entity is moving and turning toward vs. away from another entity.

4.1.4   IDENTITY

Identity uniquely describes the entities in the space. The most detailed information provides the exact identity of a person or object (e.g., "Fred," "Person A," "Fred's Cell phone"), as well as data associated with that entity. Other, less detailed forms of identity are possible, such as identifying a category precisely

(e.g., "book," "person"), or roughly ("non-digital object"), or even affiliation to a group (e.g., "family member," "visitor"). Identity information is important to discriminate one entity from another, where the required granularity of identity information depends on the envisioned system functionality. For example, crude identity categories (e.g., "a person") are sufficient if a device is supposed to react to any person approaching it, but unique identification (e.g., a person's name) might be necessary if the device is supposed to display personalized content.

4.1.5   LOCATION

In contrast to the earlier mentioned *distance*, the dimension *location* describes the qualitative and quantitative aspects of the place where the interaction takes place. Location covers both context and physical layout. *Location context* characterizes the setting of the location as a whole (such as home vs. office settings, John's bedroom), and provides meta-information such the social practice and context of use of that space by the entities seen within it (e.g., meeting room  used by the group to coordinate a particular project). *Location layout* describes the configuration of that space and its entities as a whole, such as the physical position of its fixed features (e.g., room layout, walls, entryways), or semi-fixed features (e.g., furniture positions) within it. Both types of location information are important, as the meaning applied to the four other inter-entity measures may depend on the contextual location.

4.2   APPLYING DIMENSIONS TO UBICOMP INTERACTION DESIGN

As part of designing Proxemic Interactions, developers can then use the information provided across these five dimensions to drive possible interactive behaviors of the system. The way this is done defines our Proxemic Interactions framework. Figure 4.5 summarizes the framework, where it demonstrates a possible sequence of using all five dimensions for interaction design.

First, a sensing technology (for example, a tracking system) provides spatial sensing data of tracked entities (Figure 4.5a) in the ubicomp ecology, which is used as *input*. Entities tracked can include people, devices, non-digital artifacts, and other features of the environment (left side of Figure 4.5). Next, the *location* information (Figure 4.5b) provides not only context of the setting (e.g., home vs. office), but also details about semi-fixed features (e.g., the position of a large interactive display hung on the wall) and fixed features (e.g., the doorway into the room, which acts as a boundary). Next, the *identity* information about entities allows the system either to differentiate between people and devices that are present in the ubicomp ecology, or—at a finer granularity—gives unique names of the two people and devices (Figure 4.5c). These two last steps together provide us with a list of all entities currently recognized by the system. Then, a system can determine the relative *distance* between those entities (Figure 4.5d), for example, how close any of the tablet devices are to each person, or the distance between a person and the large screen.

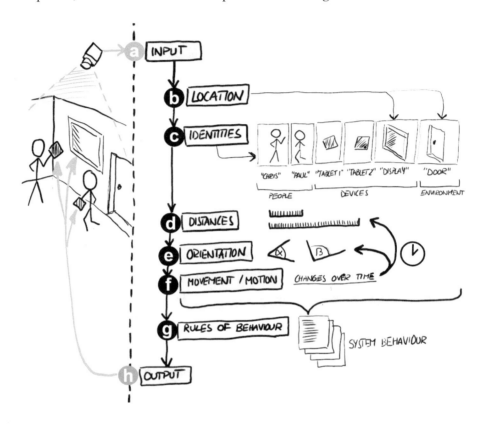

Figure 4.5: Proxemic Interactions framework.

The next step determines *orientation* between entities (Figure 4.5e); for example, if a person is facing toward the display or away from it. By determining changes of these two dimensions over time, we can determine the *movement* and *motion* information (Figure 4.5f). This provides, for instance, information about a person entering through the door and moving quickly toward the display. The information of all the five stages are then interpreted in the next step that defines the *rules of behavior* (Figure 4.5g). These rules define how the system interprets proxemic relationships between entities, and how they are translated into system actions (i.e., the reactive behavior). Depending on these rules, the system then triggers appropriate *output* actions, e.g., changing the content displayed on any of the tablets or the large interactive screen (Figure 4.5h).

Figure 4.5 illustrates a complete use of the framework. It combines all proxemic dimensions (including fine-grained changes in those dimensions as tracked over time), with a rich set of rules of behaviors to drive nuanced output. Of course, much simpler uses of the framework are possible.

For example, consider how the common hand-activated bathroom tap is viewed by the framework. Tracking is done via a range sensor that senses an object within a given range, and only a single rule of behavior is triggered (turn on tap for a limited amount of time). All other dimensions are ignored.

4.3   CONCLUSION

This chapter explained the operationalization of proxemics for ubicomp interaction design in the form of the Proxemic Interactions framework. The framework helps inform ubicomp designers about important proxemic dimensions that they can consider and apply to the design of proxemic-aware devices. In particular, we believe that knowledge of the five proxemic dimensions (distance, orientation, movement, identity, and location) can be applied broadly to ubicomp interaction. Thus our intention is to open up a new perspective onto how proxemics can be considered when designing new ubicomp systems that react seamlessly and appropriately to people's expectations.

The next chapter will explain how we can consider information in each of the five dimensions to address known ubicomp design challenges. We will also provide examples of the potential rules of behavior interpreting proxemic input. Part II of this book will then explain how to use the Proxemic Interaction framework and its five dimensions in the design of proxemic-aware systems.

CHAPTER 5

Exploiting Proxemics to Address Challenges in Ubicomp Ecologies

Other ubicomp systems have exploited a subset of the five dimensions of Proxemic Interactions we introduced in Chapter 4. Yet very few make use of all of them, let alone consider them as characterizing the interplay between entities in a ubicomp ecology. In this chapter, we describe six known ubicomp interaction design challenges. We use related work and our own applications (discussed later in this book) to detail how particular systems have used aspects of these five dimensions to address these challenges. We categorize these possible interactions into a series of Proxemic Interactions themes as part of each of the six design challenges (see also Marquardt and Greenberg, 2012).

In Section 5.1 we describe the six ubicomp interaction challenges. Next, we show the potential of using Proxemic Interactions to address these key design challenges: revealing interaction possibilities (Section 5.2), directing actions (Section 5.3), establishing connections (Section 5.4), providing feedback (Section 5.5), preventing and correcting mistakes (Section 5.6), and managing privacy and security (Section 5.7). We relate both the theory and dimensions (described in Chapter 3 and 4) to the design challenges, and situate a sampling of prior systems summarized in Chapter 2 within that setting. Finally, in Section 5.8 we discuss the use of the interaction themes and conclude.

5.1 UBICOMP INTERACTION DESIGN CHALLENGES

Designing ubicomp applications (such as those reviewed in Chapter 2) that seamlessly fit into people's environments and social practices remains a difficult task for developers. From an end user's perspective, we identify six core challenges related to designing embodied and seamless ubicomp interactions, inspired by Bellotti et al.'s (2002) design considerations for sensing systems and augmented by other analytical and reflective ubicomp discussions (e.g., Bardram and Friday, 2010; Dey, 2010). While this selection does not cover all ubicomp design challenges (e.g., scalability, graceful degradation, evaluations, see: Abowd and Mynatt, 2000; Leahu et al., 2008), we focus in particular on the ones with the highest relevance to Proxemic Interactions.

Challenge 1: Revealing interaction possibilities
Norman (1988) appropriated Gibson's (1977) notion of *affordances* to describe how an object's visuals can "suggest" how it might be used. Traditional GUIs exploited visual affordances to design interface elements that suggested their use and possible actions; they worked, because they could

assume that they were in the foreground of a user's attention, i.e., the person was watching the screen. Yet this cannot be directly applied to ubicomp, as ubicomp assumes that technology can be integrated into the everyday environment in a way that it "disappears," or is present in the just-perceptible periphery of our attention, and that it is able to fluently move in and out of the center of our attention as needed (Bardram and Friday, 2010; Buxton, 1995; Cooperstock et al., 1997; Weiser, 1991). This introduces the challenge: how can technology be designed to reveal the interaction possibilities appropriate when it is not only in the background of a person's attention, but during the transition of it moving into the foreground?

Challenge 2: Directing actions

Input to a single traditional device is straightforward, as it usually comes through a dedicated input device (e.g., a mouse, keyboard, touch surface). Yet ubicomp can be different. Input may be detached from a particular device. Possible actions can be performed through speech, gestures, eye gaze, and other alternative options. One problem is that the device has to somehow discern whether that action is actually a directive to the system, or whether it should be ignored because it is just part of a person's everyday actions (e.g., a voice command vs. social talk; a command gesture vs. a gesture or movement made in the course of doing other things) (Bellotti et al., 2002; Dey, 2010; Ju et al., 2008). The problem of directing the actions to a particular device is even more problematic when there are large quantities of devices present in the local ecology, for the system has to discern which device (or set of devices) should respond to a person's directed action.

Challenge 3: Establishing connections

Device connectivity is a significant challenge in ubicomp. Technical issues aside, the ad-hoc nature of ubiquitous computing means that people need to somehow control (albeit seamlessly) how one device connects to another device in a way that reflects their interaction needs while still safeguarding privacy and security. Within this context, Bardram and Friday (2010) give an example of transferring digital content from a personal smartphone to a large public screen. This challenge is compounded by the potential and perhaps unpredictable interplay between a large number of digital devices. Some may be personal (a smart phone), others may belong to the inhabitants of a space (a home's picture frame), and others may be public (e.g., a public wall display). Their form factor also affects their mobility, which in turn can suggest different factors affecting how they should establish connections.

Challenge 4: Providing feedback

Appropriate feedback is a mainstay of traditional GUI interaction design. Yet as ubicomp interfaces move away from the traditional desktop computer setting, it becomes even more important to provide feedback about the current status of the application, its interpretation of user input, or the occurrence of errors (Abowd et al., 2002; Bellotti et al., 2002; Dey, 2010; Ju et al., 2008). To complicate matters, ubicomp systems have to consider that people's attention in regards to the ubicomp technology might switch between foreground and background.

Challenge 5: Avoiding and correcting mistakes

When mistakes or errors happen, the system should provide options for a person to correct these mistakes (Bellotti et al., 2002; Ju et al., 2008). As many ubicomp systems use some kind of sensing technology to monitor people's actions, such errors and misinterpretation of sensor data are even more likely to occur in ubicomp settings than with traditional computers.

Challenge 6: Managing privacy and security

A large issue in ubicomp is that as the number of potential interactions with technology increase, so too do the risks to privacy and the need for greater security (Langheinrich, 2010). The question is how can the system protect privacy sensitive information and handle the access to information, while at the same time not get in the way of all the positive offerings of ubicomp mentioned in Challenges 1–5?

We now revisit each of these design challenges, where we speculate—with examples drawn from the literature reviewed in Chapter 2 and that foreshadow our own systems to be described in later chapters—how knowledge of proxemics as gathered by the 5 dimensions described in Chapter 3 can mitigate problems inherent in each challenge. These examples are merely a starting point, where their contributions are re-framed within each challenge, and where they hint at the potential of future Proxemic Interactions designs (such as those to be discussed in Part II).

5.2 REVISITING CHALLENGE 1: REVEALING INTERACTION POSSIBILITIES

To address this challenge, a system must offer possible actions (Ju et al., 2008) that afford *seamless transitions* from background to foreground interaction (Buxton, 1995). This concept is somewhat similar to how people approaching each other exchange greetings and begin communicating through various signals (eye gaze, body language, and talk), where signals and possible actions vary appropriately across this greeting phase (Kendon, 1990). Similarly, ubicomp should "greet" other entities by revealing interaction possibilities that match what is possible at the moment. Several strategies to accomplish this are described below.

5.2.1 REACTING TO THE PRESENCE AND APPROACH OF PEOPLE

At the most basic level, if a system can sense the presence and approach of people, it can use that information to reveal possible interactions.

Various prior systems do this, but only as a binary measure: if it detects a person it marks them as "present," otherwise "absent." In response to this binary measure, systems would trigger an appropriate action. Buxton (1995) describes the example of smart light switches that used motion detectors to infer presence and then turn lights on and off in response. Greenberg et al. (2011) brings up the example of a desktop computer screen that uses a proximity sensor to capture a person's distance from the display, where that information is used to either activate the screen (if the person is close) or deactivate it into a power-save mode (if the person is far or no longer detected). Both systems "reveal" interaction possibilities implicitly as the person approaches: the first by illuminating the room, and the second by seeing the desktop computer turn on and is thus ready to go.

Other systems detect and use presence information to explicitly reveal interaction possibilities. Consider *ActiveBadges*—identity tags worn by individuals—where the badge (and thus a particular person's) location is tracked at a room-level within a building (Want et al., 1992). Its inventors exploited this presence and identity information to offer personalized computing services at that person's current location, e.g., where their desktop computer display would "follow" them to other rooms and appear on nearby screens. Similarly, the EasyLiving system (Brumitt et al., 2000a, 2000b) selects custom media content when sensing the presence of a person in a particular room at home. Another popular example is a large screen that senses when a person enters a room, where the display not only turns on, but also tailors its contents to suggest its offerings (Vogel and Balakrishnan, 2004). In our media player example (introduced in Chapter 6), for example, when a person crosses a threshold into a room, a splash screen appears revealing that the large display is a media player, and then offers several videos the person could select for watching. The system intentionally displays only a small number of videos using large graphics, to make it appropriate for viewing at a distance. If one person seated on a couch is already viewing a video while another person enters, the system displays its information differently, where it reveals what is being viewed with minimal disruption to the primary viewer. In terms of our dimensions, this media player exploits both relative distance and identity to reveal appropriate interaction possibilities compared to just a binary notion of presence, i.e., it considers the room as an ecology. It uses people's *approach* across a threshold (the doorway), their *distance from the screen*, and their *presence relative to other fixed features* in the room (e.g., the couch).

5.2.2   TRANSITION FROM AWARENESS TO INTERACTION

In real life, people exploit proxemic cues as they greet and engage in social interaction. One may have peripheral awareness of the other while at a distance, become increasingly aware and engaged as the other turns toward and approaches them, and then begin to interact when within an appropriate proxemic region. Some public ambient displays apply a similar mechanism to engage people, where they trigger actions to attract a passerby's attention, and progressively show more information and interaction possibilities as the person approaches and attends the display, ideally leading to foreground interaction by direct touch (Prante et al., 2003; Vogel and Balakrishnan, 2004). The idea is that the passerby notices the public display as it *implicitly* reacts to their presence, where it captures their attention and interest (as discussed in Challenge 1). Their attention is realized by moving closer and facing the display; the system also detects and reacts to that interest (Vogel and Balakrishnan, 2004). In our media player (Chapter 6), for example, the number of videos, their size and associated text is adjusted as the person approaches the display, where it reveals more video selections and more information about those videos. A system such as this exploits distance, orientation and movement to infer a person passing by at a *larger distance*, then *turning toward* the display, then *approaching*, and finally standing directly *in front* of it.

5.2.3   SPATIAL VISUALIZATIONS OF UBICOMP ENVIRONMENTS

In the physical world, we often know what is available simply by looking around. To make this work in ubicomp, we need to explicitly visualize otherwise hidden offerings on a device's screen(s), such as when one device is within range of another, its relative position, and what can subsequently be done between them. For example, Relate Gateways (Gellersen et al., 2009) places icons at the devices' screen border to represent the type and position of surrounding devices relative to that device's position. Our own cross-device techniques, to be introduced in Chapter 7, also visualize spatial relationships to nearby personal devices: if a person points their device toward the large screen, a graphic appears as a ray-cast "projection" moving on that screen, which in turn indicates the device's position and orientation. As the mobile device approaches and is oriented toward the large display, increasing detail about that device, its contents, and its interaction possibilities are revealed. This possible reveal of information can, however, differ depending on the context of use and the fact of whether other devices are seen as public or semi-public vs. personal ones.

5.3   REVISITING CHALLENGE 2: DIRECTING ACTIONS

While Challenge 1 concerns how a ubicomp system can reveal interaction possibilities to a person, Challenge 2 addresses how a person can *direct* their input actions to a particular device.

5.3.1   DISCRETE DISTANCE ZONES FOR INTERACTION

Similar to how people tend to move closer to others when interacting (e.g., to begin a conversation), systems might accept user input only when the person is a certain distance relative to the device. Thus, to address a particular system, a person may have to approach and move closer to it. Some ambient display systems do this by realizing Hall's discrete proxemic zones as thresholds that adjust interaction possibilities according to which zone a person is in. Hello.Wall (Prante et al., 2003) introduced the notion of *distance-dependent semantics*, where the distance of an individual from the wall defined the kinds of interactions possible. While information on the large display can be seen from afar (Challenge 1), a person had to move closer to actually interact with it (e.g., to transfer information from a mobile device). Vogel and Balakrishnan (2004) extended this concept, where they defined four proxemic zones of interaction around the large display (see video: ambient display). From far to close, these ranged from ambient display, to implicit, then subtle, and finally to personal interaction with the interactive calendar application. Each of these zones allowed particular kinds of interaction with the display's contents. Similarly, Ju et al. (2008) also defined four zones around an interactive whiteboard, where she allows certain actions only when a person is standing close to it. Our media player (Chapter 6) shows yet another promising approach, where each interaction zone explicitly supports *different input modalities* that are appropriate to the person's distance from the display. When afar, people interact via pointing (ray casting), and by direct touch when in close distance. Our cross-device interaction techniques (Chapter 7) include similar capabilities, except that one points and touches with the mobile device.

5.3.2   CONSIDERING ATTENTION AND ORIENTATION

Instead of relying on only distance, the system can use other measures to infer a person's attention to it. This is the premise of *attentive user interfaces* (AUIs) that are designed to "support users' attentional capacities" (Vertegaal and Shell, 2008). In one class of AUIs, the system reaction depends on whether a person is directing his or her attention to the device as detecting eye gaze (Vertegaal and Shell, 2008), which in turn can be considered a very fine-grained measure of orientation. Our media player (Chapter 6) also exploits orientation as a measure of attention. When a person turns away from the video screen (e.g., to read a magazine or talk to another person), the system pauses video playback, and resumes when they turn back toward it. Wang's Proxemic Presenter (Section 6.10.1) is a slide presentation system that also uses the presenter's orientation as an indication of attention (Greenberg et. al, 2011). If the presenter is facing toward the audience and away from the large display, a standard slide deck is shown. However, when the presenter turns toward the display, small navigation controls and speaking notes become visible at the side of the screen closest to the presenter.

5.3.3   CONSIDERING LOCATION FEATURES

Ubicomp systems are often embedded in people's everyday environments, surrounded by other physical objects and social meanings that comprise the ecology of that place. Inspired by research in context- and location-awareness (Schilit et al., 1994), our next concept emphasizes the importance of interpreting the physical setting where an interaction takes place (Dourish, 2001a). In particular, people's relationships to fixed and semi-fixed features (as defined by Hall, 1966) can be indicators for directing actions to a particular ubicomp system. In Brumitt et al.'s (2000a) EasyLiving project, the geometric relationship of people to semi-fixed features (e.g., a couch) is considered to determine which screen is activated to display information to a person. Similarly, in our media player (Chapter 6), the ubicomp system not only monitors a person's proxemic relationship toward a device, but also to that person's distance to other fixed and semi-fixed features in the ecology. If a person selects a video and then sits on the couch, that is interpreted as an indicator that she is ready to watch the currently selected video and thus video playback begin. However, if the person instead moves to the doorway, that is interpreted as an indicator that she is no longer interested, and the system shuts down. In both cases, the distance from the person to the screen is the same, but her physical location in the room's ecology is different. These examples are a starting point of how to consider people's relationships to fixed and semi-fixed features in the environment.

5.3.4   CONSIDERING MOTION TRAJECTORIES

Going straight toward another person—or instead quickly passing by—are also proxemic cues that we implicitly interpret in everyday interactions with others. Similarly, ubicomp systems can interpret people's and device's motions for directing actions. For example, Vogel and Balakrishnan's (2004) ambient display ignores people quickly passing by, but reacts to (and gathers input) from people walking straight toward it (see video: ambient display). Motion cues can be quite fine-grained, where it can exploit distance, orientation and velocity as well as how each changes over time.

5.3.5   ADAPT TO NUMBER OF NEARBY DEVICES

A system's interpretation of a person's actions can also depend on the number of other nearby devices that it can sense. To illustrate, a user of Swindells et al.'s (2002) gesturePen triggers interaction between two devices by pointing his device to the chosen one. We can extend this to help one choose between a large number of devices by applying distance- or identity-based filtering techniques to limit the number of possible pointing targets, e.g., the system could require the person to move closer to their target up to the point where it can discriminate the desired one. For example, Ledo (2014) describes a proxemic-based hand-held remote control that shows a spatial overview of all appliances present in a living room. State information describing each appliance appears on the remote control as the contol is oriented toward the appliance. That appliance is implicitly selected to afford further interaction as the person moves toward it.

5.4   REVISITING CHALLENGE 3: ESTABLISHING CONNECTIONS BETWEEN DEVICES

As suggested by our last example, people need to somehow control how one device connects to another device within a potentially large ecology of devices in a way that seamlessly supports their interaction needs, while still safeguarding privacy and maintaining security. We do this naturally—the way we greet and move closer to one another via proxemics is essentially a negotiation to establish connections for communication.

5.4.1 CONNECTION AS A CONSEQUENCE OF CLOSE PROXIMITY

We can exploit distance, identity, and even orientation to determine proxemic relationships between devices, and then establish connections between only those that are in close proximity. As opposed to directly connecting two devices with a cable, such wireless connections facilitate the spontaneous and lightweight transfer of information. Existing systems now do this, although most do so as a binary function (e.g., close = connected). Rekimoto et al.'s (2003) combination of near-field RFID communication and wireless networks allows inter-device communication only when two mobile devices are in close proximity. Alternately, physically bumping two devices together can activate a connection: the accelerometer signal produced by bumping identifies the devices (Hinckley, 2003), and bumping can only occur as a consequence of direct touch. Another strategy exploits people's proximity to one another, where they communicate to synchronize an act that establishes the connection. One example is both people simultaneously shaking their handheld device to explicitly signal that they should be connected (Holmquist et al., 2001). Similarly, an explicit *stitching gesture* can be used, where one person starts a gesture on one device, which is then continued on the other. This can only be done if the devices are nearby (Ramos et al., 2009).

5.4.2 PROGRESSIVE CONNECTION PROCESS

While the above systems are binary in nature, progressive connection processes are also possible. Kray et al.'s (2008) *group coordination negotiation* introduced spatial regions around mobile phones to establish and break device connections or initiate data transfer. As a device moves across three discrete regions, a preview of a media transfer is first display, where transfer begins only after moving into a closer region. Our own cross-device interaction techniques (Chapter 7) are somewhat similar, but it uses a continuous rather than discrete progression over distance. In our system, when a person holds a handheld media player in her hand, a subtle notification appears on a nearby large screen to indicate the connection possibility. As he moves closer to the screen, he sees the two devices connect, where the large display progressively reveals more information about the handheld's video content as icons. As the two devices move within touch distance, a touch interface appears that allows the person to transfer digital media either through pick and drop (Rekimoto 1997) or by touching the handheld to one of the icons revealed on the large display.

5.5 REVISITING CHALLENGE 4: PROVIDING FEEDBACK

Next, we discuss how to leverage proxemics for providing continuous feedback about a system's status or any errors that occur.

5.5.1   ADJUSTING FEEDBACK OUTPUT

Due to the embedded nature of many ubicomp systems, there is often no graphical display for showing feedback to the user. Instead, output can be via visual lights, audible sounds, speech, or physically moving objects (like in many tangible user interfaces). Assuming a system knows the physical orientation and distance of a person, it can provide feedback by adjusting its output to the person that it is addressing. The Listen Reader (Back et al., 2001), for example, adjusts the volume of the audio output depending on a person's proximity to a digitally augmented book. Similarly, in our media player (Chapter 6) a person sees large preview thumbnails of available videos when at a distance. The screen continuously shows more content as the person moves closer (and thus, the person can read more information).

5.5.2   SELECTING APPROPRIATE FEEDBACK MODALITY

Furthermore a system can select the most appropriate output modality to a person (e.g., visual vs. audible) based on their proxemic relationship. For example, when the person is facing away from a large screen, the system might use an audible signal as a notification. When the person is standing closer to the system facing the screen, visual output may be used instead.

5.5.3   PROXEMIC-DEPENDENT REVEAL OF FEEDBACK

Details presented to a person can vary depending on the distance and/or orientation of the person relative to the system. He (2010), for example, introduced distance-dependent semantic zoom in an augmented reality energy viewer for the home. The feedback of energy use is adjusted based upon the viewer's proximity to rooms or appliances within a room (distance and orientation are detected through fiduciary tags). When holding the viewer outside a room's doorway, the energy use of that room as a whole is displayed. When the person moves into the room, the energy use of each appliance is seen as a colored glow around it. As the viewer moves closer to a particular appliance, details of that usage appear first as a text overlay and then as a graph.

5.6   REVISITING CHALLENGE 5: PREVENTING AND CORRECTING MISTAKES

Our next design challenge addresses the question of how a person can correct errors, such as those that result from the system misinterpretation a person's action, or by the person performing an unintended action.

5.6.1   INVERTING ACTIONS

One technique allowing a person to correct a mistake (and thus undo a system's action) is by performing the *inverse/opposite* action. The system implicitly responds by reverting to the prior state.

For example, in Vogel and Balakrishnan's (2004) ambient display setting, when a person moves closer to the screen, personal calendar information is revealed (see video: ambient display). If the person didn't want this information made public, he just steps back (and thus performs the opposite action): the personal information disappears immediately. Other proxemic dimensions can be exploited as well. For example, an action triggered by the person facing a screen can be stopped (or reverted) simply by turning away.

5.6.2 EXPLICIT ACTION TO UNDO

Ju et al. (2008) present an opposing explicit strategy to undo actions. Her application runs on the interactive whiteboard, where it implicitly responds to people's actions. This can easily result in an unwanted action (in her example: automatically moving a cluster of ink strokes to the side of the display to free up space). To correct this, the person moves closer to the screen (instead of stepping back, like in Vogel and Balakrishnan's system) and grabs the cluster of ink strokes to keep it from moving. That is, it implements an easy manual override where the person can interrupt the undesired action.

Of course, both the above techniques can be combined to override the system. In fact, Vogel and Balakrishnan (2004) used both in their system: a person can either use a set of simple hand gestures to trigger or stop certain system functions, or just step back from the screen to have the same effect.

5.6.3 PROXEMIC SAFEGUARDS

As a safeguard mechanism, actions with a high impact (e.g., deleting information, or resetting the system) could be restricted to occur only when a person is in very close proximity to a device. For example, while a person can manipulate information on an interactive whiteboard from a large distance by using remote gestures, she would have to move directly in front of the screen to delete data by (for example) direct touch. Alternatively, such actions with high impact could even require a certain proxemic relationship in *multiple* dimensions. For example, the delete action could require a person to stand in close proximity to the screen *and* be oriented toward it *and* look at the screen simultaneously. The action could also be tentative and undoable as the person remains close by, where the person then has to manually commit the changes that otherwise would be reset as they move away.

5.7 REVISITING CHALLENGE 6: MANAGING PRIVACY AND SECURITY

Managing privacy and security in ubicomp systems is difficult (Langheinrich, 2010). We review several proximity-based techniques that can mitigate some of this difficulty.

5.7.1   PROXIMITY-DEPENDENT AUTHENTICATION

Access to ubicomp systems can be granted depending on the sensed proximity of people, devices, or other objects. Bardram (2005) discussed proximity-based user authentication allowing access to computers when approached by a person. The system is implemented through authentication tokens (e.g., pens) that wirelessly authorize the access of a person once in close proximity to the computer (i.e., the person stands in front of it). The *tangible security* (Chen and Sinclair, 2008) approach uses the measured proximity between pairs of tokens to authenticate access. For example, a person obtains access to a cell phone only as long as the physical *security token* he carries remains in close proximity. If the phone is lost, strangers cannot access its contents as they do not have the security token. Mayrhofer et al. (2007) took this concept further, where his system leverages the shared knowledge (between the person and device) about spatial references to other devices in close proximity to authorize access. Furthermore, Rekimoto et al. (2003) combine near-field sensing techniques (such as RFID or Infrared) with wireless network communication to seamlessly establish device-to-device connections. Near-field communication initiates the wireless communication channel. That is, a person must not only bring his device close to the other device, but also make sure they are in line of sight before the connection is established.

5.7.2   DISTANCE-DEPENDENT INFORMATION DISCLOSURE

Another strategy uses distance between entities to determine the amount of information that is shared between them. This approach suggests that "distance implies distrust" (Fishkin et al., 2005), and vice versa: *closer proximity implies trust*. For example, the *distance-dependent disclosure RFID tags* (Marquardt et al., 2010) vary information transmitted between the tag and the reader depending on the distance between them. The closer the tag is to the reader, the more information is revealed. Similarly, Vogel and Balakrishnan's (2004) public calendar reveals a person's personal calendar information only when the person is very close to the display. The information disappears immediately once the person steps back away from the display (see video: ambient display).

5.7.3   PROXEMIC-AWARE PRIVACY MECHANISMS

While these approaches consider *distance* as a factor affecting access, the techniques could be further refined by considering other proxemic dimensions such as *orientation*, *identity*, or *location*. A person's body, face, or gaze orientation can affect the amount of information shared. For example, privacy-sensitive information shown on the display of a proxemic-aware mobile device could be visible as long as the person is looking at the screen, but hidden once looking away. Alternatively, the information might disappear once the system notices *another person* looking at the display. By considering the *identity* dimension, a system would be able to use relaxed privacy and security settings when a person is alone, but switch to more restrictive privacy and security settings when it detects any other people or devices around them (e.g., in a crowded setting). Brudy et. al.

(2014), for example, senses when a passerby is shoulder-surfing a user of a public display, where it selectively masks the information the shoulder-surfer would otherwise see (see Section 6.10.8 and video: shoulder surfing protection). By considering *location*, a mobile ubicomp device could adjust its security setting depending on the type of environment, using higher-level settings in an open office (where strangers may come by and try to access the device), but lower security level when at home (which is usually a much more trusted setting).

5.7.4   CONSIDERING PEOPLE'S EXPECTATIONS OF PERSONAL SPACE

Altman (1975) developed a theory that considers personal space as a protection mechanism for maintaining a certain level of privacy. This could be leveraged to design systems that respect people's expectations of personal space. That is, the ubicomp system can influence the simultaneous interaction of multiple people in a way that maintains such levels of privacy for everyone involved. To illustrate, let us revisit Vogel and Balakrishnan's (2004) public ambient display (see video: ambient display). When people move closer to the display, they get more details about their own personal calendar visible on the screen. Thus, people stand next to each other viewing their personal calendars. When considering Altman's theory of balancing privacy through proxemics, the system could be designed to *separate* the large screen interaction areas of the two people. For instance, the areas for viewing personal calendars could be displayed where it depends upon a minimum distance between those people. Brudy et. al. (2014) protects against shoulder-surfing by reflecting the position and orientation of a passerby on the public display (see Section 6.10.8 and video: shoulder surfing protection). The user of that display is thus aware that a passerby is shoulder-surfing. Similarly, the passerby (by seeing his reflection on the display) knows that the user is aware of his presence. In both cases, social protocol kicks in to mediate privacy.

5.8   DISCUSSION AND CONCLUSION

Overall, we concentrated on a few interaction techniques, along with example systems, to illustrate how six ubicomp interaction design challenges can be addressed by leveraging the five proxemic dimensions identified earlier. These techniques and examples are not meant to be a complete review, nor a catalog of solutions. Rather, they were chosen to inspire further ubicomp interaction designs that meet these (and perhaps other) challenges.

We also recognize that a single technique can serve different purposes across these challenges. For example, the idea of progressive reveal of information as a person approaches a display reveals interaction possibilities (Challenge 1), affords actions being directed to it (Challenge 2), is used to establish a connection (Challenge 3), provides feedback that it is responding to the person (Challenge 4), can be used to prevent and correct mistakes by inverting actions (Challenge 5), and helps people manage privacy and security simply by moving to adjust what information is visible

(Challenge 6). We believe this to be one of the strengths of Proxemic Interactions: if techniques are developed with social expectations of proxemics in mind, they can likely be applied as a universal way to mediate many challenges in ubicomp.

PART   II

Exploiting Proxemics in Ubicomp Ecologies

In this second part of this book we explore the potential of considering proxemics for interaction design in small space ubicomp ecologies. The three chapters illustrate the application of the Proxemic Interactions framework and its five dimensions (Chapter 4) for the design of novel interactions in *ubiquitous computing ecologies*. That is, in these chapters we introduce novel interaction techniques that take into account the proxemic relationships between the different entities in ubicomp ecologies—the people, devices, objects, and the environment—to mediate people's interaction with digital devices.

CHAPTER 6

Person/People-to-Device Proxemic Interactions

In this chapter, we focus on Proxemic Interactions of one person or multiple people with a large interactive display situated in a ubicomp ecology. We introduce a set of novel interaction techniques for people's interaction with large interactive screens. For the design of these techniques we consider relationships of different aspects of a small space ubicomp ecology: the relationships of a single person to a device, of multiple people to a device, and of non-digital objects to people and devices. In particular, we exploit the knowledge of distance, orientation, location, movement, and identity as part of the introduced dimensions of Proxemic Interactions (Chapter 4) to drive the possible interactions.

The remainder of the chapter is structured as follows. First, we introduce a scenario of people using a proxemic media player, an application we use as a running example throughout this chapter to explain the different interaction concepts (Section 6.1, see video: proxemic media player). This example ubicomp application reacts to nearby people and their relationship to devices, objects, and the environment. The remaining sections elaborate on general Proxemic Interactions design concepts, where the proxemic media player design serves as an example. We introduce novel interaction concepts incorporating the knowledge of the fixed and semi-fixed feature space (Section 6.2), interpret a person's directed attention extending attentive user interfaces (Section 6.3), and support fine-grained explicit interactions (Section 6.4). We then demonstrate how proxemic information can regulate interaction based either on continuous movement or by movement in and out of discrete proxemic zones (Section 6.5). In Section 6.6, we introduce the important gradual engagement design pattern, and then describe how we can apply the stages of the gradual engagement pattern to the interaction with the media player (Section 6.7). Next, we detail how the system can consider people's identity (Section 6.8). Finally, we explain how the techniques extend beyond pairwise interaction (Section 6.9).

The proxemic media player was co-developed by the authors and Till Ballendat (Ballendat et al., 2010; Greenberg et al., 2011; Ballendat, 2011). The proxemic media player and other applications described in this chapter are built atop the proxemic toolkit (Marquardt et al., 2011): software that senses spatial attributes and proxemic relationships and makes them available to a programmer (see video: proximity toolkit). The Proximity Toolkit was summarized in Section 2.5.3.

6.1   SCENARIO: THE PROXEMIC MEDIA PLAYER APPLICATION

Throughout this chapter, we use the example of people interacting with a home media player application located in a living room. Later sections, which present concepts for designing Proxemic Interactions, will use episodes from this scenario to anchor the discussion. We recommend viewing a video that shows the media player application and the interaction techniques in action, as it will make the dynamics of people to device interaction readily apparent (see video: proxemic media player).

The scenario follows Fred, who is approaching the display from a distance. We explain how the system supports Fred's implicit and explicit interaction with the digital surface as a function of his identity and his distance and orientation relative to the surface and to other features in the room. We also explain how the system responds to other proxemic dimensions such as other objects and other people in that space.

The primary interface of the interactive media player application supports browsing, selection, and playback of videos on a large wall-mounted digital surface: a 52-inch touch-sensitive SmartBoard from Smart Technologies, Inc. (Figure 6.1 top left). As summarized in Section 2.5.3, the Proximity Toolkit software tracks (via the VICON plugin and using reflective infrared markers) the position and orientation of nearby people, objects, and other digital devices (see video: proximity toolkit). All equipment is situated in a room that resembles a domestic living room.

Figure 6.1 (top) shows Fred approaching the display at four distances (a'–d'), while the four scenes below show what Fred would see at those distances. Initially, the proxemic media player is "asleep" as the room is empty. When Fred enters the room at position a' in Figure 6.1, the media player recognizes Fred and where he is standing. It activates the display, shows a short animation to indicate it is activated, and then displays four large video preview thumbnails held in Fred's media collection (Figure 6.1a). As Fred moves closer to the display at b', the video preview thumbnails and titles shrink continuously to a smaller size, thus showing an increasing number of available videos (Figure 6.1b). When Fred is very close to the surface at c', he can select a video directly by touching its thumbnail on the screen. More detailed information about the selected video is then shown on the display (Figure 6.1c), which includes a preview playback that can be played and paused (Figure 6.1c, top left), as well as its title, authors, description, and release date (Figure 6.1c, top right). When Fred moves away from the screen to sit on the couch located at d', his currently selected video track starts playing in full screen view (Figure 6.1d). If Fred had previously seen part of this video, the playback is resumed at Fred's last viewing position, otherwise it starts from the beginning.

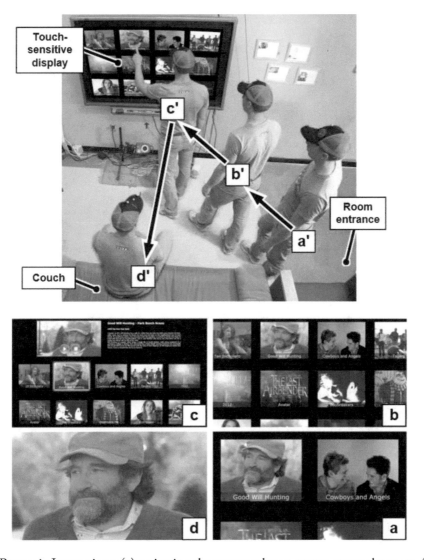

Figure 6.1: Proxemic Interactions: (a) activating the system when a person enters the room, (b) continuously revealing more content as the distance of the person to the display decreases, (c) allowing explicit interaction through direct touch when person is in close proximity, and (d) implicitly switching to full screen view when the person takes a seat (Ballendat et al. 2010).

Fred tires of this video, and decides to select a second video from the collection. He pulls out his mobile phone and points it toward the screen (Figure 6.2a). From its position and orientation, the system recognizes the phone as a pointer, and a row of preview videos appears at the bottom of the screen. A visual pointer on the screen provides feedback of the exact pointing position of Fred's phone relative to the screen. Fred then selects the desired videos by flicking the hand downward, and the video starts playing. Alternately, Fred could have used a non-digital pen to do the same interaction (Figure 6.2b).

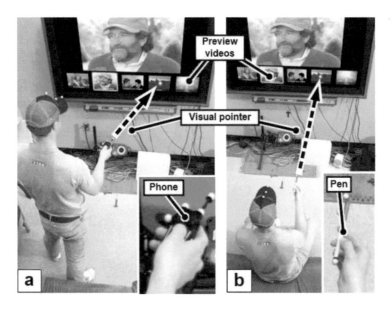

Figure 6.2: Explicit interaction triggered through distance and orientation between a person and physical artifacts: (a) cell phone, (b) pen (Ballendat et al., 2010).

Somewhat later, Fred receives a phone call. The video playback automatically pauses when he answers the phone (Figure 6.3a), but resumes playback after he finishes the call. Similarly, if Fred turns away from the screen to, for example, read a magazine, the video pauses, but then continues when Fred looks back at the screen (Figure 6.3b).

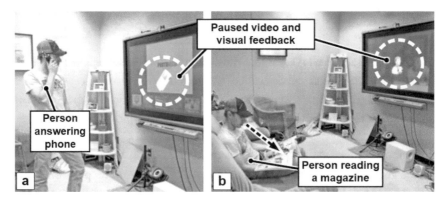

Figure 6.3: Integrating attentive interface behavior: pausing the video playback when the person is (a) answering a call or (b) reading (Ballendat et al., 2010).

As Fred watches the video while seated on the couch, George enters the room. The title of the currently playing video shows up at the top of the screen to tell George what video is being played (Figure 6.4a). When George approaches the display, more detailed information about the current video becomes visible at the side of the screen where he is standing (Figure 6.4b). When George moves directly in front of the screen (thus blocking Fred's view), the video playback pauses and the browsing screen is shown (Figure 6.4c). George gets control of the application and can now select other videos by touching the screen. The view changes back into full screen view once both sit down to watch the video (not shown, but similar to position d' at Figure 6.1).

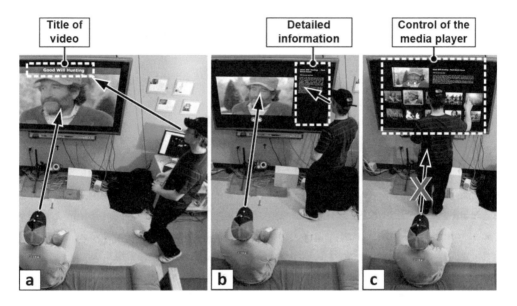

Figure 6.4: Mediating between multiple people: (a) incoming person sees basic information such as video title; (b) as one moves closer, the split view provides a more detailed video description; (c) when within reach of the display, the person gets full control (Ballendat et al. 2010).

If Fred and George start talking to each other, the video pauses until one of them looks back at the screen (Figure 6.5). When all people leave the room, the application stops the video playback and turns off the display (not shown).

While this media player is a simple application domain, it provided a fertile setting to develop and explore concepts of Proxemic Interactions.[4] In the next section we will discuss the details of Proxemic Interaction concepts associated with a single person or multiple people interacting

---

[4] We make no claim one way or another that our proxemic media player is somehow "better" than existing media players.

with a large digital surface, where these concepts apply the five input dimensions (Chapter 4) in meaningful ways to people's Proxemic Interactions with ubicomp systems.

Figure 6.5: Integrating attentive interface behavior: two people talking to each other.

6.2   INCORPORATING THE FIXED AND SEMI-FIXED FEATURE SPACE

One promise of ubicomp is to situate technology in people's everyday environments, in a way that lets people interact with information technology in their familiar places, environment, and within their social routines. Dourish framed this concept as *embodied interactions* (Dourish, 2001a); technology that is seamlessly integrated into people's everyday practices, rather than separated from them (Section 2.3). Context-aware computing is one outcome of this, where some kind of context-aware sensing (Schilit et al., 1994) provides devices with knowledge about the situation around them (Section 2.4). This sensing usually involves measuring a coarser subset of the five dimensions discussed earlier (Chapter 4), e.g., very rough positions, and other factors such as noise, light, or tilting. In this section we contribute to these concepts by introducing the notion of context-aware systems that mediate embodied interaction by understanding the proxemic relationships of people (as defined by the five dimensions) to the fixed and semi-fixed feature space surrounding them (Section 3.3).

For an interactive system (such as the interactive wall display in the media player application), knowledge about the *fixed feature space* includes the layout of the fixed aspects of the room, such as existing walls, windows, and territorial boundaries such as doors and entranceways. A fixed feature space also includes knowledge about fixed displays—such as a digital surface—located in this environment. To elaborate, knowledge about the position of the fixed entrance doors allows the system to recognize a person entering the room from the doorway (Figure 6.6a), where (as in our scenario) it takes implicit action by awakening the fixed display from standby mode. Similarly, knowing the position of the fixed display means that the interface on that display can react as a person approaches it (Figure 6.6a).

Semi-fixed features in the environment include all furniture, such as bookshelves, chairs, and tables whose position may change over time. While it is somewhat object-dependent, semi-fixed features often remain at specific physical locations, but are per se movable objects that people re-arrange to adapt to changed situations (such as moving a group of chairs around a table). Unlike fixed features whose position needs to be configured only once, knowledge about the positions of semi-fixed features must be updated over time as changes are noticed.

Knowledge of semi-fixed features can also mediate interaction. To illustrate this point, we compare two stages of a person relative to the media player's interactive surface: approaching from a distance (see Figure 6.1, position a') and watching the video when seated at the semi-fixed couch (Figure 6.1 position d'). The actual distance of the person relative to the surface is similar in both situations (Figure 6.6b), yet they suggest very different forms of interaction. The fact that the person is seated on a couch or chair facing the display becomes an indicator for watching the video. Yet standing at the same distance and then moving closer to the screen is used to infer that the person is increasingly interested in getting more information about the available videos in the media collection.

Figure 6.6: Fixed and semi-fixed features in ubicomp ecologies.

In summary, information about distance and orientation of a person *relative to* the fixed and semi-fixed feature space provides contextual cues that can mediate implicit interactions with the system. This nuanced view reflects Hall's notion that proxemics embed measures such as distance within the context of entity relationships.

6.3   INTERPRETING DIRECTED ATTENTION TO PEOPLE, OBJECTS, AND DEVICES

Proxemic Interactions can be used to extend the concept of attentive user interfaces (AUIs) that are designed to "support users' attentional capacities" (Vertegaal and Shell, 2008). In AUIs, as explained earlier in Section 2.5.2, the system reaction depends on whether a person is directing his or her attention to the device that holds the system (usually through detection of eye gaze). With Proxemic Interactions we take this AUI concept one step further, where the system is designed to also incorporate information about: what entity a person is attending to, and the importance of not only orientation (an indication of gaze) but distance as well in that context.

Attending to the system itself occurs if the device reacts to how it is being looked at. This is how most traditional AUIs work. We include an example of this behavior in the media player application: the system plays the video as long as at least one person faces the large display (Figure 6.7a), but pauses when that person looks away for a length of time (Figure 6.7b).

Figure 6.7: Interpreting directed attention to the system.

We can also differentiate these two situations by considering the transactional segment of a person (Section 3.8). Kendon (2010) explains how the fixed or semi-fixed features around a person can be the focus point of a transactional segment. For example, as long as the person is oriented toward the large display it becomes part of the current transactional segment (highlighted with a dashed outline in Figure 6.7a). Once the person turns their body and head into another direction away from the display, the transactional segment changes and does not include the display anymore.

Attention to other surrounding objects and devices. We enrich the concept of AUIs by including how a person's attention directed to *other* surrounding objects of the semi-fixed feature space can trigger implicit system reactions. In the media player system, the fact that a person is holding and facing toward a newspaper or magazine (shown in Figure 6.3b and Figure 6.8a) provides cues about the focus of this person's attention, i.e., the system infers that Fred is reading, and pauses video playback until Fred stops reading and looks back at the screen. The transactional segment shifts from the display toward the newspaper (transactional segment highlighted with a dashed outline in Figure 6.8a). If Fred had a similar gaze toward, for example, a bowl of popcorn, the video would not have paused.

A shift of attention can also be suggested by the relative distance of an object to the person. For example, the media player system detects when Fred is holding his mobile phone close to his ear (as shown in Figure 6.3a). It infers that Fred is having a phone conversation, and pauses the video until Fred moves his phone away from his head. The measurement of the relative distance of phone to the person's head, as well as their orientation toward each other, provides the necessary information for the system to implicitly react to this situation.

Figure 6.8: Interpreting directed attention to other objects or other people.

Attention to other people. We can discriminate how one person attends to other people as a means to trigger implicit system reactions. For example, consider Fred and George when they turn toward each other to converse (Figure 6.5 and Figure 6.8b). The scenario illustrates how the system implicitly reacts to this situation by pausing the video. The transactional segments of both people on the couch overlap in a face-to-face formation as illustrated in Figure 6.8b (highlighted as the area with a dashed outline). Alternatively, by knowing that both people are in a conversation (rather than just knowing that they are looking at each other), the system could have simply turned down its volume instead of pausing the video.

Of course, the reactions described above beg the question of whether the system response is an appropriate one, or whether alternate reactions (or perhaps none at all) would have been more appropriate. Should the system really pause or resume as suggested? This will be returned to later at the end of this chapter, when we discuss issues with the "rules of behavior" regarding such implicit actions.

6.4   SUPPORTING FINE-GRAINED EXPLICIT INTERACTION

Aside from *implicitly* reacting to a person's proxemic relation to other semi-fixed environment objects, these relationships can also facilitate a person's *explicit* forms of interaction with the system. In this section we introduce the concept of using physical objects as *mobile tokens* that people can use to mediate their explicit interaction with an interactive surface. The meaning of these tokens is adjusted based upon the token's identity and its distance and orientation to other entities in the space.

To illustrate this concept, consider the explicit interaction in our scenario where Fred pointed his cell phone or a pencil at the surface to view and select content (Figure 6.9). The way this works is that all mobile tracked objects are interpreted as *mobile tokens*. Three units of information cause the media player system to interpret that token as a pointing device: it is held in *front* of a person, it is roughly *oriented* toward the display, and it is within a particular *distance* from the display. Indeed, two quite different devices can serve as similar tokens: the phone in Figure 6.2a, and the pen in Figure 6.2b. It is important to note that the system is not using any of the digital capabilities of the mobile digital phone to make this inference. Rather (and as with the physical pen) the system uses only the knowledge of its identity, position, and orientation to switch to a certain interaction mode. Thus, the particular proxemic relationship between a person and a mobile token is interpreted as a *method of signaling* (Clark, 2003), as discussed in Clark's theory of pointing and placing as forms of communication. Further, the specific orientation and distance of the token to other devices (e.g., the large display) are interpreted to establish an *intrinsic connection* (Clark, 2003) to control that particular device.

Figure 6.9: Using a mobile phone as a pointer.

A key advantage is that the use of these mobile tokens as identifiers can disambiguate similar looking gestures. For example, a gesture recognition system cannot tell if the intent of a person pointing their hand toward the screen is to interact with the screen, or if it is just a gesture produced as part of a conversation. Mobile tokens, on the other hand, create a specific context to disambiguate and interpret gestures, where the distance and positions of the objects relative to the person and other objects are used to infer a certain explicit interaction mode.

Many of these behaviors can be triggered by approximate knowledge of proxemic relationships. Yet, having exact knowledge is helpful for minimizing errors that can occur where the system misinterprets a person's manipulation of a mobile token as an explicit action. For example, consider a person playing with a pen in their hand vs. pointing the pen at the screen to select an item. If proxemic measures are reasonably precise, the triggering event could rely solely on the pen being a specific distance from the person's body and a specific orientation toward the screen for a particular length of time.

Another example includes the multiple meanings held by a mobile token. Consider how the meaning of the mobile phone depends on its proxemic relation to its holder and to the display. The distance of the phone to a person's head indicates an ongoing phone conversation (Figure 6.10a), while stretching the arm holding the phone at a larger distance (relative to the person's body) and moving it toward the display shifts its meaning to an interaction pointer (Figure 6.10b). Holding the phone at a distance between these two extremes (Figure 6.10c) lets the person interact with the touch screen of the device.

In our scenario, the actual explicit interaction with the digital video content displayed on the large surface is triggered by the person through several means. Moving the position of the mobile token across the screen highlights potential media item selections. Changes of the angle of orientation allow fine-grained positioning of a pointer icon on the screen, while fast downward acceleration is used for selection. Of course, other gestures are possible.

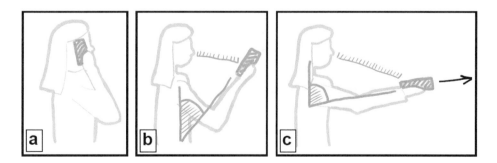

Figure 6.10: Using proxemic relationships between a person and objects (e.g., mobile phone) to infer interaction modes and disambiguate gestures.

6.5   CONTINUOUS MOVEMENTS VS. DISCRETE PROXEMIC ZONES

Another concept is that the behaviors of proxemic interfaces can react to the position and distance of the surrounding entities as either *continuous movements*, or as movements in and out of *discrete proxemic zones*.

For *continuous movement*, the calculated distances between people and devices function as input variables that continually affect the interactive system's behavior (Figure 6.11a). For example, as a person approaches the screen of the media player application, the number of visible video preview thumbnails shown continually increases with distance (see Figure 6.1a, b). To do this, the system gradually resizes the preview images to a smaller size (i.e., an animated zoom out effect); thus more content is visible as the person approaches the screen. Depending on the situation, an inverse behavior might be applied, where the system actually *zooms into* the content to make it larger when the person is approaching the screen (similar to *Lean and Zoom* (Harrison and Dey, 2008)).

With *discrete proxemic zones* we can divide the space into discrete regions (Figure 6.11b). When a person enters or leaves the thresholds of these zones, certain actions are triggered in the system. Indeed, the use of zones is inspired by the interpersonal proxemic distance zones defined by Hall (1966), and others have applied zones as a way to mediate interaction with public ambient displays (Vogel and Balakrishnan, 2004) and digital whiteboards (Ju et al., 2008).

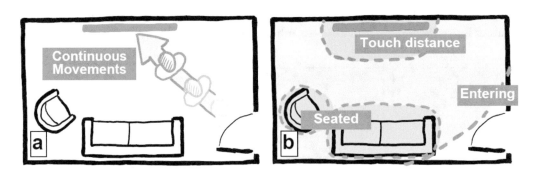

Figure 6.11: Interpreting (a) continuous movements or presence in (b) discrete zones around the large interactive display.

The media player uses discrete zones in several ways (Figure 6.11b). It uses zones to trigger an associated implicit action (e.g., activate a display screen when entering the room in zone "Entering" of Figure 6.11b). The media player also use zones to allow certain forms of explicit interaction (e.g., switching to an interface that allows direct touch interaction when the person is standing in close proximity to the screen in zone "Touch distance" of Figure 6.11b). Finally, the media player also uses zones around semi-fixed features as explained earlier in Section 6.2 (e.g., switching to full screen view of the video when sitting on the couch or a chair in zone "Seated" of Figure 6.11b).

A problem associated with discrete zones occurs when the interface rapidly switches back and forth between two states; this occurs when the person stands exactly along a border of one of the discrete zones. This jitter is solved via the concept of a *hysteresis tolerance*: the entry and exit point of each region are not at the same distance, but are two separate distances. For example, our system uses a 15–20% hysteresis tolerance for proxemic regions around the interactive wall display (percentage of the region dimension) to avoid this rapid switching.

6.6   THE GRADUAL ENGAGEMENT PATTERN

The vast majority of ubicomp interfaces are premised on the notion that a person is fully attending to them, i.e., the systems are designed to support *foreground* activities and tasks. However, a variety of systems also recognize that the person may not be directly attending to them (i.e., they are in the *background* of their attention), where they still try to be helpful by presenting an interface that selectively informs the user of information of interest.

One class of examples includes ambient displays (Mankoff et al., 2003) embedded in a physical environment. The display usually presents non-critical information unobtrusively, which a person can monitor at a distance and at the periphery of their attention (thus providing basic awareness). The display often contains a way for the person to easily transition to more in-depth information exploration if the person decides to engage with it; this normally occurs by the person approaching and directly interacting with that display. That is, such displays implicitly incorporate a binary notion of proximity: from afar, and within interaction reach.

A few early Proxemic Interactions systems provide another class of examples that use a much more refined notion of proxemics. Many of these systems commonly interpret decreasing distance and increasing mutual orientation between a person and a device within a bounded space as an indication of a person's gradually increasing interest in interacting with that device. Influential earlier work (discussed in Section 2.5.2) considered such gradual increasing engagement between a person and large interactive displays. For example, Vogel and Balakrishnan (2004) directly applied Hall's theory to a person's interaction with a public display. They defined four discrete zones around the display that affect a person's interaction when moving closer: from far to close, interactions range from ambient display of information, to implicit, subtle, and finally personal interaction (see video: ambient display). Similarly, Ju et al.'s (2008) interaction techniques with a digital whiteboard remain public and implicit from a distance, and become increasingly more private and explicit when the person moves closer to that display.

We generalize the sequence inherent in these (and other) systems as a design pattern called *gradual engagement* (Marquardt et al., 2012a; see video: gradual engagement). The basic idea is that:

- STAGE 1: background information supplied by the system provides awareness to the person about opportunities of potential interest when viewed at a distance;

- STAGE 2: the person can gradually act on particular opportunities by viewing and/or exploring its information in more detail simply by approaching it; and

- STAGE 3: the person can ultimately engage in action if so desired.

This pattern is, of course, directly inspired by proxemic theory (Chapter 3) and by the various previously described systems that reflect that pattern. Borchers (2001) also describes an even more general pattern titled "Attract-Engage-Deliver," where the difference is that our pattern incorporates proxemics as a first-class element. The pattern also characterizes what we thought was the "best" of how proxemics was previously applied to ubicomp design. The intention of this gradual engagement pattern is to characterize how we can facilitate interactions between a person or multiple people and the devices surrounding them by leveraging fine-grained proxemic measurements (e.g., distance, orientation, identity) between all entities. As a design pattern (Borchers, 2001; Tidwell, 2005), its strengths lie in (1) unifying prior work in Proxemic Interactions, (2) synthesizing essential, generalizable interaction strategies, and (3) providing a common vocabulary for discussing design solutions. Most importantly, the pattern informs and inspires future designs, and also allows for variations of the pattern applied to different domains. In this chapter we focus on the application of the gradual engagement pattern to person-to-device interactions, but as we will see later in Chapter 7, the pattern can be also applied to other relationships (e.g., device-to-device).

6.7   APPLYING THE GRADUAL ENGAGEMENT PATTERN: FROM AWARENESS TO INTERACTION

In our work, we combine both continuous movements and discrete proxemic zones to design system interfaces that move fluently from awareness, to progressive reveal, to direct explicit interaction following the gradual engagement pattern. One example illustrates this combination.

The media player begins by providing peripheral awareness information about its capabilities and content when a person enters the room (see video: proxemic media player). The system detects the presence of the person at a distance (around 4m), activates the display, displays a welcome animation, and plays a subtle acoustic signal. This indicates to the person that the system is active. Here, the system uses a discrete proxemic zone around the digital display that triggers this activation behavior. At this point, if the person just walks past the display, or does not face the display, the media player application reverts to sleep mode. If, however, the person does move closer, the system shows preview images of video content, where it progressively reveals more preview items on the screen as the person approaches the screen. Here, the system uses the continuous mapping of distance to the size and quantity of preview items shown. When the person stands within reach of the screen, we enter another discrete zone: direct touch interaction. At that distance, the person can use their hands for direct touch interaction with the screen content; thus the continuous resizing of the displayed preview thumbnails stops, as it would otherwise make selection difficult. Other applications of the gradual engagement pattern are possible, and we will illustrate several of them in Chapter 7.

6.8   LEVERAGING PEOPLE'S IDENTITY

The concepts introduced so far only require knowledge about "a person" approaching the display, but they do not require the actual identity of a person. We now discuss examples that leverage the knowledge about the actual identity of individuals.

History

Knowing which person is interacting with the system is used to continue activities that this person began in the past. For instance, when a person enters the room and immediately sits down, the media application will resume playback of the last video that a person previously watched but did not finish.

Personalization

The media player could save one's settings as a personal profile (not implemented in the current version of the proxemic media player). This could include personal configurations, idiosyncrasies of how the system should respond to that particular person, and that person's media content. For example, if a particular person were to approach the display, the media player would then display content out of that person's media library. This also raises the question of where such information is stored. While it could be on the server, privacy concerns suggest that it could also be placed on a person's mobile device. For example, our media player would only have access to the personal identity information of only those people who come in close proximity to it, where that accessed information is erased as soon as that person leaves.

Safeguards

Identifying the person interacting with the system can also function as a safeguard to restrict access (not yet implemented). For instance, children may only be allowed to access the media player application during pre-defined time slots, or access to available media content could be restricted to movies rated for their age. To take this one step further, children's viewing could be mediated by requiring the presence of others (e.g., adults or parents) in the room for either accessing particular content or for going beyond previously specified restrictions (such as the amount of time they are allowed to watch movies).

6.9   MEDIATING PEOPLE'S SIMULTANEOUS INTERACTION

Proxemic Interactions should also mediate the interaction of multiple people in the same space. In the simplest case, as long as all people are in the same proxemic state relative to the display's surface, the system's behavior could be similar to the Proxemic Interactions introduced for a single person interacting with the surface. In reality, however, we expect people to be in different proxemic stages, where the system would need to reason about how it should mediate its behavior to reflect people's simultaneous interaction possibilities.

6.9.1   MERGING MULTIPLE PROXEMIC DISTANCES

In situations where people have different proxemic distances to the interactive display of the media player application, the system can be designed to individually address people's diverse proxemic needs, albeit as a compromise.

For example, in the example scenario we saw George enter the room while Fred was watching a video (see video: proxemic media player). George wants to know what is currently playing, while Fred wants to keep watching. To compromise between these needs, the system displays the title of the currently playing video at the top of the screen, thus subtly informing George while still letting Fred watch without too much distraction (Figure 6.4a and Figure 6.12a). If George sits at the couch or on a chair, the title disappears.

If George approaches the screen instead of sitting down, the display animates and splits off a small region of the screen. This region provides further information of the video being played: its description, author information, and the release date (Figure 6.4b and Figure 6.12b). The positioning of this region also depends on George's spatial relation to the display—if he moves from the right side to the left, the information panel smoothly animates to that side of the display (Figure 6.12c).

Such a system could be annoying if, for example, that information was displayed whenever a person just happened to be approaching the screen from anywhere. Instead, our system only shows this information when a person is approaching from the fixed feature of the doorway, and only when there is another person seated.

When both people are in the same proxemic state, the views merge. For instance, both people can watch the video in full screen when seated, or both can explore and choose from the videos available when standing in front of the display.

6.9.2   HANDLING CONFLICTS

When multiple people are present within a proximity-aware application, situations will arise where the system has to handle two *conflicting* individual possibilities. For example, consider the scenario situation of Figure 6.4c (and Figure 6.12d): Fred is sitting in front of the large display watching a movie, while George moves directly in front of the display to browse a media collection.

Several strategies are possible to handle these situations. The system could favor the person in closer proximity; e.g., George standing directly in front of the display would have priority over Fred sitting at a larger distance. This is the solution shown in Figure 6.4c and Figure 6.12d, where George gets full access to the media library to select videos; a strategy that makes sense as Fred's view is already blocked. Alternately, the system could have given the video player priority, disallowing George's interaction, leaving the two to resolve this through social means (e.g., both standing up to make a selection). Or the system could create some kind of composite view, i.e., by moving the video so that Fred could still see some of it, while still giving George interactive controls in the blocked part of the screen. There is no perfect solution. These (and other possibilities) need to be considered carefully in the design of such systems.

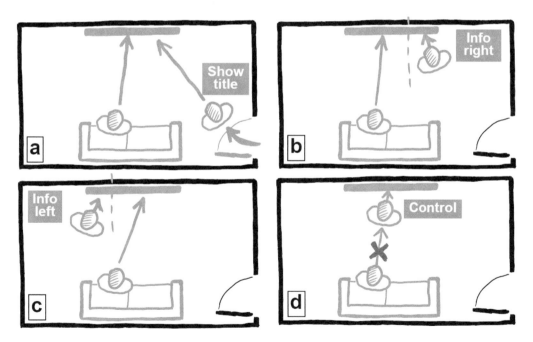

Figure 6.12: Merging multiple proxemic distances to mediate people's simultaneous interaction with the display.

To support the simultaneous interaction of multiple people in our scenario, the media player further refines the discrete zones around the large display that trigger actions once a person enters these zones (Figure 6.13). For example, the "Touch distance" zone shown in Figure 6.11b is now divided for multi-person interaction into three discrete zones (Figure 6.13 top): displaying the title when the second person enters the room, the video information when that person stands either on the left or right side of the screen, and the touch controls when the person stands directly in front of the display.

6.10   OTHER EXAMPLE APPLICATIONS

Various other faculty, students, researchers, visitors, and interns within our Interactions Laboratory at the University of Calgary became interested in the idea of Proxemic Interactions as it was being developed. They pursued their own applications: some as part of course work, some as personal explorations of the idea, and some as first-class research projects. While these projects are somewhat similar from a technological point of view in regards to the devices they use (large display + tracked person), each applies the Proxemic Interactions concepts in novel ways to a diverse set of applications and activities. We highlight a few of them here to illustrate the breadth of situations and interaction techniques amenable to Proxemic Interactions.[5]

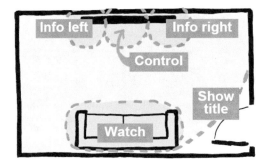

Figure 6.13: Refined discrete zones around the large display to support simultaneous interaction of multiple people.

6.10.1   VICONFACE

ViconFace, by Roberto Diaz-Marino, is a social actor—a caricature of a face that lives on a large display—whose behavior was driven by a set of simple rules inspired by Hall's proxemic zones

[5]   The application developers gave permission to summarize their work, with attribution to its primary developer. Thus we acknowledge their names and provide references if available (including video) when introducing each projects.

(Greenberg et al., 2011; Diaz-Marino and Greenberg, 2010; see video: ViconFace). Figure 6.14 illustrates several of its behaviors. We see (a) the face being lonely when no one is present, (b) happy when its friend comes into the room, all-the-while maintaining eye contact and expression as a function of distance, (c) becoming sadder as its friend moves or looks away, and (d) annoyed as his friend crosses into his intimate space. The face was also startled by sudden movements, angered by touches, and could be distracted by other objects pointed toward it. While the face was just a simple social caricature, visitors to our laboratory found it immediately understandable and compelling, where they assumed it had much more intelligence and knowledge of social rules than it actually had (its behavior repertoire was really nothing more than a simple state machine).

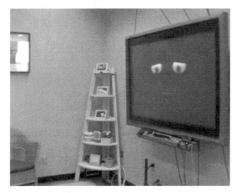
a) Lonely when no one is around,

b) it sees Rob come in, and greets him happily,

c) but is saddened when Rob looks away, and

d) finds Rob a bit too close for comfort.

Figure 6.14: ViconFace (Roberto Diaz-Marino).

6.10.2 PROXEMIC PRESENTER

Proxemic Presenter, by Miaosen Wang, is a presentation tool that reacts to the presenter's position relative to a large display (Wang, 2012; Greenberg, 2001). The focus of this project was on three specific capabilities: making it easier for a speaker to access their speaking notes; making it easier for them to move through slides, and to jump over slides by selecting one from a set of thumbnails. The Proxemic Presenter exploits distance, orientation, and identity (to discriminate the speaker from others). The sequence in Figure 6.15 shows how it works. When a speaker faces the audience, the presentation fills the screen as expected (Figure 6.15a). When the speaker stands at the side of the nearby screen and faces toward it, a small but readable pane containing speaker notes, timing information, and next/previous controls fades into view next to the speaker (Figure 6.15b). As he looks back toward the audience, the notes pane fades away. The notes pane also follows the speaker: if the speaker moves to the other side of the display and looks toward it, the pane appears at that side. If the speaker moves away from the display and then looks toward it, the notes pane does not appear. This is because the speaker is too far to read them, and showing large notes would be distracting to the audience. If the speaker shields the display from the audience by standing near and at the center of the surface, a scrollable deck of slide thumbnails appear, allowing the speaker to rapidly switch to any slide (Figure 6.15c).

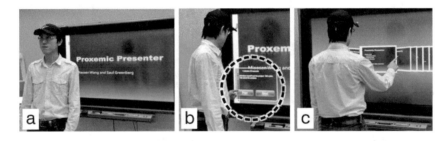

Figure 6.15: Proxemic Presenter (Miaosen Wang).

6.10.3 ATTENTIVE TRANSPARENT DISPLAY FOR MUSEUMS

Attentive Transparent Display for Museums, by Jiannan Li, is a prototype semi-transparent computer display (Figure 6.16a) positioned in front of museum artifacts that can display further information about the shown physical artifacts (Li, 2014). Depending on a person's position and their distance to the physical artifacts behind the semi-transparent display, information about these artifacts is progressively revealed and shown on the screen. The position of the displayed information is determined by ray casting from the viewer's eyes toward the physical artifact, where the ray's intersection with the transparent display sets the position for the shown information (Figure 6.16b). That is, the position the displayed information tracks the viewing angle of the person. A person can perform simple hand gestures (tracked through gloves with attached IR markers) to override actions performed by the system.

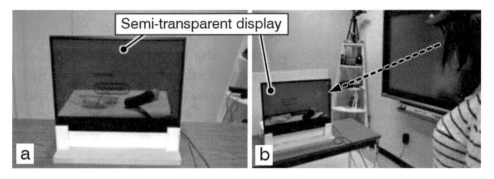

Figure 6.16: Attentive transparent display for museums (Jiannan Li).

6.10.4   PROXEMIC 3D VISUALIZATION SYSTEM

The Proxemic 3D Visualization System, by Ahmed E. Mostafa, allows a person to interact with graphical visualizations displayed on a large display (Mostafa et al., 2013a, 2013b) (see video: microseismic visualizer). It includes a proximity-based immersive navigation technique: it tracks a person's position (via the proxy of a remote control the person is holding in his hand) that directly controls how one navigates through the 3D data set shown on the display (Figure 6.17a). The system uses the proxemic properties of distance and orientation between a person and the large display to let the person coarsely navigate the 3D data set. Furthermore, as an example of the progressive reveal technique, distance and orientation also affect the details shown (i.e., more details are shown when the person orients toward the display and moves closer). This method mimics how people can walk around a 3D object to view it from different angles, and how they can see greater detail as they move closer. A person can also perform explicit gestures with a remote control to manipulate the currently displayed data set (Figure 6.17b).

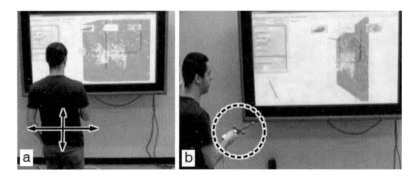

Figure 6.17: Proxemic Interactions with a 3D visualization (Ahmed E. Mostafa)

6.10.5   PROXEMIC-AWARE PONG

Proxemic-aware Pong, by Till Ballendat, is inspired by Atari's Pong game (Greenberg et al., 2011). It illustrates how Proxemic Interaction concepts can serve as a guiding strategy for the design of interactive computer games, where the proxemic relationships between the game's visual screen and one or multiple players can affect the gaming experience. Proxemic-aware Pong reacts to distance, orientation, motion and identity, where identity just distinguishes between different players. In standby mode (which displays a splash screen showing the game title), Proxemic Pong recognizes when a person enters and stands in front of the screen: it creates a paddle for that person, and starts the game. That person then controls the paddle for bouncing the ball with their body by facing forward and physically moving left and right in front of a large screen. When a second person enters the space and stands in front of the display, a second paddle is created and the game continues via turn-taking (as seen in Figure 6.18a). To penalise the player who interferes with the active player by standing in their way, Proxemic Pong grows the active player's paddle to make it easier to hit the ball.

Like Wii games, Proxemic Pong introduces exertion element into computer game play (Mueller et. al., 2014). Initially, the player's motion matches the paddle's motion. As game play continues, the system increases the ratio of the physical distance that needs to be covered to move the paddle, while also increasing the speed of the ball. This means that people have to move further and faster to hit the ball.

Proxemic Pong also exploits front to back motion. If a player moves very close to the display, the game automatically pauses; control points appear on the paddle allowing that person to adjust the paddle shape by direct touch (Figure 6.18b). If a player moves backwards and sits on the couch (i.e., the player becomes an observer), their paddle disappears and the game continues in single player mode. When both sit down on the couch or move away, the game pauses.

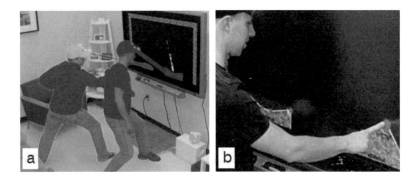

Figure 6.18: Proxemic pong game: (a) two players playing the game and (b) configuring game and changing paddle size when in close proximity to the screen (Till Ballendat).

6.10.6   PROXEMIC PEDDLER

Figure 6.19: Proxemic Peddler (Miaosen Wang).

Proxemic Peddler (by Miasoen Wang) explores how future advertisement displays might try to grab and keep a passer-by's attention (Wang et al., 2012; Wang 2012; see video: proxemic peddler). A digital advertisement board—in this case a book-selling display—reacts to the presence, distance, identity, orientation, and movements of a nearby person. The key is to do so in a non-aggressive and non-annoying manner that finds a balance between the advertiser's interest and the passer-by's interest. When no one appears within its range, it rapidly animates a book list at the bottom, where its motion is an attempt to attract the attention of a passer-by. The animation slows as soon as it detects a passer-by looking toward it (which makes the book list readable and far calmer), as illustrated in Figure 6.19, upper left. The gradual engagement pattern is applied, where additional personalized details about preferred books are displayed as the person approaches the display (Figure 6.19, upper right). If the person looks away momentarily, subtle cues are used to try to re-attract them, such as a slight shaking of the product icon (Figure 6.19, lower left). If it looks as if the person is about to leave, it tries to regain their interest by showing different products (Figure 6.19, lower right). In all cases, it gives up gracefully if it looks like the person is really not interested. More generally, Wang produced the proxemic peddler framework that describes the various attentional states of a passer-by in relation to a public advertisement display, and explains strategies to capture and preserve the attention of that person (Wang et al., 2012; Wang 2012). It includes states such as: detecting and reacting to a passer-by's initial attention and approach; digression and loss off interest; eventual departure; and an interaction history to mediate what happens over time.

6.10.7 SPALENDAR

SPALENDAR, by Xiang Anthony Chen, shows spatial visualizations of scheduled meeting locations of one's collaborators overlaid on a geographical map (Chen et al., 2012; see video: spalender). As with other ambient displays, it provides (often non-critical) information to a person while remaining in the periphery of their attention (Mankoff et al., 2003), which in turn affords opportunities for foreground interaction. Part of SPALENDAR 's interaction sequence also follows the stages of the gradual engagement pattern. A person starts by watching the display from afar (Figure 6.20a') where it shows simple flows of one's collaborators as they move between their events (Figure 6.20a). When the person approaches the display, more information about the collaborators' identities is revealed (Figure 6.20b). The identity of the person approaching the display directly affects the amount of information shown. Finally, when directly in front of the display (Figure 6.20c'), a person can use direct touch gestures to reveal detailed calendar information on demand (Figure 6.20c). A person can use hand gestures to, for example, adjust the time/date of the current information shown, or add new events to the calendar.

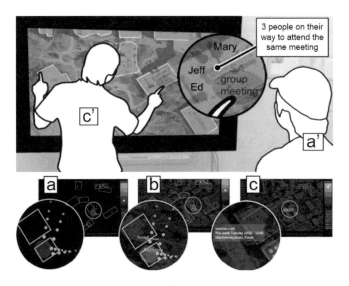

Figure 6.20: Interaction with SPALENDAR (modified from Chen et al., 2012).

6.10.8 MEDIATING SHOULDER SURFING

When people use public displays to pursue personal work, they expose their activities and sensitive data to passers-by. In most cases, such shoulder-surfing by others is likely voyeuristic vs. a deliberate attempt to steal information. Even so, safeguards are needed. Frederik Brudy developed Proxemic Interactions techniques to mitigate shoulder-surfing issues in such settings, where they sense and take action based on the spatial relationships between the passerby, the user of the display, and the display itself (Brudy et al., 2014a, 2014b; see video: shoulder surfing protection). The various techniques provide participants with awareness of shoulder-surfing moments, which in turn helps both parties regulate their behaviors and mediate further social interactions. For example, Figure 6.21 (left) illustrates how a passerby's presence, distance, orientation and gaze direction is reflected onto the display as a 3D model, where it is easily seen by the display's user. We also provide methods that protect information when shoulder-surfing is detected. Here, users can move or hide information through easy to perform explicit actions. Alternately, the system itself can mask information from the passerby's view when it detects shoulder-surfing moments. For example, Figure 6.21 (right) illustrates how the system tracks the passer-by's look direction, and greys out all portions of the screen except that shielded by the user's body.

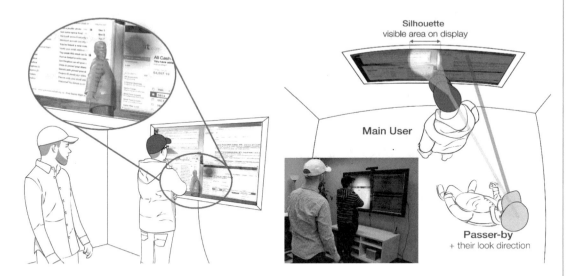

Figure 6.21: Left: mirroring a passer-by's position and orientation with a 3D-model and their gaze direction with a red dot; right: the system automatically masks out those display areas within the passer-by's look direction that are not shielded by the user's body (Brudy et al., 2014 a).

6.11   DISCUSSION AND CONCLUSION

In this chapter, we showed how Proxemic Interactions enable a multitude of implicit and explicit interactions with an interactive vertical display. We explained these interaction techniques through a scenario of people interacting with a media player application displayed on that interactive display. In particular, we explained how knowing the continuous movement of an approaching identified person along with the position, orientation, and usage of identified objects can be exploited in interface design, e.g., how the system should implicitly respond to proxemic entities and how the system can afford opportunities for explicit interactions.

The presented implementation of the proxemic-aware media player—while fully functional—serves primarily as an example that illustrates design possibilities for Proxemic Interactions between one person or multiple people and their surrounding devices. We do not suggest that the rules of behavior of the media player application are ideal, nor that they achieve the perfect balance between adjudicating proxemic information and implicit or explicit interaction. Some of the presented media player rules are clearly problematic, where the action taken may not be appropriate in certain social situations. As a simple example, the instance where the system pauses when two people turn to one another may be opposite of what those people want (e.g., when they are perhaps talking excitedly about the movie's climax). Problems such as these are likely endemic to systems that try to infer people's intentions. Instead, we see the presented techniques as a set of novel ways to consider proxemics in interaction design that can inspire future explorations of proxemic-aware technology; designing and debugging appropriate interactions based upon implicit acts (see also Schmidt, 2000), or developing design patterns such as the gradual engagement pattern comes under this exploration.

While all of the presented techniques focused on the interaction of a person (or two people) with a *single* device, we simultaneously began the exploration of how to consider proxemics to mediate device-to-device relationships. This exploration led to a series of techniques for facilitating the use of multiple devices in concert, and is the focus of the following chapter.

CHAPTER 7

Device-to-Device
Proxemic Interactions

The increasing number of digital devices in our environment, ranging from personal mobile phones to semi-public large stationary surfaces, enriches how we interact with digital content. Yet, cross-device information transfer—which should be a common operation—is surprisingly difficult. One has to know which devices can communicate, what information they contain, and how information can be exchanged.

To mitigate this problem, in this chapter we focus on applying concepts of Proxemic Interactions to mediate device-to-device operations—both between personal (e.g., tablets) and semi-public devices (e.g., digital whiteboards). In particular, we refine the gradual engagement pattern from Section 6.6 to ease the information transfer task. As we will see, the refined pattern suggests how devices can gradually engage the user by disclosing connectivity and information exchange capabilities as a function of inter-device proximity. That is, as people move and orient their personal device toward other surrounding devices, the interface progressively moves through three stages affording gradual engagement: (a) *awareness* of device presence and connectivity, (b) *reveal* of exchangeable digital content, and (c) interaction methods for *transferring* digital content between devices tuned to particular distances and device capabilities (these three stages correspond to the three parts of Figure 7.1—we discuss the details later in this chapter).

The chapter is structured as follows. First, we describe how to refine the gradual engagement pattern to address cross-device interactions (Section 7.1). Next, we briefly review related work that relates to cross-device transfer and the gradual engagement pattern (Section 7.2). The next three sections then follow the three stages of the refined design pattern: *awareness* of device presence and connectivity (Section 7.3 and Figure 7.1a), *reveal* of exchangeable digital content (Section 7.4 and Figure 7.1b), and interaction methods for *transferring* digital content between devices tuned to particular distances and device capabilities (Section 7.5 and Figure 7.1c). In each of these sections we describe particular interaction techniques, where their presentation is structured according to the three stages of the gradual engagement design pattern. We also explain how gradual engagement techniques may differ when the other device seen is personal (such as a handheld) vs. semi-public (such as a large display). Then, in Section 7.6 we briefly summarize other example systems. The remaining sections discuss sensing requirements and privacy aspects. See video: gradual engagement, which illustrates the applications and the dynamics of the various methods described in this chapter. The development of the cross-device interaction techniques was done in collaboration with Till Ballendat along with involvements by Ken Hinckely and Sebastian Boring.

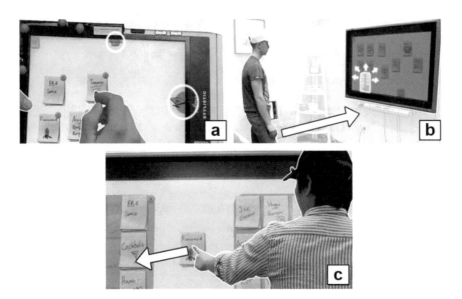

Figure 7.1: Gradual engagement pattern applied to mitigate cross-device operations: showing examples of (a) awareness of other devices via icons that spatially represent those devices, (b) progressive reveal of exchangeable content, which (c) leads to information transfer (Marquardt et al., 2012a).

7.1   APPLYING GRADUAL ENGAGEMENT TO CROSS-DEVICE INFORMATION TRANSFER

Personal mobile devices (e.g., phones, tablets) and semi-public stationary devices (e.g., information appliances, interactive surfaces) are an increasingly commonplace way for people to ubiquitously interact with digital information. Most of these devices are optimised for a seamless user experience when one uses them *individually*. Yet, using multiple devices in *concert* (such as for transferring information from a mobile phone to the device of a nearby person) is often tedious and requires executing complicated interaction sequences. This is why several projects in the area of ubiquitous computing (reviewed in Section 2.5) began introducing new techniques to facilitate transfer of content between nearby devices, e.g., (Hardy and Rukzio, 2008; Hinckley, 2003; Rekimoto, 1997). However, significant challenges remain. People do not know *which* devices can communicate with one another, *what* information they contain that is exchangeable, and *how* information can be exchanged in a controlled manner.

To mitigate these problems, we began exploring how to apply Proxemic Interactions concepts and—in particular—the gradual engagement pattern (Section 6.6) to inter-device operations. The previous application of the gradual engagement pattern (Section 6.7) primarily focused on people's interaction with large displays, where the display's content changes as a function of proxemic variables (Chapter 4). We decided to refine the *gradual engagement* design pattern by considering fine-grained proxemic relationships *between multiple devices* allowing seamless transitions from awareness to information transfer. Specifically, engagement increases continuously across *three stages* as people move and orient their personal device toward other surrounding devices (Figure 7.2):

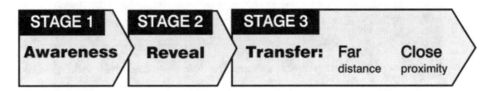

Figure 7.2: Three sequential stages of the refined gradual engagement pattern applied to cross-device operations.

Stage 1
Awareness of device presence and connectivity is provided, so that a person can understand what other devices are present and whether they can connect with one's own personal device. We leverage knowledge about proxemic relationships between devices to determine when devices connect and how they notify a person about their presence and established connections.

Stage 2
Reveal of exchangeable content is provided, so that people know what of their content can be accessed on other devices for information transfer. At this stage, a fundamental technique is progressively revealing a device's available digital content as a function of proximity.

Stage 3
Transferring digital content between devices, tuned to particular proxemic relationships and device capabilities, is provided via various strategies. Each is tailored to fit naturally within particular situations and contexts: from a distance vs. from close proximity; and transfer to a personal device vs. a semi-public device.

We illustrate the application of this gradual engagement pattern between devices as a suite of interaction techniques, all based on providing a seamless transition leading from awareness, to reveal, to interaction (see video: gradual engagement). Sensing was done through the Proximity Toolkit, where we tracked a subset of proxemic properties at high fidelity (see Section 2.5.3). We use three example applications throughout this chapter to illustrate how these various techniques leverage Proxemic Interactions and follow gradual engagement to facilitate access to digital information:

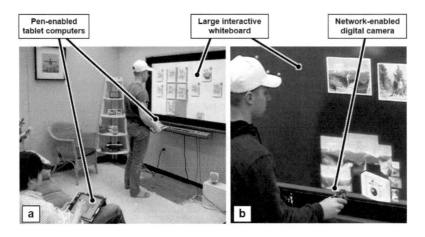

Figure 7.3: Example applications illustrating interaction concepts: (a) proxemic brainstorming, and (b) proxemic photo canvas.

- First, *proxemic brainstorming* is an interactive digital brainstorming groupware tool (Figure 7.3a). Its users can individually create, change, and manage virtual sticky notes on their personal pen-enabled tablets (e.g., see Figure 7.1a). A large whiteboard provides a public sharing space for interacting over notes, and different techniques (explained shortly) allow temporary or permanent transfer of the digital notes between all devices and thus all people in the group.

- Second, *proxemic photo canvas* (Figure 7.3b) facilitates transfer of digital photos from a network-enabled digital camera to other devices, such as a large display or a digital photo frame.

- Third, we refer back to the *proxemic media player* application from Chapter 6 to illustrate interaction concepts (see video: proxemic media player). We extended the functionality of the media player so that it recognizes nearby portable digital media players a person is using and also supports the transfer of digital media between devices.

In the main part of this chapter we will revisit each of the three stages of the refined gradual engagement pattern to introduce these techniques, where we use scenarios from each of these three applications to illustrate the techniques in action. Figure 7.4 provides an overview of all interaction techniques across the three stages of the design pattern. We list our novel or refined interaction techniques (black boxes in Figure 7.4) and refer to techniques of related work that fit into each of the three stages. Each section explain details of each particular technique. First, however, we review prior work that relates to our derivation of the gradual engagement pattern.

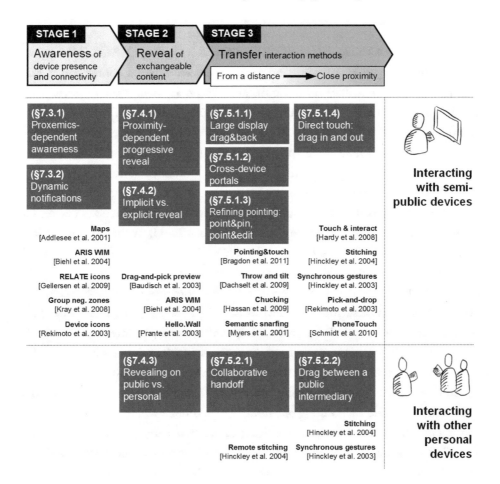

Figure 7.4: The stages of the refined gradual engagement pattern (top row) and interaction methods derived from the pattern supporting awareness and interaction in each stage: person interacting with semi-public devices (middle row) or personal devices of other people (bottom row) (modified from Marquardt et al., 2012a).

7.2   PRIOR WORK APPLIED TO GRADUAL ENGAGEMENT

We briefly sample prior work that contributed to our derivation of particular stages of the gradual engagement pattern. In our review we also refer to ubicomp systems discussed earlier in Chapter

2, but primarily focus on projects providing awareness, reveal content, or facilitating cross-device operations. Beyond the review, we also later explain how many of these prior techniques can be applied to people's interactions across all three stages of gradual engagement. Figure 7.4 summarizes how these works fit within and thus contribute to the pattern.

7.2.1   AWARENESS OF DEVICE PRESENCE AND CONNECTIVITY

Most systems define a discrete spatial region around devices, where a connection is established (and information transfer possible) once the distance becomes smaller than a certain threshold. Often, this distance depends on the actual sensing technology used (e.g., sensing range of RFID or Bluetooth).

Visualization of available devices becomes important in ubicomp environments, as an increasing number of diverse devices are present. Their presence, location, and ability to connect (or not) are rarely easily visible to a user. A few systems began exploring methods to inform a person about surrounding devices and possible connections. Most commonly, a map visualizes devices located in the environment (e.g., Sentient Computing (Addlesee et al., 2001)) or the same room (e.g., *ARIS* by (Biehl and Bailey, 2004)). Gellersen et al.'s *RELATE* Gateways provide a similar visualization, but make use of sophisticated tracking systems to dynamically update the positions of all devices (Gellersen et al., 2009). In an alternative view, icons at the border of a mobile device screen represent the type and position of surrounding devices (Gellersen et al., 2009; Rekimoto et al., 2003). Kray's *group coordination negotiation* introduced spatial regions for interaction around mobile phones (Kray et al., 2008). Their scenario used these regions to negotiate exchange of information with others. Feedback about a phone's presence in any of the regions was visualized on a tabletop.

Explicit Connections. Various systems allow people to manually associate two devices from a distance. This is usually done via pointing one device at the other. Swindells et al. (2002) uses an infrared-emitting pen to point at a device to control it. *Semantic snarfing* (Myers et al., 2001) also uses pointing to allow someone to take over temporary control of remote interfaces. Similarly, others have suggested ways to manually associate nearby devices that are all within reach. With Smart-its friends (Holmquist et al., 2001), a connection is established when two devices are shaken simultaneously and sense similar accelerometer values. In *Synchronous Gestures* people can bump devices (Hinckley, 2003)—including phones and interactive tabletops (Schmidt et al., 2010)—together to initiate a connection. In *Stitching*, users couple devices by drawing a stroke that begins on one display and ends on another (Hinckley et al., 2004). Overall, Chong et al. confirmed that proximity is one of the "big five" categories of how users associate devices (Chong and Gellersen, 2011).

7.2.2   REVEALING EXCHANGEABLE CONTENT

Several systems visualized exchangeable content. *Hello.Wall* introduced the notion of "distance-dependent semantics," where the distance (here: close, far, out of range) of a person's device from the wall screen defined the kind of information shown on the mobile display (Prante et al., 2003). The aforementioned *ARIS* shows applications running on devices located in the same room in a world-of-miniature fashion (Biehl and Bailey, 2004). In *Drag-and-Pick*, content that is located in the direction of an initial drag operation appears close to the point of interaction—even on other devices in that direction (Baudisch et al., 2003).

7.2.3   TRANSFERRING DIGITAL CONTENT

Once connected, diverse techniques allow information transfer. For example, Want's RFID-based technique allows detecting nearby objects and devices and associating/retrieving digital information (Want et al., 1999). In *Pick-and-Drop*, users pick up content on one display and place it on another with a digital pen (Rekimoto, 1997). *Touch & Interact* temporarily shift the interaction focus and content from a large display onto a mobile device (Hardy and Rukzio, 2008). Rekimoto combined near-field RFID and remote infrared communication for seamless information transfer (Rekimoto et al., 2003). Further examples for cross-device information transfer from a distance are: throwing gestures performed with a phone (Dachselt and Buchholz, 2009), touch and pointing gesture combinations (Bragdon et al., 2011), chucking motions toward the other device (Hassan et al., 2009), or *corresponding gestures* through cursor selections in multi-screen environments (Nacenta et al., 2005).

In summary, various techniques exist—most suited for particular discrete distances between devices—that fit into particular stages (but rarely all stages) of the gradual engagement pattern (see Figure 7.4). In the next three sections of this chapter, we use our design pattern to build on these earlier works. In particular, we illustrate interaction techniques that allow a person to move seamlessly from awareness at a larger distance, to gradually revealing more detail about devices and content when approaching, to direct interaction for transferring digital information between devices when standing in either close proximity or at a distance. By extending earlier work, we also consider how particular device types can influence this interaction, e.g., personal handhelds vs. semi-public stationary devices.

7.3   STAGE 1: AWARENESS OF DEVICE PRESENCE AND CONNECTIVITY

While ubicomp ecologies may contain many devices, only some of them—for a variety of reasons—are likely able to connect with a user's personal device to the point that the person can do useful work between them (such as transferring content). While these devices may sense this information (e.g., via service discovery protocols), the user is often left in the dark about these opportunities for inter-device interaction.

Consequently, we implemented methods that make a person aware of whether one's personal device and other nearby devices can detect each other's presence and if they are able to connect in a meaningful way. Building upon earlier work (Addlesee et al., 2001; Biehl and Bailey, 2004; Gellersen et al., 2009; Rekimoto et al., 2003), the basic idea is that a person sees a visual indicator—a subtle notification—that shows which devices in the surrounding environment can possibly interact with his handheld device as well as their relative position (e.g., icons in Figure 7.7). People can then subsequently move toward a particular device to either establish that connection or to reveal further information and interaction possibilities (which would occur in stages 2 and 3, discussed shortly). This is particularly important in dynamically changing or unfamiliar environments: some devices may be hidden or disguised as a non-digital device (e.g., a digital picture frame appliance), or only some of the surrounding devices may allow meaningful connections to them (e.g., while two devices may see each other over the network, they may not support the same core application of interest to the user, so there is little point in revealing their connectivity). Information about these possible connections as well as simple ways to actually establish the connection is crucial if seamless interaction across devices is to occur.

7.3.1 PROXEMIC-DEPENDENT AWARENESS

We use rules to determine when to trigger awareness of device presence and connectivity. By connection, we mean whether one device should connect to another device based on human dynamics vs. whether a device is technically capable of connecting to another. We exploit the five proxemic dimensions (Chapter 4) as sensed factors: combinations of them allow us to create nuanced rules of connection behavior.

Location informs devices if they (and the people using them) are in the same room. In almost all cases, devices present in the same room are far more relevant for interaction than the ones nearby but in another room. For example, when a person with a tablet enters a new room through the door, notifications can be triggered about other devices available in that particular room. Other devices in close proximity but in adjacent rooms—such as behind walls—are not shown. Figure 7.5a illustrates this situation, where two people and their tablets are in similar distance to the large display, but only the two devices that are in the same room connect to each other. In proxemics terms, doorways, walls and other boundaries are fixed features that further demark people's sense of social distance (Section 3.3); we believe such fixed features are applicable to how devices determine possible candidates for cross-device connections. Location also informs context; some locations (e.g., public vs. home spaces) would afford quite different connectivity semantics.

Physical distance between devices is an essential factor we exploit for determining device connection and triggering notifications. Proxemic theory states that people naturally stand close to other people they are interested in and want to communicate with. Similarly, we believe that the distance between the user's personal device and other devices in the ecology is a natural indicator of whether a connection between the two should be signalled to the user and subsequently established. Distance measurements can also be applied as a filter that prevents too many notifications in environments with a large number of digital devices. In that case, awareness information only shows a limited number of devices that have the smallest distance (e.g., the five closest devices). For example, in Figure 7.5b only the devices below a certain threshold connect to the tablet device a person is holding—all other devices in that room are ignored.

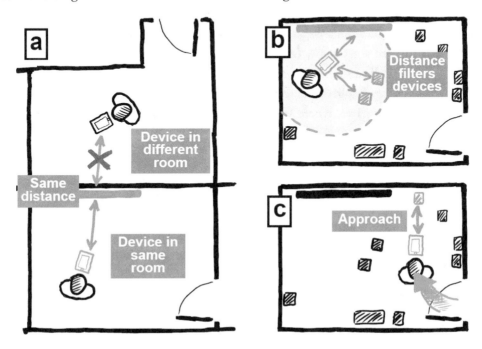

Figure 7.5: Proxemic-dependent awareness considering device's (a) location, (b) distance, and (c) movements.

Movement—the absolute or relative changes of position, orientation, speed, and acceleration of an entity over time—is an indicator of increasing or decreasing interest of one entity to another. When we are interested in something we move closer to it, while we move away when we are less interested. We can apply this to device-device connectivity. For example, if a person holding a tablet is approaching another device, we can interpret this as increasing interest of that person to connect and ultimately interact with both devices in tandem (Figure 7.5c).

Orientation of one device toward another is an additional indicator that the person wants to connect the two. This again mimics interpersonal interaction: when people interact, they orient themselves to either face the other person or stand side by side. Orientation between devices could simply be whether one device is facing toward or away from another device, or a finer measure that considers and acts upon the angle between the two (at the extreme, this becomes pointing, as in Myers et al., 2001; Swindells et al., 2002). For determining cross-device connections, we focus on all devices that are either located in front or at the sides of the device (Figure 7.6a). We assume that if a person wants to interact with a device located behind them, they turn around to face this device, and if they are uninterested, they face away. For example, the visual feedback shown in Figure 7.1a and 7.1b would appear or fade away as the person turns toward or faces away from the display.

Identity of devices functions as a filter for possible connections. Known devices can trigger the connection notification from a larger distance, while unknown devices need to be located next to each other to establish a successful (and more socially secure) connection. This technique follows the principle that "distance implies distrust" (Fishkin et al., 2005), and similarly that closer proximity between devices implies trust (although this depends on location context). Identity also distinguishes classes of devices, where (for example) connectivity to another person's personal device may be dealt with differently than to a semi-public device, as each suggests different social expectations. For example, a person's tablet computer shown on the left side of Figure 7.6b only connects to the semi-public large display (shown at the top of Figure 7.6b) but not the second person's personal tablet computer (shown at the bottom of Figure 7.6b)—even though both devices are at the same distance.

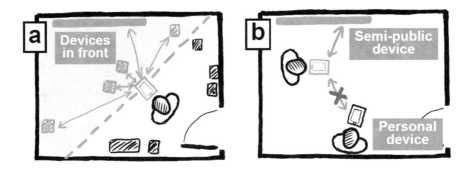

Figure 7.6: Proxemic-dependent awareness considering device's (a) orientation and (b) identity.

The combination of the five proxemic factors informs the decision about device connectivity, and the corresponding visual/auditory/tactile feedback provided, that eventually allows a user to leverage this knowledge of device presence and connectivity for further interaction.

7.3.2   DYNAMIC NOTIFICATIONS ABOUT DEVICE PRESENCE AND POSITION

Given the above, a broad variety of notification mechanisms can inform a person about the presence of other nearby devices and opportunities for interaction: audible signals, vibro-tactile haptic feedback, visual notifications, etc. Yet, given the increasing number of devices in a ubicomp ecology, we opted for a visual approach, as such notifications can be displayed in a more ambient and distinguishable manner. Visuals can portray device identity and location, and—as we will shortly see—can also serve as containers showing content (Stage 2) and act as portals for information exchange (Stage 3).

In general, all device screens in close proximity display graphical icons representing the position of surrounding connectable devices (for example see circled areas in Figure 7.1a, Figure 7.7, Figure 7.8). Each icon informs the user: where the device represented by the icon is physically located relative to the device displaying the icon; that there is a potential connection between those devices; and that devices can interact with one other (e.g., allowing information transfer). Icon appearance can be informative, such as a graphic that represents the nearby tablet. They can also be augmented with other information, such as the name of that device and/or its owner.

Figure 7.7: Icons at the edge of the screen indicate the presence and location of other devices in close proximity (Marquardt et al., 2012a).

Figure 7.7 exemplifies this in Proxemic Brainstorming: as the two people move their tablets toward each other, icons at the edge of both screens show the other devices and the name of the device's owner (see video: gradual engagement). Extending earlier work (Gellersen et al., 2009; Rekimoto et al., 2003), icon positions are continuously animated around the edge to represent the relative directional position of the corresponding device. In Figure 7.7, we see how both displays' icon positions illustrate their physical spatial relationship. Figure 7.8 is similar, except it shows how several positions are indicated in a multi-device environment: in this case, two handhelds and a large display. Again, this helps reducing ambiguity of which icon corresponds to which device in the environment.

Because icon position is dynamic, people can further identify the mapping of device icons to actual physical devices by changing their own device's distance and orientation and observing icon changes. If multiple devices are shown on a tablet's edge, for example, a person can move and/or rotate the screen and see the icons' positions updated in real-time. Naturally, the same continuous feedback applies when a person is moving closer to a cluster of devices. While approaching those devices, their corresponding icons on the tablet continuously change to reflect the new relationship between the tablet and each device. Thus, a person can move seamlessly toward and gradually engage the particular device desired for interaction.

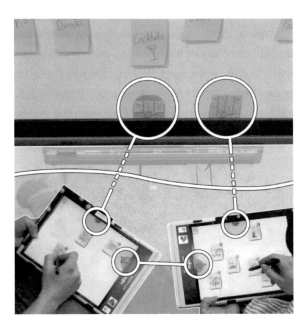

Figure 7.8: Content awareness: Proxy icons indicate the presence of nearby tablets and a large interactive display. Available content of the tablets is displayed as thumbnails atop the icons on the semi-public large display (top), but not on other people's personal devices (i.e., the two tablets at the bottom) (Marquardt et al., 2012a).

7.4 STAGE 2: REVEAL OF EXCHANGEABLE CONTENT

As proximity increases, the gradual engagement pattern suggests that devices should reveal *content* available for exchange. Knowing what content a device offers for transfer is important information for a person to decide on further interactions. In fact, revealing content available for interaction or transfer to another device creates opportunities that invite a person to discover more about this content, eventually leading to more in-depth interactions.

7.4.1 PROXIMITY-DEPENDENT PROGRESSIVE REVEAL

Importantly, revealing content is not all or none. Rather, the *distance* and *orientation* between two devices can directly affect the amount and level of detail of content awareness information shown on other devices. Our *proximity-dependent progressive reveal* technique maps the distance between devices to the amount of information shared between them. The closer two devices are, the more information is shared between them. The level of detail shown (i.e., the amount of information shared) can change either at *discrete* distance levels, *continuously* with changes in distance, or at both *discrete and continuous* levels. As well, the level of detail can change depending on the orientation between devices. Again, this can happen at discrete angles (e.g., facing to or away from another), or through continuous changes of the orientation (e.g., from 0–180°). Progressive reveal is important for three reasons. First, it presents people with opportunities as they approach another device; as with ambient displays, this could mediate the move from background peripheral awareness to foreground interaction (Vogel and Balakrishnan, 2004). Second, it gives them the chance to pull away, for example, if they see content about to be revealed that they would rather not make public. Third, it provides implicit security: in public contexts, fine details may appear in small size, and only when a person is (say) directly in front of another device, thus masking it from passersby.

The following three example scenarios illustrate both discrete and continuous approaches for progressive reveal of device content when approaching another device (see video: gradual engagement).

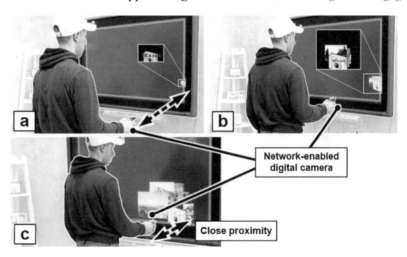

Figure 7.9: Proximity-dependent progressive reveal at discrete levels with the photo canvas: As a person approaches: (a) the large display first shows the presence of his digital camera, (b) then displays the last photo taken with the camera, and (c) a detailed view of multiple photos is revealed, all as a function of proximity.

For our first example, Figure 7.9 shows how content of the *proxemic photo canvas* is progressively revealed at *discrete* distances. Figure 7.9a reflects Stage 1: a person holding a digital camera first sees the camera icon on the large display from afar (for illustrative purposes, the icon is shown magnified as an inset in Figure 7.9a, 7.9b). Figure 7.9b, 7.9c reflect Stage 2. When the person approaches the wall display and crosses the next distance threshold (here 2m), the most recently taken photo stored in the digital camera is shown next to the camera icon (Figure 7.9b). When he moves directly in front of the wall display while holding the camera close to the screen (~30cm distance), multiple photos on the camera are revealed and shown in a spiral around the camera icon (Figure 7.9c).

In our second example, Figure 7.10 illustrates how Proxemic Brainstorming *continuously* reveals content during Stage 2—in this case multiple sticky notes located on people's tablets—as they move closer to the large display (see video: gradual engagement). The wall display shows thumbnails of all sticky notes located on the tablets above the awareness icons (Figure 7.10, right side). For the person sitting at a distance, the actual text on these notes is not yet readable, but the number of available notes is already visible. For the second person moving closer to the wall display, the thumbnails increase in size *continuously* (Figure 7.10b). For the third person standing directly in front of the display, the sticky notes are shown at full size (Figure 7.10c), allowing the person to read the text of all notes stored on the tablet and to pursue Stage 3 interactions, explained shortly.

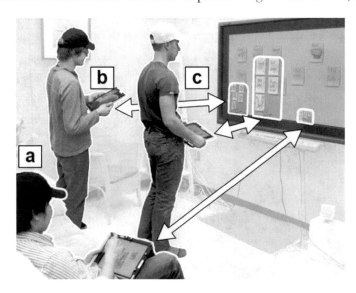

Figure 7.10: Proximity-dependent progressive reveal of personal device data of multiple users at different distances to the display: (a) minimal awareness of a person sitting further away, (b) larger, visible content of a person moving closer, and (c) large awareness icons of person standing in front of the display (Marquardt et al., 2012a).

For our third example, we illustrate how we use *discrete zones* and *continuous movements* to progressively reveal available content (see video: proxemic media player). Figure 7.11 shows how content of the *proxemic media player* (our running example from Chapter 7) is progressively revealed when other devices around it are present (see video: proxemic media player). When a person takes a portable media player out of their pocket while sitting at a distance, in stage 1 the system recognizes the device and provides awareness information through a visual icon at the border of the display (Figure 7.11a). This icon represents the portable device, where it indicates the opportunity to share content between the large surface and the portable device. If the person then orients this portable device toward the large screen, more detailed information about that device (Figure 7.11b shows the device icon) and its contents become visible (Figure 7.11c shows small thumbnail images of the video content on the device).

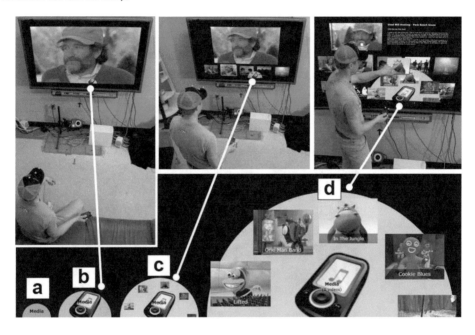

Figure 7.11: Proximity-dependent progressive reveal with proxemic media player, with increasing information available as a function of proximity: (a) awareness icon from afar, (b) more details about the device, (c) revealing content, and (d) showing large video thumbnails and titles (Ballendat et al., 2010).

All these events so far happened at discrete distance levels. Depending on the orientation between the device and the large surface, the icons continuously and instantly update their position at the border of the interactive wall screen, so that they always face the direction of the portable device. As the person moves the personal device closer to the large display, the size of the icon and the video thumbnails shown grow continuously to a large area of the screen. This is visible in Figure 7.11d, which shows the now large preview images of the videos. Finally, when the person is very close to the display, the actual titles of the portable media player's videos are shown on the screen (also visible in Figure 7.11d). When the person puts the device back in his pocket, the visualization immediately disappears and the media player continues its playback.

7.4.2 IMPLICIT VS. EXPLICIT REVEAL

The above method illustrates how content is revealed via a person's implicit actions. However, reveal can be complemented by explicit methods as well to fine-tune what is revealed. To illustrate a combination of implicit and explicit progressive reveal, we implemented a tilt-scrolling technique (a variation of Dachselt and Buchholz (2009) in Proxemic Photo Canvas, Figure 7.12). During Stage 2, a person sees a few of the camera's latest photos—organized in a spiral—progressively revealed as an implicit consequence of moving toward the display. To see more content (and while still distant from the display), the person can now explicitly tilt the camera leftward or rightward to browse through the timeline of photos. Of course, alternative forms of explicit input (e.g., hand gestures) could be considered to cause similar explicit reveal behaviors.

Figure 7.12: Explicit reveal: tilt-scrolling reveals content on digital camera.

7.4.3 REVEALING CONTENT ON PERSONAL VS. PUBLIC DEVICES

The information revealed about available content on the display of other devices should differ between *personal* and *semi-public* devices. For personal devices, we currently only provide an awareness icon of surrounding devices, but not their content. This is partially due to privacy reasons, but also size constraints: showing content on the small screens of *personal devices* may interfere with other content the user is viewing or interacting with. As we will see, we use other stage 3 methods to reveal content on personal devices during explicit information exchange.

Semi-public devices (e.g., a wall-mounted display in a meeting room), however, reveal content located on one's *personal devices* as one approaches the display. For example, the wall display in Figure 7.8 shows both tablets' awareness icons at its lower edge, where each icon now contains small thumbnail images of all Proxemic Brainstorming notes on the corresponding tablet (i.e., 3 notes on the left tablet, 12 notes on the right one). Even though these thumbnails are too small to allow for full readability, they provide awareness information about the number of notes available for sharing on each of the tablets.

7.5   STAGE 3: TECHNIQUES FOR INFORMATION TRANSFER BETWEEN DEVICES

Stage 1 and Stage 2 indicate device presence, connectivity, and available content, eventually leading to Stage 3 of the gradual engagement pattern, where a person can interact with progressively revealed content. We now present a series of novel interaction techniques (and others from related work) that allow for sharing and transferring content between devices (see video: gradual engagement).

We stress that the power of these Stage 3 techniques is that they are used in conjunction with the Stage 1 and Stage 2 methods vs. as stand-alone techniques similar to those found in the literature. Importantly, these techniques consider proxemic relationships between devices to drive the interaction, and come into play at particular points during Stage 1 and Stage 2. We are particularly interested in two contexts:

- whether information exchange is a single-person activity (based on the proximity of a handheld to a semi-public display) or a cooperative multi-person activity (based on the proximity of at least two handheld devices); and

- how they allow people to interact at different levels of proximity, e.g., from a distance vs. within reach.

7.5.1   SINGLE PERSON TRANSFER: FROM PERSONAL TO PUBLIC DEVICE

First, we present a series of techniques that primarily allow a *single person* to share content from their personal device to a public display. We begin with distance-based interactions that could be performed in the early periods of progressive reveal, to within reach interactions at later periods.

Large Display Drag and Back (From a Distance)
Large display drag and back allows a person to temporarily show digital content from their personal device on a large *public* display. The idea is that the person owns the information, but is making it more convenient for others to view it. To share content temporarily on a large display, a person can drag content onto the awareness icon representing a nearby large screen.

For example, Figure 7.13 bottom shows a person dragging a note onto that icon. As he does so, a *viewing icon* appears atop the content (here, the "eye" icon shown inside the circle of Figure 7.13) indicating that one is about to share the note on that particular public display. As the person releases the note, the content appears in full screen view on the wall display (Figure 7.13 top). To remove shared content, a person simply drags the content back from the device's awareness icon onto the tablet's canvas. Sharing also works for multiple people simultaneously: if others do similar actions, all shared content is shown side by side on the large display.

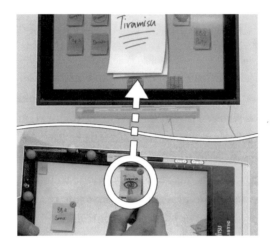

Figure 7.13: Large display drag and back: (bottom) dragging content on the wall display's awareness icon on the tablet, (top) content appears full screen on the large display (Marquardt et al., 2012a).

Cross-device Portal Drag to Transfer (From a Distance)

We can also exploit the awareness icons of Stage 1 as portals to transfer information between them via drag and drop. This extension of the *portals* concept (Voelker et al., 2011) supports transfer methods across *multiple* devices.

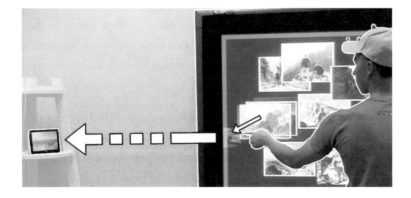

Figure 7.14: **Cross-device portal drag** (Marquardt et al., 2012a).

Figure 7.14 illustrates the Proxemic Photo Canvas on a large display and a picture frame appliance; their awareness icons are visible at their borders. A person is transferring content from the large display to the picture frame simply by dragging a photo onto the picture frame portal, which then shows that image in full size in the frame. To foreshadow what is to come, in Chapter 8 we will extend this technique to transfer information between multiple personal tablet computers that are in close proximity to one another.

Integrating and Refining Pointing Techniques: Point & Pin and Point & Edit (From a Distance)

Considering all stages of the gradual engagement pattern also helps us integrate and refine existing gestural interaction techniques for information transfer.

Figure 7.15: *Point & pin* transfers content from a distance.

For example, our *point & pin* technique lets a person copy content from the camera onto a distant public display by pointing at it and subsequently performing a throwing gesture to pin it there. This technique refines *throw & tilt* (Dachselt and Buchholz, 2009) and *chucking* (Hassan et al., 2009): the pointing ray is the extension of the stretched out arm holding the camera relative to the body, proxemic relationships of device-to-device determine recipient selection, and a preview of the most recently taken photo is shown where that ray meets the large wall display (i.e., an explicit Stage 2 action). People can "throw" photos by forward-accelerating the hand holding the camera, permanently copying that photo onto the screen at that position (Figure 7.15). The technique also works on a digital picture frame, where the photo is then shown full screen in the frame.

In a similar fashion, we integrated the *point & edit* technique as a refinement of semantic snarfing (Myers et al., 2001) and *touch+air* pointing gestures (Bragdon et al., 2011). While content on a large display is convenient for viewing, editing may be more efficient on one's portable device. To select content for transferring back to the tablet, the tablet itself can function as a distant pointing device. As shown in Figure 7.16, a person holds the tablet away from his body and points it toward the display, where the specific proxemic relationship of person and device is triggering the pointing mode. The system calculates the intersection of the pointing ray with the large display's surface. This action highlights the note (with a colored border) that is closest to that intersection point. To transfer the note to the tablet temporarily for editing purposes, the person taps on the tablet's screen. To place back the note on the large display, the person points at a position on the display and again taps the tablet's screen to confirm.

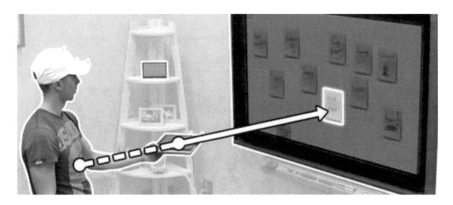

Figure 7.16: *Point & edit* technique to select and edit content from a distance.

Direct Touch: Drag In and Out (Close Proximity)

In this technique, illustrated in Figure 7.17, the tablet's content is progressively revealed in Stage 2 by growing it in size directly in front of the approaching person. (The area also follows the person's side-by-side movements). When within direct touch distance to the large display, this content becomes interactive, i.e., it allows that person to access his tablet's content by directly touching the large display. In particular, a person transfers content between the two devices (tablet & large display) by dragging items into or out of their personal area.

Figure 7.17a and 7.17b illustrate how Proxemic Brainstorming and Photo Canvas allow one to drag notes and photos to an empty region on the screen, which transfers them across devices. While both progressively revealed their contents in visually different ways, the transfer operation is identical.

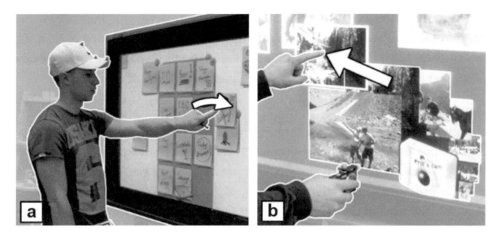

Figure 7.17: **Drag in and out in close proximity** (Marquardt et al., 2012a).

Again, we can integrate refinements of existing techniques at this stage. For example, inspired by *PhoneTouch* (Schmidt et al., 2010), the tablet itself can now be used as a physical pointing and selection device. Touching the device on the large screen will pick up or drop off information (Figure 7.18). Considering proxemics refines this technique: the pointing function of the tablet becomes active when a person stands within touch distance, and holds the tablet in a way that one of its corners points at content on the large display. As the device moves toward the display, a projected pointer highlights the currently selected note (thus providing continuous feedback before touching). When the person touches a note with a corner of the tablet, the note is picked up and temporarily transferred to the tablet device for editing. After editing, a person can quickly place that note back to a given position on the large display by touching that position with a corner of the tablet.

Figure 7.18: Touching the device on the large screen will pick up or drop off information.

7.5.2 COLLABORATIVE TRANSFER

The next suite of techniques is tailored to multiple people collaboratively sharing content with each other through their *personal* devices, possibly including a large display. Unlike the single user techniques, these include coordination protocols that influence how handoffs are achieved.

Collaborative Handoff (From a Distance)

In collaborative work scenarios, people may want to share or give digital information to another person. Often, this requires tedious sequences of tasks such as sending files by email or copying and retrieving content using portable media. Our notion of a *proxemic-aware collaborative handoff* (inspired by collaborative stitching by Hinckley et al., 2004), represents a simpler method for transferring content between devices. The idea is that one person starts the gesture on his personal device, and a second person continues this gesture on his personal device to complete the handover process. That is, one person cannot transfer information without cooperation from the other person. Both must also be in close proximity before these techniques are activated. We expect people to monitor each other's actions in a way that mediates their social protocols.

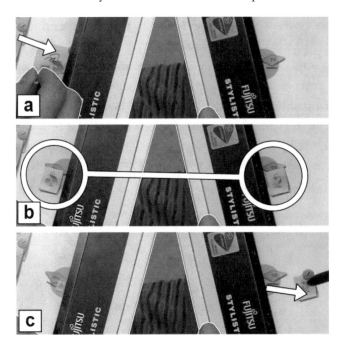

Figure 7.19: Collaborative handoff: (a) dragging content onto awareness icon representing the other tablet, (b) content appears on 2nd tablet, and (c) dragging content off the icon transfers it (Marquardt et al., 2012a).

Figure 7.19 illustrates an example of content exchange in the Proxemic Brainstorming application between two people who have moved their tablets beside each other. As before, both are aware of connection availability via progressive reveal, where in this case the awareness icon size is larger as people move closer. Similar to our previously described "portal drag to transfer," a person can initiate content sharing by dragging a sticky note onto the awareness icon of the second person's tablet (Figure 7.19a). What is different is that a thumbnail of the content then appears on the second tablet, so that it is temporarily visible on both screens (Figure 7.19b). If the second person drags the thumbnail image from the awareness icon onto his screen (thus *continuing* the first person's drag operation), the thumbnail on the first person's tablet disappears and the content is now permanently stored on the second person's device (Figure 7.19c). Through this continuation of the gesture that was started by the first person, the second person "accepts" the content transfer action. If the person does not accept, the transfer is not performed. As well, if the transfer has not yet been accepted (i.e., phase 2; Figure 7.19b), the first person can cancel the transfer by dragging the content back onto his or her screen.

Drag between a Public Intermediary (Close Proximity)
Two people can use the shared screen area of the large public display as a way to hand off content. The idea is that because information on that display is public, it implicitly gives permission to both actors to exchange information between their devices.

Figure 7.20 illustrates this. Two people are standing in direct touch distance in front of a large wall display with their tablet device in hand. Via progressive reveal, the personal content of both their devices are visible on the wall display as two interaction areas—one per person—in positions that reflect the side-by-side locations of both people (see the rectangular grey boxes containing sticky notes on the screen in Figure 7.20). The large interaction areas on the screen make it easy to view and modify content.

Two different versions illustrate different ways of performing the transfer. In the handoff version, a person can drag a note to the shared public area (i.e., the regions not covered by individual interaction areas) on the large display (Figure 7.20a, 7.20b), but not into the other person's area. The second person accepts that transfer by picking up this note and dragging it to his own interaction area (Figure 7.20c, 7.20d).

The second version does not require this handoff, relying instead on social protocol as augmented by the high visibility of all actions. Here, a person can move (or take) a note directly from one tablet to another by dragging it from one interaction area straight to the other.

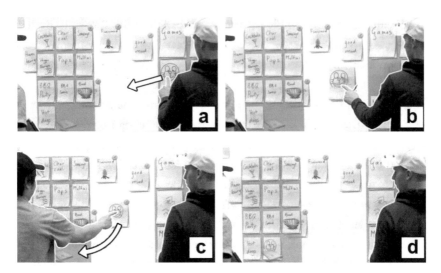

Figure 7.20: Drag between a public intermediary: (a) person drags note out of his personal interaction area, (b) using the empty space between the interaction areas as a clipboard. (c) Second person drags note into his interaction space of the tablet, and (d) the note is now moved to his tablet (Marquardt et al., 2012a).

7.6   OTHER EXAMPLE APPLICATIONS

As with Section 6.10, we briefly describe several projects by others in our laboratory. The first set illustrates the diversity of systems that consider the relations between devices. The second set includes relationships with non-digital objects. A final example includes human-robot interaction.

7.6.1   PROXEMICANVAS

ProxemiCanvas, by Xiang Anthony Chen, is an interactive drawing application in which drawing canvases displayed on people's portable computers gradually merge as a function of proxemic relationships between people and devices. For instance, from close to far distance, this ranges from: merged workspaces when very close (i.e., a merged canvas in Figure 7.21a); awareness of other people's work when sitting nearby (i.e., seeing another person's drawing cursor, Figure 7.21b); gradually less shared information when moving away (i.e., the edge of the other person's canvas is visible in Figure 7.21c); and finally no shared information when turning away (e.g., when people are sitting far apart or back to back). Technically, the system tracks the position, identity, movement, and orientation of both people's notebook computers and maps those values to various degrees of coupled workspaces.

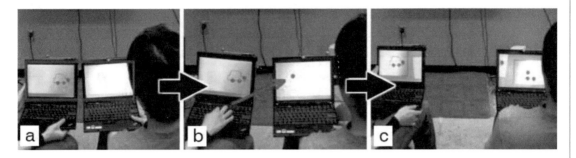

Figure 7.21: ProxemiCanvas facilitates collaborative drawing (Xiang Anthony Chen).

7.6.2   MULTI-DEVICE VIEWER FOR MEDICAL IMAGES

Multi-device Viewer for Medical Images, by Francisco Marinho Moreira Rodrigues and Teddy Seyez, lets a person browse through 3D volumetric medical data sets by moving a tablet in 3D space above a tabletop (Seyed et al., 2013). While the tabletop displays a static top-down projection of the medical dataset (e.g., a person's torso as shown in Figure 7.22), the tablet PC shows a visualization of a 2D slice cut through the 3D data set. The tablet's visualization is continuously updated when moving the tablet through the volume above the tabletop. See also Spindler et. al. (2014), who describe a generalizable form of this idea.

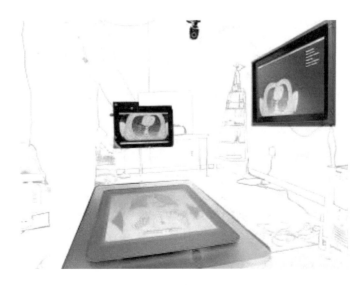

Figure 7.22: Multi-device viewer for medical images (Francisco Marinho Moreira Rodrigues).

7.6.3   PROXEMIC REMOTE CONTROLS

Proxemic remote controls, by David Ledo, leverages *Proxemic Interactions* strategies to facilitate the control of multiple appliances within a ubicomp ecology via a mobile device (Ledo and Greenberg, 2013, Ledo 2014; see video proxemic remote control). The remote control is used to discover what appliances are available, to select a particular appliance, and then to gradually engage with that appliance to view its state and ultimately to control it.

Initially, a person can discover what appliances are controllable by scanning the remote around the room. The remote's display shows the presence and location of all appliances around the border (akin to a bird's eye overview). This overview is dynamic, where appliance positions are correctly tracked and visualized. As the control faces somewhat toward a particular appliance, a larger graphic of that appliance and its state appears around its center. The user can then select that appliance simply by staying oriented toward it, and gradually engage with that appliance to view its details and to control it.

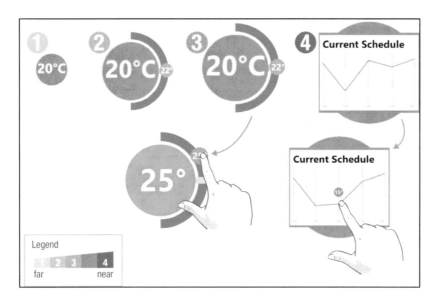

Figure 7.23: Thermostat interface, showing a series of progressively revealed interaction controls on the remote control's screen (David Ledo).

The example shown in Figure 7.23 illustrates gradual engagement with a thermostat on the wall, where the graphic sketches what appears at the center of the screen. When the thermostat interface is first revealed on the remote control, it initially shows only the current temperature of the room (step 1). As the remote is moved closer, the thermostat interface changes to include a grey circle that indicates the current temperature setting that the room is adjusting toward (step 2). As the remote moves even closer, the temperature setting changes to blue to indicate that it can now be controlled interactively (step 3, top). A user can now drag the blue circle to change the room temperature setting, which is reflected on the interface to accommodate for finger occlusion (step 3, bottom). When the person moves very close to the thermostat, an interactive schedule appears that displays set points for the temperature over the day. This schedule can then be manually modified through a dragging gesture. At any time, the user can manually override gradual engagement by locking the display to its current settings, and manually changing the level of detail displayed. They can also directly select appliances from the overview for further viewing.

7.6.4 SPATIAL MUSIC EXPERIENCE

Spatial Music Experience, by Matthew Dunlap, is an interactive music installation. The kinds of synthesizer sounds generated by the computer and their volume is determined by the proxemic relationships of people and physical objects in the space (Figure 7.24a). Generated sounds react fluently as people move and perform gestures in the space, as well as when they grab and move physical objects toward each other (e.g., the drums in Figure 7.24b).

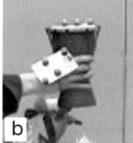

Figure 7.24: Spatial Music Experience (Matthew Dunlap)

7.6.5 TIP-ME-LENS

Tip-me-lens, by Bon Adriel Aseniero, is a mobile recommender system used to inform a customer's buying decisions while browsing products on a shelf (Aseniero et al., 2013; see video: tip-me-lens). It uses augmented reality techniques to superimpose additional information on the phone's display (Figure 7.25a) about the store items on the shelf in front of the person (Figure 7.25b). Depending on a person's distance to the shelf, the information displayed on the screen varies. Following the gradual engagement pattern, more detailed information about the products (e.g., nutritional information of food items, Figure 7.25c) is revealed once a person approaches and moves closer to the display.

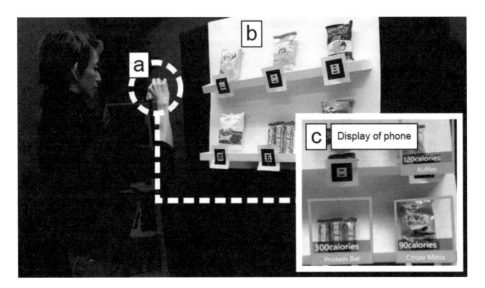

Figure 7.25: Tip-me-lens mobile recommender system (Aseniero et al., 2013)

7.6.6 THE GREETING ROBOT

The *proxemic-aware robot*, by Brendan Heenan and Setareh Aghel Manesh, is a humanoid robot that simulates social intelligence when greeting people (Heenan et al., 2014; see video: greetings robot). The robot's design models human-to-human greeting behaviors as observed and developed by Kendon (1990), which in turn incorporates behaviors that reflect proxemic theory and the gradual engagement pattern. The robot tracks the presence, proximity, and orientation of people around it. The robot then reacts to various greeting cues to enact the greetings process. When it sights a person's presence (Figure 7.26a), it stands and looks at them (Figure 7.26b). When it detects mutual gaze, it performs a distance salutation such as a wave (Figure 7.26c), head toss, and/or vocalization. It begins approaching the person, where (as people do) it avoids eye contact as it passes through the social zone. When it moves through the personal and then intimate zone, it resumes eye contact, faces its body toward the person, and performs a close salutation (such as a handshake). It then steps back to the personal zone, after which conversation could occur. During all these stages, it monitors how the person is moving (e.g., toward or away from it) and reacts accordingly, e.g., by abandoning the greeting if the person does not appear to want to engage with it.

a. sighting: *looks at person*   b. distance salutation: *stands*   c. distance saluation: *waves*
                                     & faces person

Figure 7.26: Initial greetings behavior during human-robot interaction (Heenan et al., 2014).

7.7   DISCUSSION

In this section we discuss how the gradual engagement pattern applies to larger ecologies of people and devices, how we can address privacy concerns, and how to apply the pattern with different available tracking hardware.

7.7.1   LARGE ECOLOGIES OF PEOPLE AND DEVICES

We believe the gradual engagement pattern will be increasingly relevant as ubicomp ecologies emerge with larger numbers of personal and public devices featuring different form factors and capabilities. As shown, the pattern and the techniques we derived support a variety of 1-to-1 (e.g., *collaborative handoff, cross-portal drag*) and 1-to-many (e.g., *progressive reveal, large display drag and back*) collaborative settings. A major advantage of using the stages of gradual engagement is that it leads to an implicit *filtering* of choices presented to a user. For example, following the pattern prevents a system showing an overwhelming number of icons of all present devices in a large ecology, but instead fosters a design that only reveals the device presence between neighbors. Nevertheless, future work may extend our techniques to offer alternative 1-to-many and many-to-many sharing possibilities, e.g., by allowing dragging content on multiple device icons to share transfer content to all devices of a group.

7.7.2   GRADUAL ENGAGEMENT AND PRIVACY

We recognize that the gradual engagement pattern for cross-device transfer can introduce privacy concerns in some situations. Thus, designs must incorporate safeguards to guarantee privacy of people's personal information. First, as mentioned in Stage 1, location information is essential to drive sharing behavior. For example, while it is likely to have loose sharing between devices at home, only restricted sharing might be desired in the office, and no sharing (but maybe only device awareness) in public settings. Second, implicit protection rules can be applied to prevent sharing. For example, a device in a person's pocket stays invisible, but shares content when the person takes it out and points it toward other devices. For example, Marquardt et al. (2010) followed this principle with their light-sensitive RFID tags (that are often integrated in credit cards or transit passes) that are deactivated when inside of a person's pocket and are only active when taken outside of the pocket. Third, explicit actions and commands on the device can allow a person to manually stop sharing and close inter-device connections at any time (e.g., by pressing a button). Fourth, designs should leverage existing social practices by allowing people to predict and control what they reveal to others. For example, Stage 1 reveals opportunities for information sharing. No actual information is revealed until Stage 2—and even that is gradually done, where the reveal grows as the proxemic distance lessens. Using this feedback, a person can decide at any point to stop sensitive information display.

Of course, privacy in Proxemic Interactions is a rich and fertile area for future work. While beyond the scope of this book, it is vital that it is addressed.

7.7.3   PATTERN APPLIED TO DIFFERENT TRACKING HARDWARE

The principles of the gradual engagement design pattern can be applied to interactive systems using diverse high- and low-fidelity tracking systems. While the technology can limit or enhance how the design pattern is applied in a particular situation, the pattern itself goes beyond any specific technology. At the high-fidelity end of the spectrum of possible hardware, our implementation uses an infrared-based motion capturing system provided via our Proximity Toolkit (see also video: proximity toolkit). The precise tracking information it provides of people and devices' distance or orientation, as listed in Section 2.5.3, allowed us to explore a large part of possible kinds of interactions. Such a system, however, is not yet suitable for wide deployments due to its expense, its complexity in incorporating it into the room setting, and its requirement for tracking markers.

At the opposite side of the spectrum, a possible low-fidelity system using sensor fusion of depth-camera streams and wireless-radio signals for distance and orientation measurements can similarly integrate gradual engagement methods. Despite its lower tracking fidelity, it would allow for applying diverse methods across all three stages of the pattern, such as progressive reveal, cross-device portals, and/or collaborative handoff.

Many other tracking systems would support gradual engagement as well. For example, eye-tracker-based systems can provide interaction awareness, reveal information, and offer interaction methods depending on people's attention through eye contact. Likewise, a system using GPS-based positioning and digital compass data could apply the pattern in a larger-scale outdoor deployment. Even simple proximity sensors (such as those found in bathrooms) can indicate approximate distances of something in front of it. Overall, the gradual engagement pattern has the potential of being applied to many other proxemic-aware systems with diverse tracking capabilities along this low-/high-fidelity spectrum.

7.8   CONCLUSION

We believe that proxemic-aware interaction techniques following the gradual engagement pattern can help us design future ubicomp systems to support the information transfer process in a way that more appropriately reacts to people's social understanding of personal space. We argued that gradual engagement is an essential prerequisite of such systems. We believe this pattern will be increasingly relevant as ubicomp ecologies emerge with an increasing number of personal and public devices of all different form factors and capabilities. Besides the application to cross-device transfers discussed in this chapter, the generalized gradual engagement pattern can be applied to other areas, e.g., interactive advertisements or games. In a similar way, these applications could benefit from (1) giving awareness notifications about presence, (2) reveal of content or possible interactions, and (3) providing a range of interaction techniques appropriate to the particular contexts as defined by distance, orientation, and group engagement.

The gradual engagement pattern and our derived set of techniques for mediating cross-device operations we introduced is not a complete or exhaustive set, nor do they handle all issues that will likely emerge (such as privacy). Rather, they are a starting point suggesting further interaction techniques that consider the gradual engagement pattern during ubicomp system design.

Overall, this chapter demonstrated how to consider device-to-device proxemics in interaction design. Our design of particular interaction techniques was informed by the proxemic theories reviewed in Chapter 3, the identified proxemic dimensions in Chapter 4, and the gradual engagement pattern in Section 6.6. In our next chapter, we drive this research further, where we consider both the *proxemics of people* and the *proxemics of devices* in order to facilitate small group collaboration.

CHAPTER 8

Considering Person-to-Person and Device-to-Device Proxemics

In this chapter we now combine strategies introduced in the last two chapters, where we consider *person-to-person* proxemics (through small group F-formations) and *device-to-device* proxemic relationships, both which will be used to facilitate sharing of digital content between digital devices. In particular, we introduce GROUPTOGETHER as a system that explores cross-device interaction combining the two sociological constructs of proxemics (Section 3.2–3.7) and F-formations (Section 3.8), refined through a third construct named *micro-mobility* that describes how people orient and tilt devices toward one another to promote fine-grained sharing during co-present collaboration (see video: GROUPTOGETHER). Our work was also informed by an observational study we conducted of people working together with mock-ups of mobile displays. We explain how we designed a number of cross-device interaction techniques that support nuanced gradations of sharing, from the subtle to the overt, with the goal of minimizing the transaction costs—and social disruption—of sharing information across a small-group ecology of digital devices and situated displays.

The techniques are unique in that they consider device-to-device relationships as well as human-to-human relationships—that is, the context of the social group to mediate interaction. For example, in Figure 8.1a the two people on the left standing side by side engage in a collaborative discussion and share content on their tablet devices. The third person on the right—although standing very close by—is outside this social group and thus excluded from the lightweight federation of devices.

The chapter first briefly revisits related work and the theory of micro-mobility that motivate our work (Section 8.1). Next, we present an observational study, which informs the behaviors that serve as the building blocks of our interaction techniques (Section 8.2). We then explain the GROUPTOGETHER system and detail the interaction techniques (Section 8.3), focusing initially on the micro-mobility aspects (Section 8.4.1–8.4.4). We then describe how we extend these techniques to federated devices held by users in F-formations consisting of two or more persons (Section 8.4.5), and how we consider the case where the F-formation encompasses a digital whiteboard (Section 8.4.6). We close with a discussion of salient issues raised by this research (Section 8.5). A video illustrates the applications and the dynamics of the GROUPTOGETHER system and its interaction techniques described in this chapter (see video: GROUPTOGETHER).

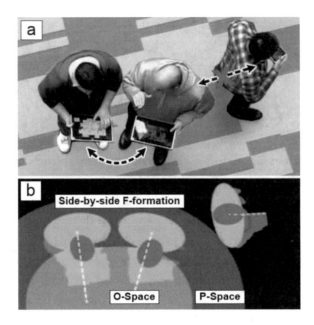

Figure 8.1: (a) F-Formation between multiple people as they collaborate, (b) grouped formations as tracked by the GROUPTOGETHER system.

8.1   USING THEORY TO MOTIVATE GROUP INTERACTION TECHNIQUES

Despite the ongoing proliferation of devices and form-factors such as slates and electronic white-boards, technology often hinders (rather than helps) informal small-group interactions. Whereas natural human conversation is fluid and dynamic, discussions that rely on digital content—slides, documents, clippings—often remain stilted due to the awkwardness of manipulating, sharing, and displaying information on and across multiple devices. To address these shortcomings, we leverage three highly related sociological constructs that have been observed in human-human social activity to inform our designs of novel cross-device interaction techniques: (1) *proxemics*, (2) *F-formations*, and (3) *micro-mobility*.

First, we consider the interpersonal *proxemic* relationships between people as they engage, and between devices as they are used by people. We argued throughout this book that computing systems—which are carried about as well as embedded in the world around us—could be enhanced by sensing proxemic relationships (via distance, orientation, movement, identity, and location) between all entities in a ubicomp ecology. In Chapter 6 we focused on possible interactions between a person and a large interactive surface, where the system responds to movement, proximity, and orientation of one person or multiple people in relation to the environment. In Chapter 7 we applied Proxemic Interactions concepts to device-to-device interaction, where we used the information about entities' orientation, distance, motion, location, and identity as a way to gradually engage people with opportunities for information exchange across devices. In this chapter we focus on new device interactions afforded by micro-mobility (defined shortly) as mediated by the proxemics between people and devices and the group's social context of the F-formation (described next).

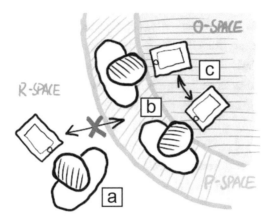

Figure 8.2: Sensing F-formations of both the people and the devices they carry to automatically federate devices and mediate cross-device interaction.

Second, we consider the dynamics of small-group gatherings as defined by *F-formations*. In particular, our system observes proxemic relationships and F-formations of both the people and the devices they carry to automatically federate devices and mediate cross-device interaction in a way that corresponds to real-time social groupings. Physically nearby people in the R-space (Figure 8.2a), especially those facing away, are recognized as socially distant from the current assemblage of users that are present in the P-space (Figure 8.2b) and therefore can be excluded from the exchange. If people within the F-formation then orient their devices toward (say) the central O-space shown in Figure 8.2c (i.e., using micro-mobility), the system can offer lightweight ways to share device contents across the group.

Third, we consider how people employ *micro-mobility* of physical artifacts to afford nuanced collaboration. The *micro-mobility* of physical artifacts is the fine-grained orientation and repositioning of objects so that they may be fully viewed, partially viewed, or concealed from other persons. For example, Luff and Heath (1998) reported on patient-doctor consultations via paper records and observed how individuals rely on the micro-mobility of these physical artifacts to facilitate communication. The doctor might gesture at a record, orient it such that it invites the patient to view material, or

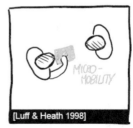

pull it back to give the doctor time to read information. These subtle manipulations of the paper record afford the shifting demands of an activity. Thus micro-mobility posits that orienting an artifact toward other persons, moving it closer to them, or even subtly tilting it toward or away from that person affords powerful and nuanced ways for individuals to share (or not share) information, as well as to fluidly manage the focus of conversation and make their intentions clear to others.

Luff and Heath (1998) introduced micro-mobility and its implications for the design of groupware systems mostly as a cautionary tale, i.e., that new technologies may disrupt the natural movement of artifacts necessary for effective communication. Micro-mobility has since been applied to other areas, particularly the spacing and orientation of digital objects on tabletop systems to denote personal territoriality as well as groupings of objects (Everitt et al., 2006). Other related techniques include adjusting the posture of dual-screen devices (Hinckley et al., 2009), bumping and pouring (Hinckley, 2003), stitching (Ramos et al., 2009), and "chucking" content from one device to another (Hassan et al., 2009) (also see our earlier discussion in Section 2.5).

The work in this chapter differs from this prior work and extends our interaction techniques from Chapter 6 and Chapter 7 in several ways. First, we apply the above concepts of proxemics, F-formations, and micro-mobility in unison. By explicitly incorporating sensing mechanisms for both interpersonal proxemics (via F-formations) as well as device-to-device orientation and identification (via micro-mobility), our system embraces these approaches in a hybrid design. Second, our focus is on cross-device interaction methods, and in particular how to decide when devices should be federated (by sensing F-formations) and how that information should be shared (by sensing micro-mobility).

8.2   DESIGN STUDY: PROXEMICS OF PEOPLE AND DEVICES

Our belief is that ubiquitous computing environments can sense social proximity of people in the form of F-formations, the device-to-device assemblages, as well as the micro-mobility of physical devices used by the group of people. Previous efforts have explored techniques for mediating cross-device interaction (we reviewed techniques in Section 2.5), sometimes informed by proxemics or a more general notion of proximity sensing.

Because past work did not apply the multiple lenses of proxemics, F-formations, and micro-mobility in unison, we performed our own design study, which helped us to narrow down the important aspects of proxemics, F-formations, and micro-mobility that we can then leverage in our interaction designs. Participants performed joint activities, consisting of both cooperative and competitive tasks, using mocked-up handheld displays representing sizes for slate, readers, and phones. Participants used these displays to enact tasks including collaborative, competitive, confidential, and co-present but individual activities (details are reported in Marquardt et al., 2012b). We report only study results here, where we observed the following behaviors (B1–B8) that illustrate interpersonal postures, movements, and gestures that people naturally exhibit in such situations.

B1. *Device as extension of person:* Participants treated the devices as part of their person. They were reluctant to bring displays into direct contact or to touch one another's displays (though they sometimes did so, albeit briefly). Users clearly exhibited a notion of "personal space" surrounding their devices, but the dimensions of the socially acceptable device-space was compressed as compared to normal interpersonal distances.

B2. *Distance and shape of F-formations vary by task:* In the presence of hand-held devices, the task influenced the choice of formation, reinforcing related findings from the proxemic literature, such as Sommer's (1969) observations of task-dependent preferred seating arrangements. For collaborative tasks that required synthesis of information across displays, users moved close together and adopted side-by-side formations. For parallel individual work, users moved apart, often in L-shaped formations. For competitive or private tasks, users often moved face-to-face, as well as further apart.

B3. *Movement of devices in and out of focal zone:* Users extended displays into the o-space defined by their joint gaze when discussing content. Displays that are not the topic of communication are moved into p-space at the user's side, with the display often facing inward. We observed fluent changes of device position and tilting angles that participants performed to bring devices into the focal zone of the o-space.

B4. *Incidental tilting:* As long as a display was not oriented toward the other person, users seemed largely oblivious to the particular tilt angles of their device. That is, any particular tilt angle is not a definitive cue in and of itself, but rather has to be interpreted in the context of the F-formation.

B5. *Pointing while tilting within the o-space:* People often pointed to an item while tilting the display toward the other person. That is, people often discuss *specific pieces of content* rather than the entire display.

B6. *Reorientation with gradation in response:* As with micro-mobility (Luff and Heath, 1998), we observed subtle tilting and reorientation to nonverbally indicate when people wanted to say something about their display. Larger, more overt movement of the display to a compromise viewpoint was a powerful cue to redirect the other person's attention. That is, people employed a gradation in response, from the subtle to the overt, to suit the current communicative need.

B7. *Avoid persistent spatial invasion:* In the few cases when users gestured at each other's display, such intrusions always remained brief, typically just a second or two. Users often want to indicate referents on the other's display, yet doing so may be uncomfortable. This suggests cross-device interactions should avoid direct interaction with another user's display (such as those proposed by Ramos et al., 2009).

B8. *Matching device pose while side-by-side:* When actively working on a joint task, users tended to mirror the tilt angle of one another's slates, suggesting that equal tilt angles offer a context where it might be useful to reduce the barriers to sharing across devices.

Our intent is not to mimic B1–B8 in our designs per se, but rather to use them as buildingblocks, or points of departure for our explorations. Furthermore, some of the above points—while perhaps obvious in retrospect—did not strike us as important observations until after we had completed our initial implementation and preliminary usability study. We will return later to these observed behaviors as we discuss the strengths, weaknesses, and possible extensions to our techniques.

8.3   GROUPTOGETHER SYSTEM: DETECTING FEDERATIONS

We built the GROUPTOGETHER system to explore our envisioned interaction concepts in action (see video: GROUPTOGETHER). We implemented a prototype informal information workspace where users can freely arrange collected content (photos, sketches, clippings, etc.) on an interactive canvas. We implemented the application for both tablets and digital whiteboards, and each instance of the application may connect to other devices nearby, as mediated by our sensing of F-formations and device micro-mobility. We chose this application context because collecting and loosely organizing content is a common need of information workers, such as during active reading (e.g., Hinckley et al., 2009).

The GROUPTOGETHER system automatically realizes the federation of devices (i.e., connecting to the devices nearby) by tracking people and devices through a hybrid of on-device sensors as well as extrinsic sensors in the environment. Implementation details are found in Marquardt, Hinckley et al. (2012b). It senses various f-formation patterns to detect if people are within an f-formation; if they are, it "connects" their devices together (e.g., as in Figure 8.1a+b). It recognizes the type of f-formation (e.g., side-by-side) and what spaces people and their devices are in (e.g., p-space and o-space). Depending on these attributes, it affords particular interaction techniques, discussed next.

8.4   INTERACTION TECHNIQUES

The interaction techniques we designed for the GROUPTOGETHER system facilitate transient sharing, copying, transfer, and reference to digital information across federated devices. These actions suit our application context and allow us to explore various possibilities in order to generate design insights. In particular, the system offers multiple ways to support co-located collaborative activity, ranging from the subtle to the more overt, with various and nuanced semantics of what it means to *share* content. For clarity, in the following we refer to a two-user F-formation involving handheld devices: the user initiating the interaction is the *sender*; and the other person is the *recipient*. We later describe how our techniques work with more than two people, and also with a large display.

We developed four interaction techniques facilitating the sharing of digital information between the devices of people standing in an F-formation. These techniques are directly inspired by behaviors B1–B8 as noted above, and as we discuss each technique we will refer back to these behaviors to reinforce our rationale, design considerations, and behavioral constraints. Note, however, that B1 and B2 are more meta-observations underlying all our techniques: they validate our preconception that there exists a proxemics of devices (B1), reinforce our design approach (devices must be proximal, but do not have to touch any other device; again B1), and furthermore that a variety of F-formation structures must be properly sensed and supported in a consistent manner by the interaction techniques (B2). Furthermore, while in the following descriptions of specific techniques we primarily focus on micro-mobility gestures, keep in mind that these gestures are only active when the user is currently sensed as standing in an F-formation. We do not claim that these techniques are the only ones possible, or even that they are the best techniques. Their purpose is to illustrate how our study findings can inform and inspire several reasonable interaction methods. Other methods are certainly possible.

8.4.1   TILT-TO-PREVIEW SELECTED CONTENT

The *Tilt-to-Preview* technique provides an extremely lightweight way to *transiently share* selected digital content across devices. The receiving user can then elect to grab a copy of the transiently shared information.

Following the example of behavior B5, *Pointing while tilting within the o-space*, the sender shares a selected piece of content by holding his finger on said content while simultaneously tipping the slate slightly (by a minimum of 10°, Figure 8.3a). This gesture is only active when the tablet is held up within o-space. When triggered it causes a transient semi-transparent representation of the selected item to appear on the display of all devices in the current F-formation (on the right tablet in Figure 8.3a). To make it easy for recipients to identify who is offering an item, an animation slides in the shared item from the side of the screen where the sender is standing.

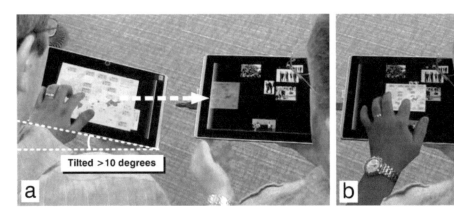

Figure 8.3: (a) Tilting tablet and touching content to transfer temporary copy, (b) touch copy on second tablet to keep permanent copy (Marquardt et al., 2012b).

We employ a tilt threshold of 10°: during pilot testing we found this angle well beyond the *incidental tilting* (B4) that users typically exhibit while holding a slate. Tipping a slate beyond this threshold serves both as a gesture to trigger the behavior as well as a social cue observable to the recipient (and any other people nearby) that the sender wishes to share something. The gesture therefore also leverages observation B6, *Reorientation with gradation in response*, with a fairly subtle overture. Note also that the recipient can ignore such an overture merely by leaving his tablet down, in p-space (as in B3, *Movement in/out of focal zone*), or accept it by holding the tablet up.

When the sender lets go of the transiently shared content, it disappears from the recipient's screen. However, the recipient can choose to keep a *copy* of the transiently shared content by touching a finger down and grabbing it while it remains visible (Figure 8.3b). This precludes any need for either user to reach onto the other's display, in accordance with observation B7 (*Avoid persistent spatial invasion*).

In two-person F-formations, the sender just tips the slate toward the o-space between them and the other user. If there are more than two people in the F-formation, the user can tip the slate toward the o-space at the center of the formation, where all then receive and see that content. As before, all participants of the current F-formation can opt to keep the shared content on their own devices by touching the semi-transparent preview on their screen.

8.4.2 FACE-TO-MIRROR THE FULL SCREEN

As noted in B6, *Reorientation with gradation in response*, we observed both subtle and overt tipping gestures in the course of our design study. As we observed there, a user can employ a larger tilt as a more demanding nonverbal request to interrupt the current thread of conversation and introduce something else. We also noticed that users often employed larger tilts to show content to their more distant partner in face-to-face formations (B2, but not pictured).

Face-to-Mirror explores how we might provide digital affordances based on these observed behaviors. Using this technique, a person can share the full screen view of the primary digital content displayed on their screen to the other tablets in the social group of an F-formation.

When a person holds their tablet vertically (at an angle larger than 70°), the interactive canvas is mirrored, at full-screen scale, to the display of all other tablets of the group (Figure 8.4). Note that unlike Tilt-to-Preview, this is a pure tilting gesture; the user does not have to touch the screen to explicitly select content. Thus, while the tilting motion is larger, the transaction cost of sharing is potentially lower because the required action is simply "show your screen to the others." Again, the tilting motion is large enough that incidental tilting (B4) is not an issue with this technique, and furthermore we only observed the *Tilting while pointing* behavior (B5) in the context of more subtle tilting motions, so requiring pointing during Face-to-Mirror would run counter to our design study observations.

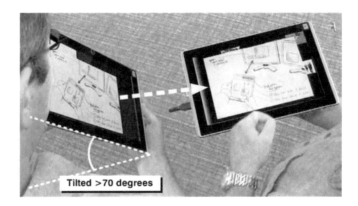

Figure 8.4: Holding tablet vertically (angle larger than 70°) shows a full screen copy on the other tablet (Marquardt et al., 2012b).

As with Tilt-to-Preview, Face-to-Mirror begins as a transient sharing technique that ends when the sender moves his slate away from the vertical posture, but where recipients can retain a copy by grabbing the mirrored item.

8.4.3   PORTALS

The above two techniques both share either a transient representation of an item, or a permanent copy if the recipient touches down and grabs it. To explore an alternative semantic of *transferring* content from one device to another (that is, moving rather than copying content), we implemented the *Portals* technique.

When tilting a tablet (more than 10°) toward the device of any other group member, a tinted edge appears along the shared screen edge of the two slates (Figure 8.5a). By dragging an item through this edge and releasing the touch, the item is (permanently) transferred to the other device (Figure 8.5b). A continuous cross-display animation reinforces the metaphor of the gesture: the content slides off the sender's screen, and slides into the recipient's screen. The recipient can then drag, resize, and otherwise manipulate the content that was transferred to their tablet (Figure 8.5c). As with Tilt-to-Preview, the recipient will only receive items sent through a Portal if his tablet is held up in o-space (as opposed to moving it down to p-space), as observed in B3.

Note that in one sense the gesture for Portals is a hybrid of Tilt-to-Preview and Face-to-Mirror: the user performs a fairly subtle (>10°) tilting motion (like Tilt-to-Preview) to create the portal, but does not have to touch the screen while doing so. On the one hand this means that Portals may be more prone to incidental tilting (B4). On the other hand, the feedback for Portals (a visually unobtrusive tinting along the matching edge of the devices) as well as the semantics of using the Portal (a transfer only occurs if the user explicitly passes an item through the shared edge of the Portal) means that there is very little impact if accidental activation of a Portal does occur.

Figure 8.5: Moving content from one slate to another: (a) dragging content through the tinted edge of screen, (b) item moves onto the other slate, and (c) the recipient repositions the item (Marquardt et al., 2012b).

8.4.4 CROSS-DEVICE PINCH-TO-ZOOM

Cross-Device Pinch-to-Zoom was motivated in part by B8, *Matching pose while side-by-side*. Here, we explore ways that users can explicitly share items when the slates are not tilted (e.g., as shown in Figure 8.6a), but just held together side-by-side in o-space (B3 and B7) and at the same relatively flat angle (B8).

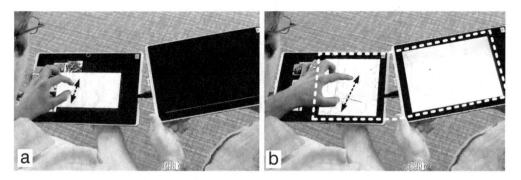

Figure 8.6: Cross-Device Pinch-to-Zoom: (a) the sender begins pinch-to-zoom on the first slate; (b) the zoomed content is displayed on surrounding slates that are part of the F-formation (Marquardt et al., 2012b).

This technique allows viewing content across multiple tablet devices when using a pinch-to-zoom gesture. As typical of freeform canvas interfaces, a person can use a two-finger pinch gesture to enlarge any content on the screen (Figure 8.6a). But since our technique leverages the GROUPTOGETHER system's knowledge of F-formations and the pose of nearby devices, when the sender enlarges the zoomed content beyond the visible area of the slate's display, the remaining content expands onto the surrounding tablets in o-space (Figure 8.6b). That is, while the person zooms in, the content is displayed on the combined screen area of the tablets that form a particular F-formation (i.e., a larger cross-device virtual canvas is created).

8.4.5   PROPAGATION THROUGH F-FORMATIONS

While the above interactions illustrate how our ideas apply to two-person F-formations, the techniques also apply to larger groups (Figure 8.7). For *Tilt-to-Preview* and *Face-to-Mirror*, for example, a person can share content with the entire group by tilting their tablet toward the center of the formation (i.e., toward o-space) rather than just tilting toward a single person.

Furthermore, we implemented the techniques described above for all three types of F-formations (side-by-side, face-to-face, and corner-to-corner). While it would be possible to support assemblage-specific gestures, we felt that this might not be intuitive to users. However, we do adapt the feedback on the screen (e.g., placement of the tinting indicating an active Portal) to match the spatial arrangement of users.

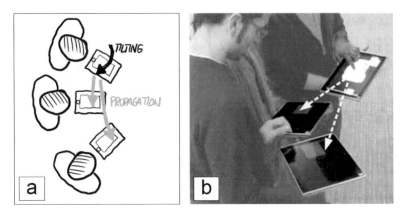

Figure 8.7: Shared content propagates to devices of all members of the current F-formation (Marquardt et al., 2012b).

Likewise, users who are sensed as external to the F-formation cannot participate in group interactions, unless of course they move to stand within the group. While it might be interesting to explore various techniques for beyond-arms-reach interaction (Bragdon et al., 2011)—for example, to allow distant persons to send items to an F-formation, or to the digital whiteboard—by the same token in the context of GROUPTOGETHER this would go against the simplicity of the natural human behaviors that we observed in our design study, so we chose not to pursue such mechanisms here.

8.4.6 A DIGITAL WHITEBOARD AS PART OF AN F-FORMATION

Because F-formations can implicitly encompass fixed or semi-fixed features of the environment (Section 3.3), we included a large screen digital whiteboard in our system as an exemplar.

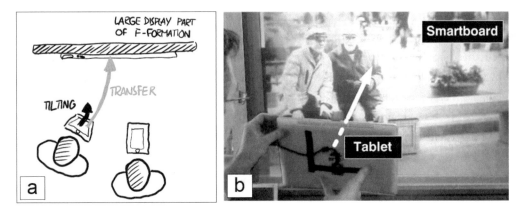

Figure 8.8: Using the Face-to-Mirror technique with a large digital whiteboard display sensed as part of an F-formation (Marquardt et al., 2012b).

Users within a sensed F-formation can share content with the digital whiteboard in a manner analogous to sharing content to slates held by other participants. For example, consider the *Face-to-Mirror* technique. A person can hold their tablet vertically toward the large display, and a temporary copy of the tablet's content appears on the large screen (Figure 8.8). Similarly, a person standing next to the whiteboard can use the Portals technique to move content to the large display by first tilting their tablet toward the large display and then begin dragging content onto the edge of the slate facing toward the whiteboard.

Our implementation considers the digital whiteboard in a manner similar to the human participants in an F-formation; that is, it has a particular position and a facing vector. When it falls along the perimeter of p-space it is treated as part of the F-formation, but if it falls outside the huddle, in r-space, it is not. For example, if a circle of users stands in front of the digital whiteboard, with one user's back to the display, and another user performs a Face-to-Mirror gesture, the content will be mirrored to the F-formation but not to the whiteboard. But if the same circle expands to encompass the whiteboard, then the content would be sent to the whiteboard as well.

8.5 DISCUSSION AND FUTURE WORK

While our system explored a number of novel ideas, it is clear that much more could be done. For example, we explored a pair of techniques—*Tilt-to-Preview* and *Face-to-Mirror*—that looked at two extremes in gradation of response (B6). But from our observational studies, as well as from the commentary of Luff & Heath (1998), it is clear that people's use of micro-mobility is more nuanced still. Therefore, it would be interesting to explore similarly nuanced techniques that explore this continuum further. These might include both implicit ways of using device tilt and motion for context sensing, as well as explicit gestures or posturing of devices (as explored with the techniques in this chapter) to support finely delineated notions of sharing content.

The observations in our design study, as well as those resulting from an informal evaluation of our implementation (Marquardt et al., 2012b), strongly suggest that people treat handheld objects as extensions of their person (B1). Yet by the same token the sociological rules governing "object territoriality" are clearly not the same as those governing our physical bodies. To our knowledge the notion of object territoriality has never been systematically studied, which suggests the need for further experimental and observational studies to better understand behavioral principles that might inform interaction design for micro-mobility and F-formations.

8.6 CONCLUSION

In this chapter we have described GROUPTOGETHER, a sensing system that jointly brings into play the sociological constructs of micro-mobility and F-formations. We summarized a design study that enumerates a number of behaviors illustrating how these combined notions of the *prox-*

emics of people and *the proxemics of devices* surface during joint activity. We then demonstrated how the attributes sensed by our system can leverage these behaviors to enable a number of novel interactions that leverage both the micro-mobility of devices and the social structure of F-formations.

We believe we have only just scratched the surface of a potentially rich space of such techniques. As mobile devices become thinner, lighter, and more flexible, the opportunities to explore these types of socially situated interactions should continue to expand. These should be welcome developments for the many contexts where users need to share and discuss digital artifacts while remaining fully engaged in the seamless flow of social exchange with friends and colleagues.

CHAPTER 9

Dark Patterns

Authors of ubicomp papers concerning innovative design ideas tend to forward their central idea in a positive light. True critical perspectives are rarely offered. When they are, they tend toward a few cautionary lines in the discussion, or relegated to future work where its actual use would be examined. The problem is that many of our new innovations involve designing for situations that are extremely sensitive to intentional or unintentional abuse (e.g., privacy, distraction, and intrusion concerns). The same is especially true of Proxemic Interactions. Rather than wait until some future field study indicating potential harms (where it may be too late to address emerging concerns), we should consider the "dark side" of Proxemic Interactions at the outset.

It is clear, at least intuitively, that there is a dark side to Proxemic Interactions. For example, Proxemic Interactions rely on sensing people and their devices within the surrounding environment. While the systems shown earlier in this book illustrate how sensed dimensions would be valuable to system design, such sensing—as well as the inevitable inaccuracy of interpreting and translating that information into action—immediately raises concerns by experts and non-experts alike about privacy, errors, distraction, and intrusion. In addition, dystopian visions of the future hint at abuses of such technologies. A well-known example is the movie *Minority Report* that illustrates how a character is selectively bombarded by targeted advertisements as he moves in a public space.

In this chapter, we revisit the idea of Proxemic Interactions. Our goal is to present a critical perspective—the dark side—of this technology (Greenberg et al., 2014a; Boring et al., 2014). Our method is to articulate potential dark patterns indicating how we think this technology can be—and likely will be—abused, and anti-patterns in which the resulting behavior occurs as an unintended negative side effect. To avoid being overly broad, we focus our scope somewhat to people's Proxemic Interactions with large (and mostly public) displays, although we do illustrate other examples as needed.

9.1 DARK PATTERNS

Architect Christopher Alexander introduced the notion of design patterns: a documented reusable and proven solution to an architectural design problem (Alexander et al., 1977). Design patterns are typically derived by examining existing solutions to design problems (which may include "folk" solutions) and generalizing them. Design patterns were later advocated as a way of describing common solutions to typical software engineering problems (Gamma et al., 1994), and to interaction design problems (Borchers, 2001). The gradual engagement pattern introduced in Chapter 6 is an example.

A *dark pattern* is a special kind of pattern defined by Brignull (2011) and Brignull et al. (2013) as:

> *"a type of user interface that appears to have been carefully crafted to trick users into doing things [where these user interfaces] are carefully crafted with a solid understanding of human psychology, and they do not have the user's interests in mind."*

Brignull's specific goal in identifying dark patterns was to recognize and name companies, and describe their dark practices so that people would be aware of dark patterns in an interface, and to shame the companies using them.

Highly related to dark patterns are *anti-patterns* that indicate a design failure or non-solution (Koenig, 1995), or an otherwise bad design choice. While dark patterns are intentional, anti-patterns are designs that unintentionally result in a negative experience or even harm.

In the remainder of this chapter, we combine the notion of dark patterns and anti-patterns to articulate not only possible deceptions and misuses of Proxemic Interactions (dark patterns), but also problems that may appear even when the designer has reasonable intentions (anti-patterns). While the novelty of Proxemic Interactions makes pattern elicitation somewhat of a thought exercise (albeit grounded in existing examples where possible), we believe this approach to be appropriate for forecasting—and ideally mitigating—the dark side of our future technologies before actual deceptive patterns become widespread. We now turn to our patterns. Afterward, we discuss how many of our patterns arise from several foundational issues.

9.2   THE CAPTIVE AUDIENCE

The person enters a particular area to pursue an activity that takes a given time, and that does not involve the system. The system senses the person at that location, and begins an unsolicited (and potentially undesired) action based on the fact that the person is now captive.

Unlike desktop computers, technology can be spatially located in an environment to leverage a person's expected routines. When done for beneficial purposes, the technology enhances or supports what the person normally does at that location, which is one of the basic premises of this book. The captive audience pattern instead exploits a person's expected patterns and routine for its own purposes, where the system knows that the person cannot leave without stopping what they otherwise intended to do.

Novo Ad (www.novoad.com), for example, produces advertising mirrors that display video ads on mirror-like screens. The Novo Ad website on its Advertising Mirror page states:

"the system serves as a mirror screen which identifies figures standing in front of it and switches itself automatically on. At start-up the screen displays a 6 second long ad on a full screen, which is later reduced to ¼ of the screen."

Novo Ad identifies public washrooms as one of the prime locations for their displays (see video at YouTube ID: PXwbacfAwnY) as sketched in Figure 9.1. The woman becomes the captive audience, as her primary task is to use the sink and mirror for grooming. The video ad, which starts on her approach, is the unsolicited system action. Other captive locations listed by Novo Ad include dressing rooms and elevators.

Figure 9.1: Novo Ad screenshot (sketch by David Ledo; from Greenberg et al., 2014a).

Captive Media, a British company, takes this one step further (www.captivemedia.co.uk). They estimate that a man using a urinal is captive for ~55 seconds. They place screens directly above the urinal (Figure 9.2, left), and use proximity and "stream" sensors "to detect the position of a man's stream as he pees" (Figure 9.2, right). This information is then used to activate advertising-sponsored pee-controlled games as illustrated in Figure 9.2 left. Later, we discuss how Captive Media has various positive policies in place to mitigate dark pattern effects, where it tries to balance the benefits to product user (by game play) and the client (by effective advertising).

Sensors are not even needed to enact this pattern. Some ATMs, for example, employ the captive audience pattern in a particularly effective way, at least for the advertiser. By displaying advertisements when they know customers are waiting to receive cash or have their bankcard returned, they exploit that the captive customer cannot leave or divert their attention without risking loss of the desired transaction or even one's bankcard.

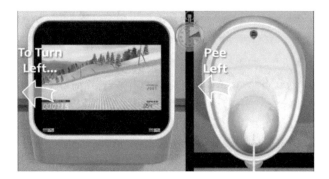

Figure 9.2: Captive Media screenshot (see video at YouTube ID: XLQoh8YCqo4), ©Captive Media, with permission.

"15 Million Merits," the second episode of the dystopian Black Mirror Channel 4 television series, also includes several examples of the captive audience pattern. It portrays a future where each person's bedroom is built out of display walls that are always on when that person is present (as sketched in Figure 9.3). They can only be turned off temporarily when a person makes a payment, or by leaving the room.

Figure 9.3: Scene from Black Mirror (sketch by David Ledo; from Greenberg et al., 2014a).

9.3   THE ATTENTION GRABBER

The person happens to pass by the field of view of a strategically located system. The system takes deliberate action to attract and keep that person's attention.

Attracting attention of a passerby is an exceedingly common strategy used by anyone selling a product or service: the goal is to turn the passerby into a customer. Carnival barkers, greeters in establishment doorways, and aggressive street peddlers all verbally address a passerby to try to get them to enter into a conversation and ultimately into a sales transaction. Establishments use storefronts and windows to advertise their wares. Flashing lights and myriads of public signage and billboards (some electronic and digital) commonly compete for the passerby's attention.

Proxemic-aware public devices are perfectly poised to grab attention of passersby. Like barkers and greeters, they can sense the passerby as an opportunity, as well as gauge how well their attention-getting strategies are working by how the person responds. For example, turning to face the device, or stopping, or approaching the display all suggest that a person's attention is momentarily acquired.

The dystopian future depicted in the movie *Minority Report* contains a scene that popularized this scenario. Multiple advertising walls detect the protagonist John Anderton moving through a crowded hallway. All walls vie for his attention in a visual and audio cacophony. The ad wall for Guinness Draught, for example, shouts his name along with a directed message: "John Anderton, you could use a Guinness right about now!"

An example of an existing simple but compelling public display in this genre is the Cheil Worldwide Nikon D700 Guerrilla-Style Billboard (as sketched in Figure 9.4). Located in a busy subway station in Korea, it displays life-size images of paparazzi that appear to be competing for the passerby's attention. When the passerby is detected in front of the billboard, lights flash (as in Figure 9.4) to simulate flashing cameras. The red carpet leads to a store that sells the type of cameras being used.

Figure 9.4: The Nikon D700 Billboard (sketch by David Ledo; from Greenberg et al., 2014a).

Within advertising and marketing, this pattern is commonly referred to as AIDA, an acronym for: attract Attention, maintain Interest, create Desire, and lead customers to Action (Strong, 1925). Wang et al.'s Proxemic Peddler and Proxemic Framework (Wang et. al., 2012, Wang 2012), described in Section 6.10.6 and illustrated in Figure 6.19, is actually an application of AIDA to proximity-sensing digital displays. While its design tries to find a trade-off that benefits both advertiser and user, its design is unquestionably based upon attempts to attract and keep the passerby's attention.

Commercial interest in attention-grabbing systems is increasing. For example, Apple's iBeacon is an experiment that recognizes a person (via her iPhone) at specific locations in an Apple store. Notifications about a particular nearby product are then sent and displayed on that person's phone.

While the above examples illustrate how proxemic displays can grab attention in an entertaining and perhaps subtle manner, they can also be obnoxious. An earlier version of Wang et. al's (2012) Proxemic Peddler system displayed flashing graphics and shouted out loud audio messages to the passerby. The more the display was ignored, the more insistent it became. The Black Mirror episode mentioned previously includes an extreme example of a fascist Attention Grabber pattern within the context of a Captive Audience pattern: the display wall shown in Figure 9.3 detects when the person is trying to shut out the displayed information by sensing if that person's eyes are closed, or turned away. If so, it plays increasingly annoying sounds and messages to force the person to look at the content.

9.4   BAIT AND SWITCH

The system baits the viewer with something that is (from the viewer's perspective) desirable, but the system then switches it to something else after the person directs his or her attention to it and moves closer.

Brignull et al. (2013) characterize this pattern as follows:

> *"The user sets out to do one thing, but a different, undesirable thing happens instead. This is one of the oldest tricks in the book, and it is very broad in nature…"*

Consider the case where a public display has gained a viewer's attention because the viewer is in fact interested in the "bait" being displayed (e.g., an apparently incredible offer). The viewer "opts-in" by approaching the display. In turn, the display recognizes the viewer's interest and offers further enticing details concerning its content. The viewer's attention becomes increasingly focused. Once the viewer is fully drawn in, the system then switches to something else. A typical "switch" would be to an inferior or more costly product purportedly because the initially advertised product is no longer available. Another switch may require the viewer to sign up to some otherwise unwanted service before the viewer can proceed (which could also become a security issue). Yet another switch is the introduction of other content (i.e., unexpected advertising) in this process.

A compelling (and in this case useful) bait-and-switch example was developed by Amnesty International, where they created a bus-stop display that detects when people are looking at it (see video at YouTube id: DQl_pnuNskQ). When noone's gaze is directed at it, it displays a scene showing domestic violence, which is viewable out of the corner of one's eye (Figure 9.5, left). Yet when a person turns to look at the display directly, it changes into a photo of the couple pretending to be happy (Figure 9.5, right). A slight delay is introduced so that people can get a glimpse of the switch-over. This example is also relevant to the Attention Grabber pattern.

Figure 9.5: Amnesty International Eye Tracking (sketch by David Ledo; from Greenberg et al., 2014a).

Bait and switch also exists in other proxemic-aware systems that do not use public displays. Consider public wireless networks such as those at airports. They detect travellers within its range, and offer the bait of what appears to be free-of-charge wireless. Yet once a traveller is apparently connected, the network may require the traveller to give up information by signing into some service. Alternately, the offered "free" service may be so slow that the alternate higher quality pay service is the only realistic offering.

9.5   MAKING PERSONAL INFORMATION PUBLIC

As the person enters a particular area, the system makes that person's personal information publicly visible.

One of the appeals of Proxemic Interactions is to make personal information readily available on nearby devices. Vogel and Balakrishnan's (2004) original work on ambient displays illustrated how a public ambient display reveals both public and personal information as a person approaches it. Personal information includes calendars, notifications, and directed messages, which can then be manipulated by that person (see video: ambient display).

Their system is intended to be helpful. Yet the basic issue is that other onlookers can see that personal information. Vogel and Balakrishnan (2004) tried to mitigate this by describing how the person's body could physically shield personal information presented directly in front, and how the person could hide information through an explicit gesture.

The previously mentioned scene from *Minority Report*, with its myriads of advertising walls, make a passerby's private information public as a byproduct of their clamor for attention. We see its Guinness advertising wall (amongst others) publicly identify the protagonist by shouting out his name. In that scene, another advertising wall for a credit card visually displays both the protagonist's name and personal information about him (that he has been a member since 2037).

Making personal information public could be an intentional design goal rather than an unintended side effect. An example is the guerilla-style bus stop display produced for the Fitness First health club chain in Rotterdam (Figure 9.6). The bench nearby the display contains a weight sensor, where the commuter's weight is then publicly displayed on the bus stop's wall. Its purpose is purportedly to motivate people to join the health club by intentionally publicizing their weights and offering them a price reduction fee of their weight in Euros in return.

Figure 9.6: The Fitness First health club display. © Dutch ad agency N=5, with permission.

9.6 WE NEVER FORGET

In day-to-day life, proximity is an ephemeral phenomenon. The proxemic relationship between parties dissolves as soon as they separate. In contrast, systems can tag any Proxemic Interactions as indicating a permanent, persistent (and undesirable) relationship that is never forgotten.

The "we never forget" pattern occurs when systems maintain a history of peoples' past proxemic connections, where that history is used to re-establish connections, to trigger information exchange, and/or to recreate prior contexts (e.g., showing the last-displayed information). When used beneficially, the idea is to remember details that make it easy to pick up where one has left off. Unfortunately, this might be completely inappropriate in a different context.

For instance, mobile devices—when brought into range of other devices—typically remember any entered credentials (such as a passphrase) that allow both to connect to one another. This can be a tremendous convenience: when that device comes back into range, those credentials are reused automatically to re-establish the connection, minimizing user load. Remembered WiFi hotspots automatically re-establish network connections when a device returns to a location, while Bluetooth pairings ease device-to-device interconnections, such as how a person's mobile phone is linked to a hands-free system in that person's car. Similarly, various interaction techniques trigger pairings and information exchange when proxemic-aware devices are brought close together, e.g., by bringing mobile devices together to enable information reveal and exchange as described in Section 7.1.

On the other hand, this approach can fail for several reasons. First, people may do a one-off connection to a device they otherwise do not control or trust (e.g., a one-time transaction with a public display). If that person happens to pass by that other device at a later time, there is no reason for that connection to be re-established (particularly if there is some risk involved). Second, security is compromised. If (say) one's mobile phone is stolen, the thief may be able to explore nearby locations to see if he or she can access other devices or networks without entering any credentials.

Third, circumstances change even with trusted devices. For example, a person that previously used a conference room display to show some personal photos on his phone to visiting friends could have these photos reappear inappropriately on the display while walking past it with her work colleagues. Or, consider the case of cell phones paired to one's Bluetooth car system, where it automatically displays incoming calls and redirects audio to the car's speakers. We can easily imagine what could happen on a family trip when an incoming call from one's secret lover is broadcast for all to see on the radio consul and the lover's greeting heard if accepted. As another example, a manager and an employee may be working physically close together, where they pair their laptops to work on a project report. A week later, the manager and employee sit next to each other in a meeting discussing the team's progress. As their laptops get close to each other again, the manager's laptop automatically shares the currently opened document, which, in this case, is a sensitive spreadsheet with the wages of all team members.

Fourth, a person may be unaware that he or she is again sharing his or her device's data with another person that they had previously shared with. This absence of reciprocity (if you share with me, I should know that I share with you) is a known problem in groupware, where one of the parties may be unaware that one's data is being shared with others. To remedy this, such systems should provide awareness of other users and their actions (Bellotti and Edwards, 2001). When proxemic connections are established, the system needs to inform its users about what information is being shared and when, and to whom this information is made available (who is making a connection?)

(Pierce et al., 2003). Likewise, users need to know what will happen to their information once it is shared (Bellotti and Edwards, 2001), and what happens once the connection is destroyed.

Finally, credentials obtained in one setting may be remembered by the system and inappropriately applied to other settings. This "one login for all" is an increasingly common practice in other systems, such as Facebook or Google. The danger, of course, is that a person who has established a single proxemic connection to (say) a particular display may not want that connection to occur when they happen to pass by other associated displays.

9.7   DISGUISED DATA COLLECTION

Information gathered to provide a certain service is abused to build a rich user profile, without the consent of users.

Systems that track proxemic relationships have access to large quantities of data about the behavior of their users. Public advertising displays that track the user's distance, location, orientation, and movement are a goldmine for marketers, who can exploit this information to figure out which ads users are looking at and for how long. Fortunately, personal risk is somewhat mitigated as long as the person is not equipped with technology that can be tapped to uniquely identify oneself (e.g., broadcasting cell phones, RFID chips, smart cards).

Unfortunately, many public displays rely on some form of computer vision to track proxemic relationships. Given that the installation has access to images of its users anyway, it is entirely plausible to use image analysis to try and uniquely identify users. Systems such as these would make the targeted advertisements from Minority Report a reality. Indeed, there are already commercial systems, such as the Aware-Live Technologies Look product (http://www.aware-live.com/), that use computer vision to identify characteristics of its users including gender, approximate age, and a classification in marketing segments (e.g., Generation X). Similar to the AIDA model mentioned earlier, Aware-Live's mantra is "recognize [demographics], analyze [to make intelligent decisions] and engage [to interact with customers in a precise manner]."

Similarly, free WiFi services can collect a person's location inside stores by tracking the signal strength and IP of their device to different WiFi hotspots. For example, Euclid Analytics offers services that measure walk-by traffic, visit duration, and even brand loyalty (http://euclidanalytics.com/). If the store offers the WiFi service, it can potentially track their browsing behavior via web server proxies.

These and other data collection approaches can be combined to build an even richer user profile. Indeed, this would allow systems to exploit the user's proxemic history, thereby leveraging the "We Never Forget" pattern. Just like so-called "loyalty" cards track a person's shopping behaviors, the user's location could be tracked when they walk past different advertising displays and locations, where the personal profile is both constructed by and shared between these systems, thereby allowing information to "chase" the moving person.

9.8 THE SOCIAL NETWORK OF PROXEMIC CONTACTS/ UNINTENDED RELATIONSHIPS

The system tracks your proxemic relations with others and constructs a social network on the assumption that you are somehow socially related, when there is no relationship.

Proxemics assumes that increasing social engagement (and thus a social relationship) is typically accompanied by decreasing physical distance, mutual orientation, etc. That is, social engagement leads to people adjusting these factors to their mutual benefit. Proxemic Interactions systems do this somewhat backwards. They assume that some sensed phenomena (decreasing physical distance, mutual orientation, etc.) signal a social relationship, i.e., it treats the sensed phenomenon as causal. This assumption is not always correct. In real life, strangers may approach and even glance at each other, but no social relationship exists between them. Moreover, not all relationships are reciprocal: while one person believes they have a relation to another, the other may not reciprocate at the same strength, if at all.

The assumption that all Proxemic Interactions imply a social relationship is problematic for a variety of reasons. Perhaps the most worrisome is that the underlying system may be trying to infer one's social network from proxemic events between two people, where strangers are included. This scenario is not at all farfetched. In 2013, Edward Snowden revealed the U.S. National Security Agency's controversial practice of tracking phone call metadata records (the number dialed, a cell phone's location, time, and duration of call, etc.). They used this information to compile sophisticated social network diagrams of Americans, ostensibly to identify and target terrorist networks. Even if one accepts this practice, innocent parties may be inadvertently included as "false positives" in one's social network, perhaps due to erroneous (wrong numbers) or innocuous calls.

It would be just as straightforward to create an equivalent social network by sensing one's proximity to others. These too could easily include unintended relationships. For example, matches between location and time information in cell phone metadata records can be used to determine those people in the same proxemic vicinity. Eagle et. al. (2009) compared observational data from mobile phones with self-report data, and concluded that they could accurately infer 95% of friendships based on observational data alone. This also means that 1 in 20 are not friendships (i.e., they are false positives). Other technologies can provide even more accurate data of one's proximity to another and thus record that as a potential relationship, e.g., facial recognition systems identifying co-located people in a public place, or passing by the front of an identity-sensing device (such as a large display).

Once created, the social network could be used for a variety of dark purposes. Authorities could exploit the social network to identify potential "suspects" by their inferred association to an unsavory character. Marketers could use that social network to identify a potential target audience by their association with a known demographic fitting that profile. Spammers and phishers could exploit it for their own deceptive purposes. In all cases, the agencies involved may not care that "false positives" are included, where they may be treated as collateral damage or simply as noise. While algorithms could perhaps detect and minimize the number of false positives, the social network will always include some unintended relationships.

9.9   THE MILK FACTOR

The proxemic system forces you to move through or go to a specific location in order to get a service.

The rules of Proxemic Interactions, which we use in our everyday lives, can be misused to force people to move to or from a specific location. In non-computer scenarios, this can be seen in the design of supermarket spaces. Products that are purchased frequently (e.g., milk, or bread) are located in distant areas of the store. Thus, shoppers are forced to walk through isles with goods, which leads to increased visibility of promoted items and impulse purchases.

Proxemic interactions systems can force people to position themselves in specific places by limiting access to functionality to particular locations. For example, all zone-based proxemic displays invoke certain types of interactions at specific distances. While most research systems do this with good intensions (such as many of those described in prior chapters), all require its user to stand within specific boundaries.

This can have unintended consequences. MirrorSpace (Roussel et al., 2004) is a video conferencing system that mitigates privacy: images are blurred when the person is far away and only become sharp and identifiable when they stand close to the display. If the person needs to be in another corner of the room while talking over the link, they lose fidelity. In the video player by Dostal et al. (2013), the motivation for limiting visibility of information is to allow some viewers to watch a film with subtitles from a position on the right side of the sitting area, while simultaneously allowing others to watch the same film without the subtitles on the left side of the sitting area. This forces people to sit in particular locations if they want to see a movie a particular way (vs. sitting on the floor).

A commercial example that exploits people having to go to a specific location is the Design Studio S vending machine in Japan (www.designss.com/products/2010/09/01/vendingmachine.html?ctg jp). When potential customers are far, the vending machines show advertising images tailored to the season, time of day, and temperature. However, to see what drinks are available for purchase, the potential customer must approach the area in front of the vending machine, which only then shows a drinks menu. However, at that point the vending machine uses its camera to covertly perform a computer vision-based analysis of the nearby customer to establish their approximate age and gender, as in the Disguised Data Collection pattern. This data is used to "subtly" offer targeted drinks selections. Demographic and sales data is uploaded (without consent) to the company's servers for further analytics and marketing use. This is a clear example of a dark pattern: the customer cannot even see the range of drinks for sale, which forces them to move close enough to the machine to make covert data collection possible. This also raises the specter of price discrimination (already practiced on some websites), where an identified demographic may be charged differently depending on their ability to pay.

9.10   DISCUSSION

The patterns we discussed are a sampling rather than an exhaustive list. Even so, they reveal several common root problems that can be exploited as dark patterns. In the following, we discuss these root problems in more detail.

Opt-in/opt-out choices are particularly problematic in proxemic-aware systems. The overall problem is that a person implicitly opts-in simply by entering a space and approaching the proxemic-aware entity, regardless of whether the person actually intends to opt into the situation. Currently, opt-out requires the person to leave that area, which may not be a reasonable choice for them (e.g., as in the Captive Audience). Opt-out may further inflict uncertainty about what will happen to traces of bygone interactions (e.g., trails of personal information on public displays, as in Making Personal Information Public and We Never Forget).

There is a clear trade-off. Implicit opt-in strategies are popular because they both simplify interaction (from the user's perspective) and increase engagement (from the vendor's perspective). Yet their high potential for misuse is problematic (e.g., as in the Disguised Data Collection or Unintended Relationships pattern). At the very least, Proxemic Interactions systems must have a way to opt-out if interaction is not desired. Leaving the space, while simple, may not always be a practical option. Explicit user actions are also possible, such as invoking a particular gesture to opt out (Ju et al., 2008), or turning off services on personal devices. Yet these require both learning and extra work.

Physical space is imbued with dual meanings. People's practices and expectations of the physical space can be quite different from the meaning and practice applied by the technology. This means that a person may approach a location for one reason, but as a consequence they are exposed to the system exploiting their approach for another reason (e.g., simply wanting to walk past a display as in the Attention Grabber pattern).

In many of the discussed patterns, a user's context plays an important role. For example, being surrounded by many commuters in a subway may form highly Unintended Relationships simply due to the close proximity of others.

One possible solution is to gather more contextual information to better infer whether a person is using the physical space as is, or whether they actually have an interest in the system. For example, an Attention Grabber can sense a person's speed to determine whether they are in a hurry, and thus let them pass by undisturbed. Unintended Relationships can be avoided by comparing its collected data to other data sources that mine friendship data, such as social network data. Of course, this introduces other concerns.

Ownership of the physical space is ambiguous. A person looking for a quiet corner may consider that space as temporarily their own, but if this happens in a public area, their presence can still be exploited. Yet a public display may consider the installation space around itself as its own, where any person (and the devices they carry) in that space becomes fair game. While people have social rules that dictate what happens when interacting in private, personal, or public space, technology can easily violate those rules (e.g., an obnoxious display invades a person's privacy with targeted advertising as in the Attention Grabber pattern).

We believe it is crucial to define who owns the space around a proxemic interaction system. This is particularly true for public spaces that people perceive as owned by them. Yet, the definition of a public space is somewhat vague. Consider the urinal in the Captive Audience pattern: a company running public restrooms may own this space, but the person using it would consider it a private enclave. Ultimately, there has to be some control and rules for who is allowed to do what in a given space. At the very least, the system must make it clear (e.g., by its visuals, or by marking) that it has taken a certain amount of space for its own use.

Attention is inherently sought after in Proxemic Interactions. The gradual engagement design pattern discussed in Sections 6.6 and 7.1 suggests that Proxemic Interactions gradually reveal information as entities approach one another (e.g., as in the Making Personal Information Public pattern). Whether done subtly or blatantly (as in the Attention Grabber pattern), attention of the person is demanded—even if that person has no intent to interact with the system.

The problem is that a user's context (and his or her willingness to pay attention to the system respectively) again plays an important role. That is, people should be able to move through a space with a proxemic system installed without being affected by it if they (maybe explicitly) opted out of being part of the system.

Accidental proxemics occurs when people unintentionally enter what could be interpreted as a proxemic relationship. They may approach and even orient themselves toward something with no real intent of engaging with the system. Yet inferences of such a relationship leads to problems, such as engaging people without consent in the Captured Audience, and the accidental sharing of private information in the We Never Forget pattern. If the approach is due to another reason (e.g., just walking past a display), it becomes relatively hard to discriminate that action from an intentional opt-in to use the system.

When proxemic systems interpret any approach action as the start of a proxemic relationship, users cannot enter a space without triggering the system (similar to the Midas Touch problem, Velichkovsky et al., 1997). For example, smart keys for various cars now allow one to automatically unlock and lock the doors of a car when approaching or leaving the car. However, the person cannot physically verify that the doors are locked, as approaching the car again will unlock them.

Accidental proxemics is a particularly nasty variation of opting in vs. opting out. Similar to the other root problems, avoiding accidental proxemics is difficult if intention is sensed implicitly. No matter how carefully done, the system will sometimes get it wrong.

Ideally, Proxemic Interactions systems must strike a delicate balance between implicit and explicit interaction, and by making users aware of what is happening (Ju et. al., 2008). While the solution is to intervene and override the proxemic system's behavior if it does not correspond with their intentions, it demands that they do extra explicit work.

9.11   CONCLUSION

In this chapter, we reconsidered the vision of Proxemic Interactions through a critical lens. We identified potential dark patterns demonstrating how proxemic systems can abuse people either intentionally or unintentionally. Based on these patterns, we discussed several common root problems and speculated on potential solutions. Solutions are at best tentative, but we hope that they could evolve into a code of conduct taken into account by designers, with the goal of both lowering the risk of intentional abuse and unintentional design flaws.

Unfortunately, this may be easier said than done. At least two parties are involved in Proxemic Interactions systems: the party deploying the system vs. the system's users. Both may have quite different intentions and desires. For example, if the goal of system stakeholders is to acquire a person's attention, the actual users may have little chance of opting out. Thus legislation may play a role, as it has in other cases of a mismatch in interests. For example, governmental authorities have (to some extent) enforced rules to better protect users from the excesses of online e-commerce systems, and to limit spammers and phishers.

Another and perhaps much better solution is to consider Proxemic Interactions systems design from a mutually beneficial perspective. No company wants to be viewed negatively, and we expect good companies will pay attention to how potentially dark patterns can be turned into a good (or at the worst a neutral) pattern that balances benefits to the company, client, and product user. This already happens in the advertising industry, where the best ads provide value to its viewers (e.g., humor, engagement, interest, etc.) as part of its service. Indeed, several of our examples already do this. The Nikon D700 Billboard of Figure 9.4 is an example of an entertaining and novel guerrilla ad that invokes curiosity; its cost is also small—the red carpet suggesting the direction to the store selling the displayed cameras. Proxemic Peddler (Figure 6.15) uses subtle rather than aggressive visuals to strike a balance between how it senses and reacts to people's attention vs. loss of interest. The Amnesty International campaign in Figure 9.5 presents an important (albeit disturbing) social message to the public.

Captive Media offers a particularly positive example of institutional awareness. Their representative told us how their policy deeply considers mutual benefits. They consider Captive Media's urinal (Figure 9.2) primarily as an interactive entertainment device into which they incorporate some advertising: it enlivens a time that is otherwise boring, and they see it serving as a social ice-breaker (e.g., bars, hotel events). During actual urinal use, they advocate that the majority of time is for game play, with only a fraction of the time for advertisements—that is, the cost of play is small. When acting as an ambient display, they advocate that it must display entertaining content at least 50% of the time. They also advocate outfitting only a portion of the urinals in a bathroom with their display, thus allowing people to opt out. Finally, they collect experience reactions, where they found that Captive Media users are overwhelmingly positive.

Yet this is still early times. Even if Proxemic Interactions systems were designed to avoid abuse, problems will inevitably cause user frustration, likely due to well-known issues in implicit interaction (Bellotti et al., 2002). This remains a grand challenge.

CHAPTER 10

Conclusion

This book opened with the idea that:

we can leverage information about people's and devices' fine-grained proxemic relationships for the design of novel interaction techniques in ubicomp ecologies.

The overarching goal of this book was to elaborate on this idea. In particular, we wanted to inform the design of future proxemic-aware devices that—similar to people's natural expectations and use of proxemics—allow increasing connectivity and interaction possibilities when in proximity to people, other devices, or objects. Overall, the book explored how the fine-grained knowledge of proxemic relationships between the entities in small-space ubicomp ecologies (people, devices, objects) can be exploited in interaction design.

10.1   WHAT WAS LEARNED

Let's reconsider what the book and its chapters delivered.

The four chapters in Part I largely concerned background and theory that related proxemics to ubiquitous computing, where it introduced the notion of Proxemic Interactions.

Chapter 2 introduced ubiquitous computing (ubicomp), and in particular the idea and challenges of creating ubiquitous computing ecologies. It introduced several theories and practices underpinning the design of such ecologies, including context awareness and embodied interaction. It then touched upon the central notion of this book: that ubicomp system design can also consider the spatial relationships—the proxemics—of the entities within its ecology. To bring these ideas to life, the chapter described example systems as done by various researchers that uses some form of spatial relationship to manage interaction.

Chapter 3 provided a comprehensive analytical survey of relevant proxemic literature, where it synthesized key theories about people's use and understanding of personal space and proxemics.

Chapter 4 argued that these theories can help design, where they can (a) allow thinking in structured ways during the design process, (b) provide a clear vocabulary for discussing designs, and (c) allow generating novel ideas through design dimensions and constructs. In particular, it operationalized proxemics for ubicomp interaction design. It is one thing to provide theory, but translating that theory about interpersonal behaviors into technical design practice is quite a different matter. This translation was done through the Proxemic Interactions framework. The framework identified five key dimensions of measured proxemic relationships that can be considered to mediate people's interactions with ubicomp systems: distance, orientation, movement, identity, and location. The chapter then explained how to use information from these five dimensions to guide the design of novel interaction techniques.

Chapter 5 described six important ubicomp interaction design challenges: (1) revealing interaction possibilities; (2) directing actions; (3) establishing connections; (4) providing feedback; (5) avoiding and correcting mistakes; and (6) managing privacy and security. It then revisited each of these challenges, where it elaborates, at a high level, various ways that proxemic theory and Proxemic Interactions can be applied to ubicomp design to meet those challenges.

Next, the four chapters in Part II described how the Proxemic Interactions framework can be exploited in a range of small-space ubicomp ecologies. Its first three chapter introduced novel interaction techniques that take into account the proxemic relationships between the different entities in ubicomp ecologies—the people, devices, objects, and the environment—to mediate people's interaction with digital devices. Each chapter described tested applications to illustrate in detail how the design of these techniques exploited particular dimensions of Proxemic Interactions: distance, orientation, location, movement, and identity.

Chapter 6 focused on the Proxemic Interactions between people and a large interactive display. It introduced the proxemic media player as its testbed application, where it reacts to nearby people as well as people's proxemic relationships to the environment and to the devices and objects they carry. This includes interaction methods that incorporate: the fixed and semi-fixed features of the environment; how people direct their attention; explicit actions by the person such as pointing; and continuous vs. discrete movements of people and their devices. The chapter also introduces the *gradual engagement design pattern* that captures a "best practice" of proxemic-based ubicomp design. It also showed how such systems can leverage identity, and how it can mediate people's simultaneous interaction.

Chapter 7 focused on applying concepts of Proxemic Interactions to mediate device-to-device operations, such as between personal (e.g., tablets) and semi-public devices (e.g., digital whiteboards). In particular, it refined and applied the gradual engagement pattern to ease the information transfer task. The pattern described how the interface progressively moves through three stages: (a) *awareness* of device presence and connectivity, (b) *reveal* of exchangeable digital content, and (c) interaction methods for *transferring* digital content between devices tuned to particular distances and device capabilities. It reviewed prior systems that used some parts or all of this pattern, and introduced a variety of novel interaction methods embedded within several of our own testbed applications.

Chapter 8 turned to small group interaction. It explained how proxemics combined with F-formation theory can help identify small groups and its person-to-person relationships. It also explained how micro-mobility can help identify device-to-device relationships, i.e., how people orient and tilt devices toward one another to promote fine-grained sharing during co-present collaboration. It introduced GROUPTOGETHER as a system containing a set of interaction techniques affording cross-device interaction techniques that support nuanced gradations of sharing, from the subtle to the overt, with the goal of minimizing the transaction costs—and social disruption—of sharing information across a small-group ecology of digital devices and situated displays. More generally, the chapter illustrates how theories can be combined to influence design.

Chapter 9 reconsidered Proxemic Interactions from a critical perspective. Its primary concern is that Proxemic Interactions can be mis-appropriated, either deliberately or unintentionally, to produce systems that are not in the best interest of its users. It described several *dark patterns* that identify ways that such systems could be crafted, along with the root problems leading to these patterns. It also discussed why these systems are problematic and hinted at possible solutions.

10.2   POTENTIAL DIRECTIONS FOR FUTURE WORK

In this section, we describe possible directions for research extending the work presented in this book.

10.2.1 DEFINING RULES OF BEHAVIOR

One of the unsolved issues in Proxemic Interactions is how one can configure the *rules of behavior*, i.e., how the system should react to the proxemic information it gathers. While computers can take action based on its inference of the proxemic dynamics, it will sometimes get it wrong. Creating meaningful behaviors and repairing mistakes will, we believe, become a central issue in the design of such systems. Even with this caveat, we believe that Proxemic Interactions will become a powerful way to realize embodied interaction, where—ideally—the system naturally responds to people's social expectations and practices in their everyday environments, and where mistakes are easily repaired or of little consequence.

As one approach to address the difficult challenge for defining appropriate rules of behavior, future work could also investigate end-user programming methods for reconfiguring existing or creating new behaviors. Balancing ease-of-use vs. potential expressiveness, and finding the right building blocks for such a non-expert tool interface, would be key challenges for these explorations.

10.2.2 OTHER FACTORS INFLUENCING PROXEMIC BEHAVIOR

While going beyond the scope of this book, people's perception of proxemic relationships is also influenced by other factors such as gender, cultures, age, work hierarchies, and other factors (Hall, 1966). These differences also affect the design of Proxemic Interactions. For example, we can imagine a system that requires people to stand in very close proximity to each other to collaboratively interact with an interactive surface, e.g., to exchange digital documents. This close proximity might be perceived as adequate by some, but as too intimate by others. Therefore, the design of Proxemic Interactions has to consider these variations in proxemic perception. In this regard, the presented explorations in this book serve just as examples that illustrate design possibilities for Proxemic Interactions. We do not suggest that the rules of behavior we described are ideal, nor that they achieve the perfect balance between adjudicating proxemic information and implicit or explicit interaction. Future research should further investigate the impact of these other factors influencing the proxemic behavior, and explore how to address this in ubicomp system designs.

10.2.3   PATTERN LANGUAGE OF PROXEMIC INTERACTIONS

Our gradual engagement pattern is just a starting point suggesting further exploration of proxemic patterns in interaction design. These patterns would then also unify prior work, synthesize essential, generalizable interaction strategies, and provide a common vocabulary for discussing design solutions. Most importantly, the patterns inform and inspire future designs, but also allow for variations of the pattern applied to different domains. A possible outcome could be a Proxemic Interactions Pattern Language—a collection of proxemic patterns that not only describe the essential patterns themselves, but also the inter-relations between—similar to Christopher Alexander's seminal architectural pattern language (Alexander et al., 1977).

10.2.4   VIOLATING PROXEMIC EXPECTATIONS

Despite our belief in the importance to consider proxemic theories and people's expectations of personal space in interaction design, as a contradicting possibility one could imagine interaction designs that deliberately violate expectations of proxemics. Violations of a person's personal space as defined by proxemics do not always cause negative reactions (Burgoon and Hale, 1988). Thus, depending on the context and design of ubicomp applications, deliberate violations of personal space (such as requiring people to stand in close/intimate distance) might be an integral part of the user experience itself (for example, in games or public interactive art installations).

10.2.5   SAFEGUARDING ABUSES

While Proxemic Interactions afford many benefits, they can easily be abused. Security and privacy are an issue. Abuses, such as those illustrated by dark patterns, are not only possible but should be expected. A serious question is whether we can safeguard against these abuses, perhaps by making those safeguards an inherent part of the technology. However, we are still in the early stages. We do not yet understand the full risks of this technology, let alone how we can produce effective safeguards.

10.2.6   INTERACTIONS IN LARGE-SCALE, CLUTTERED UBICOMP ECOLOGIES

The research described in this book concentrated on interactions in small space environments. An interesting question to answer in future work would be how we can apply proxemics to mitigate challenges of people's interactions in cluttered environments with 10's or 100's of devices present simultaneously. This research challenge would address multiple challenges in ubicomp interaction, such as handling scalability, providing meaningful feedback through visualizations, and exploring people's interactions in these ubicomp device ecologies.

10.2.7 PROXEMIC INTERACTIONS IN PUBLIC SPACES, BUILDINGS, CITIES

The ubicomp settings in this book were largely based on small spaces, such as rooms in domestic settings, offices, and small meeting rooms. We recognize that ubicomp systems designed for public spaces, building- and city-wide deployments could also leverage proxemics. This is a very ripe area for future work, with many possibilities.

10.2.8 TECHNICAL CHALLENGES

Most of the systems described in this book rely on particular technologies. Some are quite simple and affordable (e.g., infrared range sensors such as those used for bathroom faucets), but are extremely limited in the proxemic information they can obtain. While tracking systems do exist that can capture rich information (e.g., motion capture systems), they tend to be extremely expensive. Another important factor is how these systems fit within the ecosystem. Many require embedding technology into the environment, such as embedding sensors or tracking systems into a room's infrastructure. This is impractical in most settings. Another issue is robustness: some sensing systems are notoriously poor or error-prone, leading to poor confidence in the readings they produce. Ideally, future sensing technologies will be affordable, reliable, rich in the information they produce, will use little power, and will be small enough to embed into our devices, into wearables, and into our environment. They will detect each other, determine their proxemic relationships, and deliver that information to applications that can exploit that information. However, no such technology yet exists.

10.2.9 OTHER CONCERNS

The suggested future research above touches upon many possible directions. As often is the case with new interaction paradigms in the early stages, the area is wide open. There are many other possibilities to explore proxemics in interaction design: application-specific issues and opportunities, qualitative studies about people's use and perception of proxemic-aware systems, or new hardware developments—which again both restrict and expand what can be done.

10.3 THE FUTURE IS HERE

William Gibson once said, "The future is already here — it's just not very evenly distributed." This aptly describes how technology, including Proxemic Interactions, emerges into the everyday world over time. Proxemic Interactions was an esoteric topic 10 years ago, where only a few researchers considered it. As we wrote this book, interest in Proxemic Interactions has grown considerably within the human-computer interaction and ubicomp community. For example, a group of 29 researchers interested in the area, and from a variety of backgrounds and nationalities, met at an invited workshop in Dagstuhl, Germany, to explore themes in Proxemic Interactions. A full report of its activities and outcomes can be found in Greenberg et al., 2014b. When we checked to see who was citing our own work in Proxemic Interactions, we saw myriads of other articles in the area, some using proxemics in ways quite novel ways and situations. As hinted at in Chapter 9, systems incorporating some form of proxemic awareness are now being deployed into the wild, for example, as commercial products or guerrilla advertisements. We are certain that there are many more such systems out there. To rephrase Gibson, Proxemic Interactions are already here. They're just not very evenly distributed.

10.4 CLOSING REMARKS

With an increasing number of digital devices available around us to facilitate our everyday tasks, it also becomes increasingly important to find interaction strategies that let us more naturally and easily connect to and interact with these devices. We believe that Proxemic Interactions has great potential for designing such interactions, as it can exploit people's expectations of how they and their devices should interact within particular ecologies as they move toward each other. We hope the work presented in this book will inspire researchers to consider proxemic measures between all entities in ubicomp ecologies—the people, devices, and other objects—to design interactive systems that match closer to our natural understanding and expectations of proxemics.

References

Abowd, G.D., Atkeson, C.G., Hong, J., Long, S., Kooper, R., Pinkerton, M., 1997. Cyberguide: A Mobile Context-Aware Tour Guide. *Wireless Networking* 3, 421–433. DOI: 10.1023/A:1019194325861.

Abowd, G.D., Mynatt, E.D., 2000. Charting Past, Present, and Future Research in Ubiquitous Computing. *ACM Transactions on Computer-Human Interaction* 7, 29–58. DOI: 10.1145/344949.344988.

Abowd, G.D., Mynatt, E.D., Rodden, T., 2002. The Human Experience [of Ubiquitous Computing]. *IEEE Pervasive Computing* 1, 48–57. DOI: 10.1109/MPRV.2002.993144.

Adams, L., Zuckerman, D., 1991. The Effect of Lighting Conditions on Personal Space Requirements. *The Journal of General Psychology* 118, 335–340. DOI: 10.1080/00221309.1991.9917794.

Addlesee, M., Curwen, R., Hodges, S., Newman, J., Steggles, P., Ward, A., Hopper, A., 2001. Implementing a Sentient Computing System. *Computer* 34, 50–56. DOI: 10.1109/2.940013.

Aiello, J.R., 1987. Human Spatial Behavior. Stokols, D., Altman, I. (Eds.), *Handbook of Environmental Psychology*. John Wiley & Sons, New York, pp. 359–504.

Aiello, J.R., Aiello, T.D.C., 1974. The Development of Personal Space: Proxemic Behavior of Children 6 through 16. *Hum. Ecol.* 2, 177–189. DOI: 10.1007/BF01531420.

Alexander, C., Ishikawa, S., Silverstein, M., 1977. *A Pattern Language: Towns, Buildings, Construction*. Oxford University Press.

Altman, I., 1975. *The Environment and Social Behavior: Privacy, Personal Space, Territory, and Crowding*. Brooks/Cole Publishing Company, Monterey, California.

Annett, M., Grossman, T., Wigdor, D., Fitzmaurice, G., 2011. Medusa: A Proximity-Aware Multi-Touch Tabletop. *Proceedings of the 24th Annual ACM Symposium on User Interface Software and Technology, UIST '11*. ACM, New York, NY, USA, pp. 337–346. DOI: 10.1145/2047196.2047240.

Antifakos, S., Schiele, B., 2002. Beyond Position Awareness. *Personal Ubiquitous Computing* 6, 313–317. DOI: 10.1007/s007790200034.

Argyle, M., Dean, J., 1965. Eye-Contact, Distance and Affiliation. *Sociometry* 28, 289–304. DOI: 10.2307/2786027.

Aseniero, B.A., Tang, A., Carpendale, S., Greenberg, S., 2013. Showing Real-time Recommendations to explore the stages of Reflection and Action (No. 2013-1040-07). Technical Report #2013-1040–07, Department of Computer Science, University of Calgary, Calgary, Alberta, Canada. Includes video figure.

Back, M., Cohen, J., Gold, R., Harrison, S., Minneman, S., 2001. Listen Reader: An Electronically Augmented Paper-Based Book. *Proceedings of the SIGCHI Conference on Human Factors in Computing Systems, CHI '01*. ACM, New York, NY, USA, pp. 23–29. DOI: 10.1145/365024.365031.

Baldassare, M., 1978. Human Spatial Behavior. *Annu. Rev. Sociol.* 4, 29–56. DOI: 10.1146/annurev.so.04.080178.000333.

Ballendat, T., 2011. Visualization of and interaction with digital devices around large surfaces as a function of proximity. Master's thesis, Institut fur Informatik, Ludwig-Maximilians-Universitat Munchen, Munich, Germany, February.

Ballendat, T., Marquardt, N., Greenberg, S., 2010. Proxemic Interaction: Designing for a proximity and orientation-aware environment. *Proceedings of the ACM Conference on Interactive Tabletops and Surfaces, ITS' 10. ACM*, New York, NY, USA, pp. 121–130. DOI: 10.1145/1936652.1936676.

Bardram, E., 2005. The Trouble with Login: On Usability and Computer Security in Ubiquitous Computing. *Personal and Ubiquitous Computing* 9, 357–367. DOI: 10.1007/s00779-005-0347-6.

Bardram, J., Friday, A., 2010. Ubiquitous Computing Systems In: Krumm, J. (Ed.), *Ubiquitous Computing Fundamental*s. CRC Press, Boca Raton, Florida, USA, pp. 37–94.

Baudisch, P., Cutrell, E., Robbins, D., Czerwinski, M., Tandler, P., T, P., Bederson, B., Zierlinger, A., 2003. Drag-and-Pop and Drag-and-Pick: techniques for accessing remote screen content on touch- and pen-operated systems. *Proceedings of IFIP TC13 International Conference on Human-Computer Interaction, INTERACT '03*. IOS Press, pp. 57–64.

Beaudouin-Lafon, M., 2004. Designing interaction, not interfaces. *Proceedings of the Working Conference on Advanced Visual Interfaces, AVI '04.* ACM, New York, NY, USA, pp. 15–22. DOI: 10.1145/989863.989865.

Bechtel, R.B., Churchman, A., 2002. *Handbook of Environmental Psychology*. John Wiley and Sons.

Bellotti, V., Back, M., Edwards, W.K., Grinter, R.E., Henderson, A., Lopes, C., 2002. Making sense of sensing systems: five questions for designers and researchers. *Proceedings of the 20th ACM Conference on Human Factors in Computing Systems, CHI '02*. ACM, New York, NY, USA, pp. 415–422. DOI: 10.1145/503376.503450.

Bellotti, V., Edwards, K., 2001. Intelligibility and Accountability: Human considerations in context-aware systems. *Human–Computer Interaction*, 16(2–4), 193-212. DOI: 10.1207/S15327051HCI16234_05.

Bell, P.A., Greene, T., Fisher, J., Baum, A.S., 2005. *Environmental Psychology*, 5th ed. Psychology Press.

Bennett, F., Richardson, T., Harter, A., 1994. Teleporting-Making Applications Mobile. *Proceedings of the Workshop on Mobile Computing Systems and Applications*. IEEE Computer Society, pp. 82–84. DOI: 10.1109/WMCSA.1994.36.

Biehl, J.T., Bailey, B.P., 2004. ARIS: an interface for application relocation in an interactive space. *Proceedings of Graphics Interface, GI '04*. Canadian Human-Computer Communications Society, London, Ontario, Canada, pp. 107–116.

Borchers, J., 2001. *A Pattern Approach to Interaction Design*. Wiley, New York, NY, USA.

Boring, S., Baur, D., Butz, A., Gustafson, S., Baudisch, P., 2010. Touch projector: mobile interaction through video. *Proceedings of the 28th International Conference on Human Factors in Computing Systems, CHI '10*. ACM, New York, NY, USA, pp. 2287–2296. DOI: 10.1145/1753326.1753671.

Boring, S., Greenberg, S., Vermeulen, J, Dostal J., Marquardt, N., 2014. The dark patterns of proxemic sensing. *IEEE Computer* 47(8), 56–60. IEEE, August. DOI: 10.1109/MC.2014.223.

Bragdon, A., DeLine, R., Hinckley, K., Morris, M.R., 2011. Code space: touch + air gesture hybrid interactions for supporting developer meetings. *Proceedings of the ACM International Conference on Interactive Tabletops and Surfaces, ITS '11*. ACM, New York, NY, USA, pp. 212–221. DOI: 10.1145/2076354.2076393.

Brave, S., Ishii, H., Dahley, A., 1998. Tangible Interfaces for Remote Collaboration and Communication. *Proceedings of the ACM Conference on Computer Supported Cooperative Work, CSCW '98*. ACM, New York, NY, USA, pp. 169–178. DOI: 10.1145/289444.289491.

Brignull, H., Miquel, M., Rosenberg, J., 2013. Dark patterns library, http://darkpatterns.org. Retrieved Nov. 2013.

Brignull, H., 2011. Dark patterns: Deception vs. honesty in UI design. *Interaction Design, Usability*, 338.

Brudy, F., Ledo, D., Greenberg, S., Butz, A., 2014a. Is anyone looking? Mitigating shoulder surfing on public displays through awareness and protection. *Proceedings of the 3rd International Symposium on Pervasive Displays, PerDisp '14*, ACM, New York, NY, USA, pp. 1–6. DOI: 10.1145/2611009.2611028.

Brudy, F., Ledo, D., Greenberg, S., 2014b. Is anyone looking? Mediating shoulder surfing on public displays (the video). ACM SIGCHI 2014 Video Showcase (Juried), *Proceedings of Extended Abstracts, CHI '14*, ACM, New York, NY, USA. DOI: 10.1145/2559206.2579528.

Brumitt, B., Krumm, J., Meyers, B., Shafer, S., 2000a. Ubiquitous computing and the role of geometry. Personal Communications, *IEEE* 7, 41–43. DOI: 10.1109/98.878536.

Brumitt, B., Meyers, B., Krumm, J., Kern, A., Shafer, S., 2000b. Easy Living: Technologies for Intelligent Environments. *Proceedings of the Second International Symposium on Handheld and Ubiquitous Computing, HUC '00*. Springer, pp. 12–27. DOI: 10.1007/3-540-39959-3_2.

Burgoon, J.K., Hale, J.L., 1988. Nonverbal Expectancy Violations: Model Elaboration and Application to Immediacy Behaviors. *Communication Monographs* 55, 58–79. DOI: 10.1080/03637758809376158.

Buxton, W.A.S., 1995. Integrating the Periphery and Context: A New Model of Telematics. *Proceedings of Graphics Interface, GI '95*. Canadian Human-Computer Communications Society, pp. 239–246.

Buxton, W.A.S., 1997. Living in Augmented Reality: Ubiquitous Media and Reactive Environments. Finn, K., Sellen, A., Wilber, S. (Eds.), *Video Mediated Communication*. Lawrence Erlbaum Associates, Inc., Hillsdale, NJ, USA, pp. 363–384.

Chen, X., Boring, S., Carpendale, S., Tang, A., Greenberg, S., 2012. SPALENDAR: Visualizing a Group's Calendar Events over a Geographic Space on a Public Display. *Proceedings of the 11th International Working Conference on Advanced Visual Interfaces, AVI '12*. ACM. DOI: 10.1145/2254556.2254686.

Chen, Y., Sinclair, M., 2008. Tangible security for mobile devices. *Proceedings of the 5th Annual International Conference on Mobile and Ubiquitous Systems: Computing, Networking, and Services, MobiQuitous '08*. ICST, Dublin, Ireland, pp. 1–4.

Chong, M.K., Gellersen, H., 2011. How users associate wireless devices. *Proceedings of the 2011 Annual Conference on Human Factors in Computing Systems, CHI '11*. ACM, New York, NY, USA, pp. 1909–1918. DOI: 10.1145/2470654.2466207.

Chong, M.K., Mayrhofer, R., Gellersen, H., 2014. A survey of user interaction for spontaneous device association. *ACM Computing Surveys* 47 (1). DOI: 10.1145/2597768.

Ciolek, T.M., 1983. The proxemics lexicon: A first approximation. *J Nonverbal Behav* 8, 55–79. DOI: 10.1007/BF00986330.

Ciolek, T.M., Kendon, A., 1980. Environment and the Spatial Arrangement of Conversational Encounters. *Sociological Inquiry* 50, 237–271. DOI: 10.1111/j.1475-682X.1980.tb00022.x.

Clark, H.H., 2003. Pointing and Placing. Kita, S. (Ed.), *Pointing. Where Language, Culture, and Cognition Meet*. Erlbaum, Hillsdale, NJ, USA, pp. 243–268.

Cooperstock, J.R., Fels, S.S., Buxton, W.A.S., Smith, K.C., 1997. Reactive Environments: Throwing Away Your Keyboard and Mouse. *Communications of the ACM* 40, 65–73. DOI: 10.1145/260750.260774.

Coulouris, G., Dollimore, J., Kindberg, T., Blair, G., 2011. *Distributed Systems: Concepts and Design*, 5th ed. Addison-Wesley.

Dachselt, R., Buchholz, R., 2009. Natural throw and tilt interaction between mobile phones and distant displays. *Proceedings of the 27th International Conference Extended Abstracts on Human Factors in Computing Systems, CHI EA '09*. ACM, New York, NY, USA, pp. 3253–3258. DOI: 10.1145/1520340.1520467.

Dey, A.K., 2010. Context-Aware Computing. Krumm, J. (Ed.), *Ubiquitous Computing Fundamentals*. CRC Press, Boca Raton, Florida, USA, pp. 285–319. DOI: 10.1207/S15327051HCI16234_02.

Dey, A.K., Abowd, G.D., Salber, D., 2001. A conceptual framework and a toolkit for supporting the rapid prototyping of context-aware applications. *Human-Computer Interaction* 16, 97–166. DOI: 10.1207/S15327051HCI16234_02.

Diaz-Marino, R., Greenberg, S., 2010. The Proximity Toolkit and ViconFace: The video. Video Showcase, DVD. *Proceedings of the ACM Conference on Human Factors in Computing Systems, ACM CHI'10*, ACM, New York, NY, USA. DOI: 10.1145/1753846.1754233.

Dostal, J., Kristensson, P., Quigley, A., 2013. Multi-view proxemics: Distance and position sensitive Interaction. *Proceedings of the 2nd ACM International Symposium on Pervasive Displays, PerDis '13*, ACM, New York, NY, USA, pp. 1–6. DOI: 10.1145/2491568.2491570.

Dourish, P., 2001a. *Where the Action Is: The Foundations of Embodied Interaction*. The MIT Press.

Dourish, P., 2001b. Seeking a foundation for context-aware computing. *Human-Computer Interaction* 16, 229–241. DOI: 10.1207/S15327051HCI16234_07.

Duke, M.P., Nowicki, S., 1972. A New Measure and Social-Learning Model for Interpersonal Distance. *Journal of Experimental Research in Personality* 6, 119–132.

Dunbar, R.I.M., Duncan, N.D.C., Nettle, D., 1995. Size and structure of freely forming conversational groups. *Human Nature* 6, 67–78. DOI: 10.1007/BF02734136.

Eagle, N., Pentland, A., Lazer, D., 2009. Inferring friendship network structure by using mobile phone data. *Proceedings of the National Academy of Science of the United States of America*, 106(36), pp. 15274–15278. DOI: 10.1073/pnas.0900282106.

Erickson, T., 2002. Some problems with the notion of context-aware computing. *Communications of the ACM* 45, 102–104. DOI: 10.1145/503124.503154.

Evans, G.W., Lepore, S.J., Schroeder, A., 1996. The Role of Interior Design Elements in Human Responses to Crowding. *Journal of Personality and Social Psychology* 70, 41–46. DOI: 10.1037/0022-3514.70.1.41.

Everitt, K., Shen, C., Ryall, K., Forlines, C., 2006. MultiSpace: enabling electronic document micro-mobility in table-centric, multi-device environments. Shen, C. (Ed.), *Proceedings of First IEEE International Workshop on Horizontal Interactive Human-Computer Systems, TABLETOP '06*. IEEE, pp. 27–34. DOI: 10.1109/TABLETOP.2006.23.

Fishkin, K.P., Roy, S., Jiang, B., 2005. *Some Methods for Privacy in RFID Communication. Security in Ad-Hoc and Sensor Networks, Lecture Notes in Computer Science*. Springer, pp. 42–53. DOI: 10.1007/978-3-540-30496-8_5.

Fitzmaurice, G.W., 1993. Situated information spaces and spatially aware palmtop computers. *Communications of the ACM* 36, 39–49. DOI: 10.1145/159544.159566.

Gamma, E., Helm, R., Johnson, R., Vlissides, J., 1994. *Design patterns: Elements of reusable object-oriented software*. Pearson.

Gellersen, H., Fischer, C., Guinard, D., Gostner, R., Kortuem, G., Kray, C., Rukzio, E., Streng, S., 2009. Supporting device discovery and spontaneous interaction with spatial references. *Personal Ubiquitous Computing* 13, 255–264. DOI: 10.1007/s00779-008-0206-3.

Gibson, J., 1977. The Theory of Affordances. Shaw, R., University of Minnesota. (Eds.), *Perceiving, Acting, and Knowing: Toward an Ecological Psychology*. Lawrence Erlbaum Associates, Hillsdale, NJ, USA.

Gifford, R., 1997. *Environmental Psychology: Principles and Practice*, 2nd ed. Prentice-Hall, Inc.

Greenberg, S., 2001. Context as a dynamic construct. *Human-Computer Interaction* 16, 257–268. DOI: 10.1207/S15327051HCI16234_09.

Greenberg, S., Boring, S., Vermeulen, J., Dostal, J., 2014a. Dark patterns in proxemic interactions: A critical perspective. *Proceedings of the ACM Conference on Designing Interactive Systems, DIS '14*. ACM, New York, NY, USA, pp. 523–532. DOI: 10.1145/2598510.2598541.

Greenberg, S., Hornbaek, K., Quigley, A., Reiterer H., Radle, R., 2014b. Proxemics in Human-Computer Interaction (Dagstuhl Seminar 13452). *Dagstuhl Report Series*, Volume 3, Issue 11. Dagstuhl, Germany, Schloss Dagstuhl—Leibniz-Zentrum fur Informatik, Dagstuhl Publishing, pp. 29–57, February.

Greenberg, S., Kuzuoka, H., 2001. Using Digital but Physical Surrogates to Mediate Awareness, Communication and Privacy in Media Spaces. *Personal Technologies* 3, 182–198. DOI: 10.1007/BF01540552.

Greenberg, S., Marquardt, N., Ballendat, T., Diaz-Marino, R., Wang, M., 2011. Proxemic Interactions: The New Ubicomp? *ACM Interactions* 18, 42–50, ACM. DOI: 10.1145/1897239.1897250.

Hall, E.T., 1963. A system for the notation of proxemic behavior. *American Anthropologist* 65, 1003–1026. DOI: 10.1525/aa.1963.65.5.02a00020.

Hall, E.T., 1966. *The Hidden Dimension*, 1st ed. Doubleday, Garden City, NY.

Hall, E.T., 1968. Proxemics. *Current Anthropology* 9, 83–108. DOI: 10.1086/200975.

Hardy, R., Rukzio, E., 2008. Touch & interact: touch-based interaction of mobile phones with displays. *Proceedings of the 10th International Conference on Human Computer Interaction with Mobile Devices and Services, MobileHCI '08*. ACM, pp. 245–254. DOI: 10.1145/1409240.1409267.

Harrison, C., Dey, A.K., 2008. Lean and zoom: proximity-aware user interface and content magnification. *Proceeding of the 26th SIGCHI Conference on Human Factors in Computing Systems, CHI '08*. ACM, New York, NY, USA, pp. 507–510. DOI: 10.1145/1357054.1357135.

Harrison, S., Dourish, P., 1996. Re-place-ing space: the roles of place and space in collaborative systems. *Proceedings of the 1996 ACM Conference on Computer Supported Cooperative Work, CSCW '96*. ACM Press, New York, NY, USA, pp. 67–76. DOI: 10.1145/240080.240193.

Hassan, N., Rahman, M.M., Irani, P., Graham, P., 2009. Chucking: A One-Handed Document Sharing Technique. *Proceedings of the 12th IFIP TC 13 International Conference on Human-Computer Interaction, INTERACT '09*. Springer, Berlin, Heidelberg, pp. 264–278.

Hayduk, L.A., 1985. Personal space: The conceptual and measurement implications of structural equation models. *Canadian Journal of Behavioral Science/Revue canadienne des sciences du comportement* 17, 140–149. DOI: 10.1037/h0080132.

Hediger, H., 1950. *Wild Animals in Captivity*. Butterworths Scientific Publications.

He, H.A., 2010. One Size Does Not Fit All: Extending the Transtheoretical Model to Energy FeedbackTechnology Design. MSc Thesis, Department of Computer Science, University of Calgary, Calgary, Alberta, Canada.

Heenan, B., Greenberg, S., Aghel Manesh, S., Sharlin, E., 2014. Designing Social Greetings in Human Robot Interaction. *Proceedings of the ACM Conference on Designing Interactive*

System, ACM DIS '14, ACM, New York, NY, USA, pp. 855–864. Includes video figure. DOI: 10.1145/2598510.2598513.

Hinckley, K., 2003. Synchronous gestures for multiple persons and computers. *Proceedings of the 16th Annual ACM Symposium on User Interface Software and Technology, UIST '03*. ACM, New York, NY, USA, pp. 149–158. DOI: 10.1145/964696.964713.

Hinckley, K., Dixon, M., Sarin, R., Guimbretiere, F., Balakrishnan, R., 2009. Codex: A Dual Screen Tablet Computer. *Proceedings of the ACM Conference on Human Factors in Computing Systems, CHI '09*. ACM, New York, NY, USA, pp. 1933–1942. DOI: 10.1145/1518701.1518996.

Hinckley, K., Pierce, J., Sinclair, M., Horvitz, E., 2000. Sensing techniques for mobile interaction. *Proceedings of the 13th Annual ACM Symposium on User Interface Software and Technology, UIST '00*. ACM, New York, NY, USA, pp. 91–100. DOI: 10.1145/354401.354417.

Hinckley, K., Ramos, G., Guimbretiere, F., Baudisch, P., Smith, M., 2004. Stitching: pen gestures that span multiple displays. *Proceedings of the Working Conference on Advanced Visual Interfaces, AVI '04*. ACM, New York, NY, USA, pp. 23–31. DOI: 10.1145/989863.989866.

Holmquist, L., Mattern, F., Schiele, B., Alahuhta, P., Beigl, M., Gellersen, H.-W., 2001. Smart-Its Friends: A Technique for Users to Easily Establish Connections between Smart Artifacts. *Proceedings of Third International Conference on Ubiquitous Computing, UbiComp '01*. Springer, p. 116. DOI: 10.1007/3-540-45427-6_10.

Ishii, H., Kobayashi, M., Arita, K., 1994. Iterative design of seamless collaboration media. *Communications of the ACM* 37, 83–97. DOI: 10.1145/179606.179687.

Ishii, H., Ullmer, B., 1997. Tangible Bits: Toward Seamless Interfaces Between People, Bits and Atoms. *Proceedings of the ACM Conference on Human Factors in Computing Systems, CHI '97*. ACM, New York, NY, USA, pp. 234–241. DOI: 10.1145/258549.258715.

Ju, W., Lee, B.A., Klemmer, S.R., 2008. Range: exploring implicit interaction through electronic whiteboard design. *Proceedings of the ACM Conference on Computer Supported Cooperative Work, CSCW '08*. ACM, New York, NY, USA, pp. 17–26. DOI: 10.1145/1460563.1460569.

Katz, D., 1937. *Animals and Men: Studies in Comparative Psychology*. Longmans, Green.

Kendon, A., 1990. *Conducting Interaction: Patterns of Behavior in Focused Encounters*. Cambridge University Press.

Kendon, A., 2010. Spacing and orientation in co-present interaction. *Proceedings of Development of Multimodal Interfaces: Active Listening and Synchrony*. Presented at the Lecture Notes in Computer Science, Springer, pp. 1–15. DOI: 10.1007/978-3-642-12397-9_1.

Knowles, E.S., 1989. An affiliative conflict theory of personal and group spatial behavior. Paulus, P.B. (Ed.), *Psychology of Group Influence*. L. Erlbaum, Hillsdale, NJ.

Koenig, A.,1995. Patterns and antipatterns. *J. Object-Oriented Programming*, 8 (1): 46–48.

Kraut, R., Egido, C., Galegher, J., 1988. Patterns of contact and communication in scientific research collaboration. *Proceedings of the 1988 ACM Conference on Computer-Supported Cooperative Work, CSCW '88*. ACM, New York, NY, USA, pp. 1–12. DOI: 10.1145/62266.62267.

Kray, C., Rohs, M., Hook, J., Kratz, S., 2008. Group Coordination and Negotiation through Spatial Proximity Regions around Mobile Devices on Augmented Tabletops. *3rd IEEE International Workshop on Horizontal Interactive Human Computer Systems, TABLETOP '08*. IEEE, pp. 1–8. DOI: 10.1109/TABLETOP.2008.4660176.

Krueger, M.W., Gionfriddo, T., Hinrichsen, K., 1985. VIDEOPLACE—An Artificial Reality. *SIGCHI Bull.* 16, 35–40. DOI: 10.1145/1165385.317463.

Langheinrich, M., 2010. Privacy in Ubiquitous Computing. Krumm, J. (Ed.), *Ubiquitous Computing Fundamentals*. CRC Press, Boca Raton, Florida, USA, pp. 37–94.

Leahu, L., Sengers, P., Mateas, M., 2008. Interactionist AI and the promise of ubicomp, or, how to put your box in the world without putting the world in your box. *Proceedings of the 10th International Conference on Ubiquitous Computing, UbiComp '08*. ACM, New York, NY, USA, pp. 134–143. DOI: 10.1145/1409635.1409654.

Ledo, D., 2014. Remote control design for a ubiquitous computing ecology. MSc Thesis, Department of Computer Science, University of Calgary, Calgary, Alberta, Canada.

Ledo, D., Greenberg, S., 2013. Mobile Proxemic Awareness and Control: Exploring the Design Space for Interaction with a Single Appliance. *Proceedings ACM CHI 2013 Video Program, CHI EA '13*. ACM, New York, NY, USA, pp. 2831–2832. DOI: 10.1145/2468356.2479534.

Li, J., 2014. Two-sided transparent display as a collaborative medium. Master's thesis, Department of Computer Science, University of Calgary, Calgary, Alberta, Canada.

Luff, P., Heath, C., 1998. Mobility in collaboration. *Proceedings of the ACM Conference on Computer Supported Cooperative Work, CSCW'98*. ACM, pp. 305–314. DOI: 10.1145/289444.289505.

Mankoff, J., Dey, A.K., Hsieh, G., Kientz, J., Lederer, S., Ames, M., 2003. Heuristic Evaluation of Ambient Displays. *Proceedings of the 21st ACM Conference on Human Factors in Computing Systems, CHI '03*. ACM, New York, NY, USA, pp. 169–176. DOI: 10.1145/642611.642642.

Marquardt, N., 2013. Proxemic interactions in ubiquitous computing ecologies. Ph.D. thesis, Department of Computer Science, University of Calgary, Calgary, Alberta, Canada, July.

Marquardt, N., Ballendat, T., Boring, S., Greenberg, S., Hinckley, K., 2012a. Gradual engagement between digital devices as a function of proximity: From awareness to progressive reveal to information transfer. *Proceedings of Interactive Tabletops and Surfaces, ITS '12*, ACM, New York, NY, USA, pp. 31–40. Includes video figure. DOI: 10.1145/2396636.2396642.

Marquardt, N., Diaz-Marino, R., Boring, S., Greenberg, S., 2011. The Proximity Toolkit: Prototyping proxemic interactions in ubiquitous computing ecologies. *ACM Symposium on User Interface Software and Technology, UIST'11*. ACM, New York, NY, USA, pp. 315–326. Includes video figure. DOI: 10.1145/2047196.2047238.

Marquardt, N., and Greenberg, S., 2012. Informing the Design of Proxemic Interactions. *IEEE Pervasive Computing*, 11(2): 14–23, April–June. DOI: 10.1109/MPRV.2012.15.

Marquardt, N., Hinckley, K., Greenberg, S., 2012b. Cross-device interaction via micro-mobility and F-formations. *ACM Symposium on User Interface Software and Technology, UIST '12*. ACM, New York, NY, USA, pp. 13–22. Includes video figure. DOI: 10.1145/2380116.2380121.

Marquardt, N., Taylor, A., Villar, N., Greenberg, S., 2010. Rethinking RFID: Awareness and Control for Interaction with RFID Systems. *Proceedings of the ACM Conference on Human Factors in Computing Systems, CHI '10*. ACM, New York, NY, USA, pp. 2307–2316. DOI: 10.1145/1753326.1753674.

Marshall, P., Rogers, Y., Pantidi, N., 2011. Using F-formations to analyze spatial patterns of interaction in physical environments. *Proceedings of the ACM 2011 Conference on Computer Supported Cooperative Work, CSCW '11*. ACM, New York, NY, USA, p. 445. DOI: 10.1145/1958824.1958893.

Mayrhofer, R., Gellersen, H., Hazas, M., 2007. Security by Spatial Reference: Using Relative Positioning to Authenticate Devices for Spontaneous Interaction. *Proceedings of the International Conference on Ubiquitous Computing, UbiComp '07*. Springer, pp. 199–216. DOI: 10.1007/978-3-540-74853-3_12.

Mentis, H.M., O'Hara, K., Sellen, A., Trivedi, R., 2012. Interaction proxemics and image use in neurosurgery. *Proceedings of the SIGCHI Conference on Human Factors in Computing Systems, CHI '12*. ACM, New York, NY, USA, pp. 927–936. DOI: 10.1145/2207676.2208536.

Merrill, D., Kalanithi, J., Maes, P., 2007. Siftables: toward sensor network user interfaces. *Proceedings of the 1st International Conference on Tangible and Embedded Interaction, TEI '07*. ACM, New York, NY, USA, pp. 75–78. DOI: 10.1145/1226969.1226984.

Mostafa, A., Greenberg, S., Brazil, E., Sharlin, E., Sousa, M., 2013a. Interacting with microseismic visualizations. *Proc. ACM CHI 2013 Extended Abstracts, CHI EA '13*. ACM, New York, NY, USA, pp. 1749–1754. DOI: 10.1145/2468356.2468670.

Mostafa, A., Greenberg, S., Brazil, E., Sharlin, E.,Sousa, M., 2013b. Interacting with microseismic visualizations, the video. *Proceedings of the ACM CHI 2013 Video Program (Juried), Conference on Human Factors in Computing Systems, CHI '13*. ACM, New York, NY, USA. DOI: 10.1145/2468356.2479540.

Mueller, F., Stellmach, S., Greenberg, S., Dippon, A., Boll, S., Garner, J., Khot, R., Naseem, A. and Altimira, D., 2014. Proxemics play: Understanding proxemics for designing digital play experiences. *Proceedings of the ACM Conference on Designing Interactive Systems, DIS '14*, ACM, New York, NY, USA, pp. 533–542. DOI: 10.1145/2598510.2598532.

Myers, B.A., Peck, C.H., Nichols, J., Kong, D., Miller, R., 2001. Interacting at a Distance Using Semantic Snarfing. *Proceedings of the 3rd International Conference on Ubiquitous Computing, UbiComp '01*. Springer, London, UK, UK, pp. 305–314. DOI: 10.1007/3-540-45427-6_26.

Nacenta, M.A., Gutwin, C., Aliakseyeu, D., Subramanian, S., 2009. There and back again: Cross-display object movement in multi-display environments, *Human-Computer Interaction* 24 (1), 170–229. DOI: 10.1080/07370020902819882.

Nacenta, M.A., Aliakseyeu, D., Subramanian, S., Gutwin, C., 2005. A comparison of techniques for multi-display reaching. *Proceedings of the SIGCHI Conference on Human Factors in Computing Systems, CHI '05*. ACM, New York, NY, USA, pp. 371–380. DOI: 10.1145/1054972.1055024.

Norman, D., 1988. *The Psychology of Everyday Things*. Basic Books, New York, NY, USA.

Nöth, W., 1995. *Handbook of Semiotics*. Indiana University Press.

Olwal, A., Feiner, S., 2009. Spatially aware handhelds for high-precision tangible interaction with large displays. *Proceedings of the 3rd International Conference on Tangible and Embedded Interaction, TEI '09*. ACM, New York, NY, USA, pp. 181–188. DOI: 10.1145/1517664.1517705.

Osmond, H., 1957. Function as the basis of psychiatric ward design. *Mental Hospitals* (Architectural Supplement) 8, 23–29.

Oulasvirta, A., Salovaara, A., 2009. Ubiquitous Computing and the Concept of Context. Ang, C.S., Zaphiris, P. (Eds.), *Human Computer Interaction: Concepts, Methodologies, Tools, and Applications*, pp. 630–634. DOI: 10.4018/978-1-87828-991-9.ch002.

Patterson, M.L., 1975. Personal Space: Time to burst the bubble? *Man-Environment Systems* 67.

Petri, H.L., Huggins, R.G., Mills, C.J., Barry, L.S., 1974. Variables Influencing the Shape of Personal Space. *Pers Soc Psychol Bull* 1, 360–361. DOI: 10.1177/0146167274001001121.

Pierce, J., Mahaney, H., Abowd, G., 2003. Opportunistic annexing for handheld devices: Opportunities and challenges. *Proceedings of Human Computer Interaction Consortium Winter Meeting, HCIC '03.*

Prante, T., Röcker, C., Streitz, N., Stenzel, R., Magerkurth, C., van Alphen, D., Plewe, D.A., 2003. Hello. Wall–Beyond Ambient Displays. Video and Adjunct. *Proceedings of Ubicomp Conference.*

Price, G.H., Dabbs, J.M., 1974. Sex, Setting, and Personal Space: Changes as Children Grow Older. *Pers Soc Psychol Bull* 1, 362–363. DOI: 10.1177/0146167274001001122.

Ramos, G., Hinckley, K., Wilson, A., Sarin, R., 2009. Synchronous Gestures in Multi-Display Environments. *Human-Computer Interaction* 24, 117–169. DOI: 10.1080/07370020902739288.

Rekimoto, J., 1997. Pick-and-drop: A Direct Manipulation Technique For Multiple Computer Environments. *Proceedings of the 10th Annual ACM Symposium on User Interface Software and Technology, UIST '97*. ACM, New York, NY, USA, pp. 31–39. DOI: 10.1145/263407.263505.

Rekimoto, J., Ayatsuka, Y., Kohno, M., Oba, H., 2003. Proximal Interactions: A Direct Manipulation Technique for Wireless Networking. *Proceedings of the IFIP International Conference on Human-Computer Interaction, INTERACT '03*. IFIP, pp. 511–518. DOI: 10.1.1.74.9849.

Rekimoto, J., Saitoh, M., 1999. Augmented surfaces: a spatially continuous work space for hybrid computing environments. *Proceedings of the SIGCHI Conference on Human Factors in Computing Systems, CHI '99*. ACM, New York, NY, USA, pp. 378–385. DOI: 10.1145/302979.303113.

Rogers, Y., 2004. New theoretical approaches for human-computer interaction. *Annual Review of Information Science and Technology* 38, 87–143. DOI: 10.1002/aris.1440380103.

Rogers, Y., 2006. Moving on from Weiser's vision of calm computing: Engaging UbiComp experiences. *Proceedings of the Eighth International Conference on Ubiquitous Computing, Ubi-Comp '06*. Springer, pp. 404–421. DOI: 10.1007/11853565_24.

Rogers, Y., 2012. *HCI Theory: Classical, Modern, and Contemporary*, 1st ed. Morgan & Claypool Publishers. DOI: 10.2200/S00418ED1V01Y201205HCI014.

Roussel, N., Evans, H., Hansen, H., 2004. Proximity as an interface for video communication. *IEEE Multimedia* 11(3), 12–16. DOI: 10.1109/MMUL.2004.15.

Sakurai, S., Itoh, Y., Kitamura, Y., Nacenta, M.A., Yamaguchi, T., Subramanian, S., Kishino, F., 2008. *Interactive Systems. Design, Specification, and Verification*. Graham, T.C., Palanque, P. (Eds.). Springer, Berlin, Heidelberg, pp. 252–266.

Schilit, B., Adams, N., Want, R., 1994. Context-Aware Computing Applications. *IEEE Workshop on Mobile Computing Systems and Applications.* IEEE, Los Alamitos, CA, USA, pp. 85–90. DOI: 10.1109/WMCSA.1994.16.

Schmidt, A., 2000. Implicit human computer interaction through context. *Personal Technologies* 4 (2–3), pp. 191–199. DOI: 10.1007/BF01324126.

Schmidt, D., Chehimi, F., Rukzio, E., Gellersen, H., 2010. PhoneTouch: a technique for direct phone interaction on surfaces. *Proceedings of the 23nd Annual ACM Symposium on User Interface Software and Technology, UIST '10.* ACM, New York, NY, USA, pp. 13–16. DOI: 10.1145/1866029.1866034.

Scott, S.D., Carpendale, M.S.T., Inkpen, K.M., 2004. Territoriality in Collaborative Tabletop Workspaces. *Proceedings of the ACM Conference on Computer-Supported Cooperative Work, CSCW'04,* ACM, New York, NY, USA, pp. 294–303. DOI: 10.1145/1031607.1031655.

Scott, S.D., Carpendale, S., 2010. Theory of Tabletop Territoriality. In C. Müller-Tomfelde (ed.), *Tabletops—Horizontal Interactive Displays*, Springer (HCI Series), (ISBN: 978-1-84996-112-7), pp. 375–406. DOI: 10.1007/978-1-84996-113-4_15.

Seyed, T., Burns, C., King, P., Rodrigues, F.M., Costa Sousa, M., Maurer, F., 2013. MRI Table Kinect: A multi-surface application for exploring volumetric medical imagery. *Proceedings of the Workshop on Safer Interaction in Medical Devices, MediCHI '13,* Paris, France.

Shneiderman, B., 2006. A Second Path to HCI Innovation: Generative Theories Tied to User Needs. *ACM CHI 2006 Workshop Position Paper*: What Is the Next Generation of Human-Computer Interaction?

Shoemaker, G., Tang, A., Booth, K.S., 2007. Shadow reaching: a new perspective on interaction for large displays. *Proceedings of the 20th Annual ACM Symposium on User Interface Software and Technology, UIST '07.* ACM, New York, NY, USA, pp. 53–56. DOI: 10.1145/1294211.1294221.

Snibbe, S.S., Raffle, H.S., 2009. Social immersive media: pursuing best practices for multi-user interactive camera/projector exhibits. *Proceedings of the 27th International Conference on Human Factors in Computing Systems, CHI '09.* ACM, New York, NY, USA, pp. 1447–1456. DOI: 10.1145/1518701.1518920.

Sommer, R., 1959. Studies in Personal Space. *Sociometry* 22, 247–260. DOI: 10.2307/2785668.

Sommer, R., 1969. *Personal Space: The Behavioral Basis of Design*. Prentice-Hall, Englewood Cliffs, NJ.

Sommer, R., 2002. Personal Space in a Digital Age. Bechtel, R.B., Churchman, A. (Eds.), *Handbook of Environmental Psychology*. John Wiley and Sons, pp. 647–660.

Spindler, M., Büschel, W., Winkler, C., Dachselt, R. 2014. Tangible displays for the masses: Spatial interaction with handheld displays by using consumer depth cameras. *Personal and Ubiquitous Computing*, Springer London, 18(5), pp. 1213–1225. DOI: 10.1007/s00779-013-0730-7.

Streitz, N.A., Geisler, J., Holmer, T., Müller-Tomfelde, C., Reischl, W., Rexroth, P., Seitz, P., Steinmetz, R., 1999. i-LAND: an interactive landscape for creativity and innovation. *Proceedings of the SIGCHI Conference on Human Factors in Computing Systems, CHI '99*. ACM, New York, NY, USA, pp. 120–127. DOI: 10.1145/302979.303010.

Streitz, N., Prante, T., Müller-Tomfelde, C., Tandler, P., Magerkurth, C., 2002. Roomware©: the second generation. *Extended Abstracts on Human Factors in Computing Systems, CHI EA '02*. ACM New York, NY, USA, pp. 506–507. DOI: 10.1145/506443.506452.

Streitz, N., Prante, T., Röcker, C., Alphen, D. van, Magerkurth, C., Stenzel, R., Plewe, D., 2003. Ambient displays and mobile devices for the creation of social architectural spaces. Public and Situated Displays—Social and Interactional Aspects of Shared Display Technologies, *The Kluwer International Series on Computer Supported Cooperative Work*. Kluwer, Dordrecht, pp. 387–409. DOI: 10.1007/978-94-017-2813-3_16.

Strong, E., 1925. *The Psychology of Selling and Advertising*, McGraw-Hill NY.

Sundstrom, E., Altman, I., 1976. Interpersonal relationships and personal space: Research review and theoretical model. *Human Ecology* 4, 47–67. DOI: 10.1007/BF01531456.

Swindells, C., Inkpen, K.M., Dill, J.C., Tory, M., 2002. That one there! Pointing to establish device identity. *Proceedings of the 15th Annual ACM Symposium on User Interface Software and Technology, UIST '02*. ACM, New York, NY, USA, pp. 151–160. DOI: 10.1145/571985.572007.

Tandler, P., Prante, T., Müller-Tomfelde, C., Streitz, N., Steinmetz, R., 2001. Connectables: dynamic coupling of displays for the flexible creation of shared workspaces. *Proceedings of the 14th Annual ACM Symposium on User Interface Software and Technology, UIST '01*. ACM, New York, NY, USA, pp. 11–20. DOI: 10.1145/502348.502351.

Terrenghi, L., Quigley, A., Dix, A., 2009. A taxonomy for and analysis of multi-person-display ecosystems. *Personal and Ubiquitous Computing* 13, 583–598. DOI: 10.1007/s00779-009-0244-5.

Tidwell, J., 2005. *Designing Interfaces: Patterns for Effective Interaction Design*. O'Reilly Media, Inc.

Ullmer, B., Ishii, H., Glas, D., 1998. mediaBlocks: physical containers, transports, and controls for online media. *Proceedings of the 25th Annual Conference on Computer Graphics and*

Interactive Techniques, SIGGRAPH '98. ACM, New York, NY, USA, pp. 379–386. DOI: 10.1145/280814.280940.

Underkoffler, J., Ishii, H., 1999. Urp: a luminous-tangible workbench for urban planning and design. *Proceedings of the SIGCHI Conference on Human Factors in Computing Systems, CHI '99*. ACM, New York, NY, USA, pp. 386–393. DOI: 10.1145/302979.303114.

Velichkovsky, B., Sprenger, A., Unema, P., 1997. Toward gaze-mediated interaction: Collecting solutions of the "midas touch problem." *Proceedings of the 6th IFIP TC.13 International Conference on Human-Computer Interaction, INTERACT '97*, Chapman and Hall, pp. 509–516.

Vertegaal, R., Shell, J.S., 2008. Attentive user interfaces: the surveillance and sousveillance of gaze-aware objects. *Social Science Information* 47, 275–298. DOI: 10.1177/0539018408092574.

Voelker, S., Weiss, M., Wacharamanotham, C., Borchers, J., 2011. Dynamic portals: a lightweight metaphor for fast object transfer on interactive surfaces. *Proceedings of the ACM International Conference on Interactive Tabletops and Surfaces, ITS '11*. ACM, New York, NY, USA, pp. 158–161. DOI: 10.1145/2076354.2076384.

Vogel, D., Balakrishnan, R., 2004. Interactive public ambient displays: transitioning from implicit to explicit, public to personal, interaction with multiple users. *Proceedings of the 17th Annual ACM Symposium on User Interface Software and Technology, UIST '04*. ACM, New York, NY, USA, pp. 137–146. DOI: 10.1145/1029632.1029656.

Wang, M., 2012. The Proxemic Peddler framework: Designing a public display that captures and preserves the attention of a passerby. Master's thesis, Department of Computer Science, University of Calgary, Calgary, Alberta, Canada, April.

Wang, M., Boring, S., Greenberg, S., 2012. A Public Advertising Display that Captures and Preserves the Attention of a Passerby. *Proceedings of the 2012 International Symposium on Pervasive Displays, PerDis '12*. ACM, New York, NY, USA. DOI: 10.1145/2307798.2307801.

Want, R., Fishkin, K.P., Gujar, A., Harrison, B.L., 1999. Bridging Physical and Virtual Worlds with Electronic Tags. *Proceedings of the ACM Conference on Human Factors in Computing Systems, CHI '99*. ACM, New York, NY, USA, pp. 370–377. DOI: 10.1145/302979.303111.

Want, R., Hopper, A., Falcão, V., Gibbons, J., 1992. The Active Badge Location System. *ACM Transactions on Information Systems* 10, 91–102. DOI: 10.1145/128756.128759.

Weiser, M., 1991. The Computer for the 21st Century. *Scientific American* 265, 94–104. DOI: 10.1038/scientificamerican0991-94.

Weiser, M., 1994. The world is not a desktop. *ACM Interactions* 1, 7–8. DOI: 10.1145/174800.174801.

Weiser, M., Brown, J.S., 1996. Designing Calm Technology. *PowerGrid Journal* 1, 1.

Wigdor, D., Shen, C., Forlines, C., Balakrishnan, R., 2006. Table-centric interactive spaces for re-al-time collaboration. *Proceedings of the Working Conference on Advanced Visual Interfaces, AVI '06*. ACM, New York, NY, USA, pp. 103–107. DOI: 10.1145/1133265.1133286.

Wilson, A.D., Benko, H., 2010. Combining multiple depth cameras and projectors for interactions on, above and between surfaces. *Proceedings of the 23nd Annual ACM Symposium on User Interface Software and Technology, UIST '10*. ACM, New York, NY, USA, pp. 273–282. DOI: 10.1145/1866029.1866073.

Author Biographies

Nicolai Marquardt is a Lecturer in Physical Computing at University College London. At the UCL Interaction center he is working in the research areas of ubiquitous computing, physical user interfaces and interactive surfaces. In particular, his research of Proxemic Interactions focuses on how to exploit knowledge about people's and devices spatial relationships in interaction design. He graduated with a Ph.D. in Computer Science from the Interactions Lab at the University of Calgary, and joined Microsoft Research in Cambridge and Redmond as an intern during his graduate studies. Together with Saul Greenberg, Sheelagh Carpendale, and Bill Buxton he is co-author of *Sketching User Experiences: The Workbook* (Morgan-Kaufmann 2012). See: http://www.nicolaimarquardt.com.

Saul Greenberg is a Full Professor and Industrial Research Chair in the Department of Computer Science at the University of Calgary. While he is a computer scientist by training, the work by Saul and his talented students typifies the cross-discipline aspects of Human Computer Interaction, Computer Supported Cooperative Work, and Ubiquitous Computing. He and his crew are well known for their development of toolkits, innovative system designs based on observations of social phenomenon, articulation of design-oriented social science theories, and refinement of evaluation methods. He is a Fellow of the ACM, received the CHCCS Achievement award, and was elected to the ACM CHI Academy for his overall contributions to the field of Human Computer Interaction. Together with Nicolai Marquardt, Sheelagh Carpendale and Bill Buxton he is the co-author of *Sketching User Experiences: The Workbook* (Morgan-Kaufmann 2012) as well several other books on Human Computer Interaction. See: http://saul.cpsc.ucalgary.ca.

Printed in the United States
by Baker & Taylor Publisher Services